# Basic Statistics for Health Information Management Technology

Carol E. Osborn, PhD, RHIA

*Associate Director*
*Department of Medical Information Management*
*Coding, Data Quality, and Compliance*
*The Ohio State University Health System*

**JONES AND BARTLETT PUBLISHERS**

*Sudbury, Massachusetts*

BOSTON    TORONTO    LONDON    SINGAPORE

# About The Author

**Carol E. Osborn, PhD, RHIA,** earned an undergraduate degree in health information management from Mercy College of Detroit, a master's degree in health sciences education and evaluation from the State University of New York at Buffalo, and a PhD in research and evaluation from Ohio State University.

Dr. Osborn has spent most of her career in the academic setting, teaching at both the University of Illinois at Chicago and at Ohio State University. She is currently Associate Director of Medical Information Management for The Ohio State University Health System. In this position, she is responsible for instruction in coding, data quality, documentation improvement, and compliance. She has also consulted in a variety of healthcare settings including acute care, specialty care, and healthcare-related organizations. She has served on The Ohio State University's Institutional Review Board for 12 years. She was part of the Allied Health Education Consulting Team to the Ministry of Health of Saudi Arabia. She has also served as a consultant to health information management (HIM) baccalaureate degree programs.

Dr. Osborn has been active in professional associations at the state and national levels. She has served as secretary, treasurer, and president of the Illinois Medical Record Association. Nationally, she has served on the Council of Education, the Sub-Panel for Accreditation of Academic Programs, and the Joint Committee on Education, and for ten years served as a member of the Panel of Accreditation Surveyors. She has authored numerous articles and book chapters for professional journals and textbooks. She is currently on the editorial review board for *Perspectives in Health Information Management*.

# PREFACE

This text was written specifically for health information technology students enrolled in associate degree programs and for practicing health information management professionals. It focuses on applying basic statistical techniques to problems in health care. The text is set up so that students can input the data for each problem using their own statistical software. It is not the intent of this book to teach the student how to use SPSS, Microsoft Excel, or any other type of statistical package or electronic spreadsheet. They are included in this text as examples; I am not endorsing any of these products.

My goal in writing this book was to introduce students and professionals to how statistical techniques can be used to describe and make inferences from healthcare data. There are many statistical books available on the market, but few are directed specifically to the health information management profession. Also, this text also includes the "traditional hospital statistics" such as the average length of stay and total inpatient service days, which are not included in other versions of this text.

# CHAPTER 1   BASIC STATISTICAL DATA USED IN ACUTE CARE FACILITIES

## KEY TERMS

Autopsy
Average daily census
Average length of stay (ALOS)
Bed count day
Bed turnover rate
Census
Consultation
Daily inpatient census
Death rate
Dichotomous variables
Direct maternal death
Discharge days
Fetal autopsy rate
Fetal death
Fetal death rate
Frequency distribution
Gross autopsy rate
Gross death rate
Hospital-acquired infection

Hospital autopsy rate
Indirect maternal death
Inpatient bed occupancy rate
Inpatient service day
Length of stay (LOS)
Maternal death rate
Net autopsy rate
Net death rate
Newborn autopsy rate
Newborn death rate
Outpatients
Postoperative infection rate
Proportion
Rate
Ratio
Surgical operation
Surgical procedure
Total length of stay
Variable

## LEARNING OBJECTIVES

At the conclusion of this chapter, you should be able to:

1. Define key terms.
2. Define hospital rates and indicators.
3. Calculate hospital measures of morbidity, mortality, and volume indicators.

It is often said that hospitals and other types of health care facilities are data rich but information poor. There are many types of databases within the facility, many contained within the organization's information warehouse. Information warehouses contain both clinical and financial information. It is the job of the health information management professional to turn the data contained in these databases into information that can be used by physicians, administrators, and other frequency measures used with dichotomous variables are ratios, proportions, and rates. All three measures are based on the same formula:

$$\text{ratio, proportion, rate} = \frac{x}{y} \times 10^n$$

In this formula, $x$ and $y$ are the two quantities being compared, and $x$ is divided by $y$. $10^n$ is read as "10 to the $n^{\text{th}}$ power." The size of $10^n$ may equal 1, 10, 100, 1000, or more, depending on the value of $n$:

$$10^0 = 1$$
$$10^1 = 10$$
$$10^2 = 10 \times 10 = 100$$
$$10^3 = 10 \times 10 \times 10 = 1000$$

## Ratios and Proportions

A ratio is a comparison between two different things. In a **ratio**, the values of a variable (such as gender: $x$ = female, $y$ = male) are expressed so that $x$ and $y$ are completely independent of each other. For example, the gender of patients discharged from a hospital is compared as:

$$\frac{\text{female}}{\text{male}}, \text{ or } \frac{x}{y}$$

In this example, the ratio represents the number of female discharges compared to the total number of male discharges.

How then would you calculate the female-to-male ratio for a hospital that discharged 457 women and 395 men during the month of July? The procedure for calculating a ratio is outlined in Exhibit 1.1.

A proportion is a particular type of ratio. A **proportion** is a ratio in which $x$ is a portion of the whole, $x + y$. In a proportion, the numerator is always included in the denominator. Exhibit 1.2 outlines the procedure for determining the proportion of hospital discharges for the month of July that was female.

## Rates

Rates are a third type of frequency measure. In health care, **rates** are often used to measure an event over time and are sometimes used as performance improvement measures. The basic formula for a rate is

$$\frac{\text{Number of cases or events occurring during a given time period} \times 10^n}{\text{Number of cases or population at risk during same time period}}$$

or

$$\frac{\text{Total number of times something did happen} \times 10^n}{\text{Total number of times something could happen}}$$

In inpatient facilities, there are many commonly computed rates. In computing the Caesarean section (C-section) rate, we count the number of C-sections performed during a given period of time; this value is placed in the numerator. The

---

**Exhibit 1.1    Calculation of a Ratio: Discharges for July 20xx**

1. Define $x$ and $y$.
   $x$ = number of female discharges
   $y$ = number of male discharges
2. Identify $x$ and $y$.
   $x = 457$
   $y = 395$
3. Set up the ratio $x/y$.
   457/395
4. Reduce the fraction so that either $x$ or $y$ equals 1.
   1.16/1

There were 1.16 female discharges for every male discharge.

---

**Exhibit 1.2    Calculation of a Proportion: Discharges for July 20xx**

1. Define $x$ and $y$.
   $x$ = number of female discharges
   $y$ = number of male discharges
2. Identify $x$ and $y$.
   $x = 457$
   $y = 395$
3. Set up the proportion
   $x/(x + y)$ or $457/(457 + 395) = 457/852$
4. Reduce the fraction so that either $x$ or $x + y$ equals 1.
   0.54/1.00

The proportion of discharges that were female is 0.54.

---

number of cases, or population at risk, is the number of women who delivered during the same time period; this number is placed in the denominator. The denominator represents the total number of times a C-section could have occurred.

By convention, inpatient hospital rates are calculated as the rate per 100 cases ($10^n = 10^2 = 10 \times 10 = 100$) and are expressed as a percentage. The method for calculating the hospital C-section rate is presented in Exhibit 1.3.

In the example, 33 of the 263 deliveries at Hospital X during the month of May were C-sections. In the formula, the numerator is the number of C-sections performed in May (a given period of time) and the denominator is the total number of deliveries (the population at risk) performed in the same time frame, including C-sections. In calculating the rate, the numerator is always included in the denominator. Also, when calculating the rate, the numerator is first multiplied by 100 and then divided by the denominator.

Because hospital rates rarely result in a whole number, they usually must be rounded either up or down to the next whole number. The hospital should set a policy on whether rates are to be reported to one or two decimal places. The division should be carried out to at least one more decimal place than desired.

In rounding, when the last number is five or greater, the preceding number should be increased by one. In contrast, when the last number is less than five, the

---

Exhibit 1.3   **Calculation of C-Section Rate for July 20xx**

---

For the month of July, 23 C-sections were performed; during the same time period, 149 women delivered. What is the C-section rate for the month of July?

1.  Define the variable of interest (numerator) and population or number of cases at risk (denominator).

    Numerator: total number of C-sections performed in July

    Denominator: total number of women who delivered in July, including C-sections

2.  Identify the numerator and denominator.

    Numerator: 23

    Denominator: 149

3.  Set up the rate.

    $(23 \times 100)/149$

4.  Multiply the numerator times 100 ($10^n = 10^2$), then divide by the denominator.

    $(2300/149) = 15.4\%$.

The C-section rate for the month of July is 15.4%.

---

preceding number should remain the same. For example, when rounding 25.56% to one decimal place, the rate becomes 25.6%. When rounding 1.563% to two decimal places, the rate becomes 1.56%. Rates of less than 1% are usually carried out to three decimal places and rounded to two. For rates less than 1%, a zero should precede the decimal to emphasize that the rate is less than 1% (for example, 0.56%).

## HOSPITAL STATISTICS

Hospitals collect data about both inpatients and outpatients on a daily basis. They use these statistics to monitor the volume of patients treated daily, weekly, monthly, or within some other specified time frame. These statistics give health care decision-makers the information they need to plan facilities and to monitor inpatient and outpatient revenue streams. For these reasons, health information management (HIM) professionals must be well versed in data collection and reporting methods. Because most of data collection and reporting are now automated, it is important to understand the underlying concepts from which these data are generated.

Standard definitions have been developed to ensure that all health care providers collect and report data in a consistent manner. The *Glossary of Health Care Terms*, developed by the American Health Information Management Association (AHIMA), is a resource commonly used to describe the types of health care events for which data are collected (The glossary is currently published as an appendix in *Calculating and Reporting Healthcare Statistics*, Horton, 2004.) The glossary includes definitions of terms related to health care corporations, health maintenance organizations (HMOs), and other health-related programs and facilities. Some basic terms that HIM professionals should be familiar with include:

- **Hospital inpatient**: A person who is provided room, board, and continuous general nursing service in an area of the hospital where patients generally stay at least overnight.
- **Hospital newborn inpatient**: An infant born in the hospital at the beginning of the current inpatient hospitalization. Newborns are usually counted separately because their care is so different from that of other patients. Infants born on the way to the hospital or at home are considered hospital inpatients, not hospital newborn inpatients.
- **Inpatient hospitalization**: The period in a person's life when they are an inpatient in a single hospital without interruption except by possible intervening leaves of absence.
- **Inpatient admission**: The formal acceptance by a hospital of a patient who is to be provided with room, board, and continuous nursing services in an area of the hospital where patients generally stay overnight.

- **Inpatient discharge**: The termination of a period of inpatient hospitalization through the formal release of the inpatient by the hospital. This designation includes patients who are discharged alive (by physician order), who are discharged against medical advice, or who died while hospitalized. Unless otherwise indicated, inpatient discharges include deaths.
- **Hospital outpatient**: A hospital patient who receives services in one or more of the outpatient facilities when not currently an inpatient or home care patient. An outpatient may be classified as either an emergency outpatient or a clinic outpatient. An emergency outpatient is admitted to the hospital's emergency department for diagnosis and treatment of a condition that requires immediate medical, dental, or other type of emergency service. A clinic outpatient is admitted to a clinical service of the clinic or hospital for diagnosis and treatment on an ambulatory basis.

## Inpatient Census Data

Even though much of the data collection process has been automated, an ongoing responsibility of the HIM professional is to verify the census data that are collected daily. The census reports patient activity for a 24-hour reporting period. Included in the census report is the number of inpatients admitted and discharged for the previous 24-hour period as well as the number of intra-hospital transfers. An intra-hospital transfer is a patient who is moved from one patient care unit (for example, the ICU) to another (the surgical unit). The usual 24-hour reporting period begins at 12:01 a.m. and ends at 12:00 midnight. In the census count, adults and children are reported separately from newborns.

However, before compiling census data, it is important to understand the related terminology. The **census** refers to the number of hospital inpatients present at any one time. For example, the census in a 300-bed hospital may be 250 patients at 2:00 p.m. on May 1, but 245 only one hour later. Because the census may change throughout the day as admissions and discharges occur, hospitals designate an official census-taking time. In most facilities, the official count takes place at midnight.

The result of the official count taken at midnight is the **daily inpatient census**. This refers to the number of inpatients present at the official census-taking time each day. Also included in the daily inpatient census are any patients who were admitted and discharged the same day. For example, if a patient was admitted to the cardiac care unit at 1:00 p.m. on May 1 and died at 4:00 p.m. on May 1, he would be counted as a patient who was both admitted and discharged the same day.

Because patients admitted and discharged the same day are not present at census-taking time, the hospital must account for them separately. If it did not, it would lose credit for the services it provided to these patients. The daily inpatient census reflects the total number of patients treated during the 24-hour period. Exhibit 1.4 displays a sample daily inpatient census report.

Exhibit 1.4    **Sample Daily Inpatient Census Report, Adults and Children**

| May 2 | |
|---|---|
| Number of patients in hospital at midnight, May 1 | 230 |
| + Number of patients admitted May 2 | +35 |
| − Number of patients discharged, including deaths, May 2 | −40 |
| Number of patients in hospital at midnight May 2 | 225 |
| + Number of patients both admitted and discharged, including deaths | + 5 |
| Daily inpatient census at midnight, May 2 | 230 |
| Total inpatient service days, May 2 | 230 |

A unit of measure that reflects the services received by one inpatient during a 24-hour period is an **inpatient service day**. The number of inpatient service days for a 24-hour period is equal to the daily inpatient census, that is, one service day for each patient treated. In Exhibit 1.5, the total number of inpatient service days for May 2 is 230.

Inpatient service days are compiled daily, weekly, monthly, and annually. They reflect the volume of services provided by the health care facility—the greater the volume of services, the greater the revenues to the facility. Daily reporting of the number of inpatient service days is an indicator of the hospital's financial condition.

As mentioned earlier, the daily inpatient census is equal to the number of inpatient service days provided for a single day. The total number of inpatient service days for a week, a month, or some other period of time can be divided by the total number of days in the given period to get the average daily inpatient census.

As an example, consider that a hospital might have a daily inpatient census of 240 for day one, 253 for day two, and 237 for day three. The total number of inpatient service days for the three-day period would be 730. When that total is divided by three days, the average daily census is 243.3. The **average daily census** is the average number of inpatients treated during a given period of time. The general formula for calculating the average daily census is:

$$\frac{\text{Total number of inpatient services for a given period}}{\text{Total number of days in the same period}}$$

In calculating the average daily census, adults and children (A&C) are reported separately from newborns (NBs). This is because the intensity of services provided to adults and children is greater than it is for newborns. To calculate the average daily census for adults and children, the general formula is modified as follows:

$$\frac{\text{Total number of inpatient service days for A\&C for a given period}}{\text{Total number of days for the same period}}$$

The formula for the average daily census for newborns is:

$$\frac{\text{Total number of inpatient service days for NBs for a given period}}{\text{Total number of days for the same period}}$$

For example, the total number of inpatient service days provided to adults and children for the week of May 1 is 1729, and the total for newborns is 119. Using the preceding formulae, the average daily census is 1729/7 = 247 for adults and children and 119/7 = 17 for newborns. The average daily census for all hospital inpatients for the week of May 1 is (1729 + 119)/7 = 264. Table 1.3 presents the various formulae for calculating the average daily census.

## Inpatient Bed Occupancy Rate

Another indicator of the hospital's financial position is the inpatient bed occupancy rate, also called the percentage of occupancy. The **inpatient bed occupancy rate** is the percentage of official beds occupied by hospital inpatients for a given period of time. In general, the greater the occupancy rate, the greater the revenues for the hospital. For a bed to be included in the official count, it must be set up, staffed, equipped, and available for patient care. The total number of inpatient service days is used in the numerator because it is equal to the daily inpatient cen-

Table 1.3  **Calculation of Average Daily Census Statistics**

| Indicator | Numerator ($x$) | Denominator ($y$) |
|---|---|---|
| Average daily inpatient census | Total number of inpatient service days for a given period | Total number of days for the same period |
| Average daily inpatient census for adults and children (A&C) | Total number of inpatient service days for A&C for a given period | Total number of days for the same period |
| Average daily inpatient census for newborns (NBs) | Total number of inpatient service days for NBs for a given period | Total number of days for the same period |

sus, or the number of patients treated daily. The denominator is the total number of bed count days. **Bed count days** are calculated by multiplying the number of days in the given period by the number of beds available during the time frame of interest.

The occupancy rate compares the number of patients treated over a given period of time to the total number of beds available for that same period of time. If 200 patients occupied 280 beds on May 2, the inpatient bed occupancy rate would be $(200/280) \times 100 = 71.4\%$. If the rate was calculated for two or more days, the number of beds would be multiplied by the number of days in that particular time frame.

If we were to calculate the rate for seven days, we would divide the total number of inpatient service days by the total bed count days for that period. For example, if 1729 inpatient service days were provided during the week of May 1, the number of beds (280) would be multiplied by the number of days (7), and the inpatient bed occupancy rate for that week would be $[1729/(280 \times 7)] \times 100 = 88.2\%$.

The denominator in the previous formula is actually the total possible number of inpatient service days. That is, if every available bed in the hospital were occupied every single day, this value would be the maximum number of inpatient service days that could be provided. This is an important concept, especially when the official bed count changes for a given reporting period. For example, if the bed count changes from 280 to 300 beds, the bed occupancy rate must reflect this change. The total number of inpatient beds multiplied by the total number of days in the reporting period is called the total number of bed count days.

The general formula for the inpatient bed occupancy rate is:

$$\frac{\text{Total number of inpatient service days for a given period} \times 100}{\text{Total number of inpatient bed count days for the same period}}$$

For example, in May the total number of inpatient service days provided was 7582. The bed count for the month of May changed from 280 to 300 beds on May 20. To calculate the inpatient bed occupancy rate for May, it is necessary to determine the total number of bed count days. May has 31 days, so the total number of bed count days is calculated as:

Number of beds, May 1–May 19 = 280 × 19 days = 5320 bed count days
Number of beds, May 20–May 31 = 300 × 12 days = 3600 bed count days
5320 + 3600 = 8920 bed count days

The inpatient bed occupancy rate for the month of May is $(7582/8920) \times 100 = 85.0\%$.

As with the average daily census, the inpatient bed occupancy rate for adults and children is reported separately from that of newborns. To calculate the total

Table 1.4  **Calculation of Inpatient Bed Occupancy Rates**

| Rate | Numerator × 100 | Denominator |
|------|-----------------|-------------|
| Inpatient bed occupancy rate | Total number of inpatient service days for a given period | Total number of inpatient bed count days for the same period |
| Inpatient bed occupancy rate for adults and children (A&C) | Total number of inpatient service days for A&C for a given period | Total number of inpatient bed count days for A&C for the same period |
| Inpatient bed occupancy rate for newborns (NBs) | Total number of NBs inpatient service days for a given period | Total number of bassinet bed count days for the same period |

number of bed count days for newborns, the official count for newborn bassinets is used. Table 1.4 reviews how to calculate inpatient bed occupancy rates.

It is possible for the inpatient bed occupancy to be greater than 100%. This occurs when the hospital faces an epidemic or disaster. In this type of situation, hospitals set up temporary beds that are not normally included in the official bed count. As an example, Critical Care Hospital experienced an excessive number of admissions in January because of an outbreak of influenza. In January, the official bed count was 150 beds. On January 5, the daily inpatient census was 156. Therefore, the inpatient bed occupancy rate for January 5 was $(156/150) \times 100 = 104\%$.

## Bed Turnover Rate

The **bed turnover rate** is a measure of hospital utilization. It includes the number of times each hospital bed changes occupants. The formula for the bed turnover rate is:

$$\frac{\text{Total number of discharges (including deaths) for a given time period}}{\text{Average bed count for the same period}}$$

For example, Critical Care Hospital experienced 2060 discharges and deaths for the month of April. Its bed count for April averaged 677. The bed turnover rate is therefore $2060 / 677 = 3.0$. The interpretation is that, on average, each hospital bed had three occupants during April.

## Length of Stay Data

The **length of stay (LOS)** is calculated for each patient after he or she is discharged from the hospital. It refers to the number of calendar days from the day of patient admission to the day of discharge. When the patient is admitted and discharged in the same month, the LOS is determined by subtracting the date of admission from the date of discharge. For example, the LOS for a patient admitted on May 12 and discharged on May 17 is five days (17 − 12 = 5).

When the patient is admitted in one month and discharged in another, the calculations must be adjusted. One way to calculate the LOS in this case is to subtract the date of admission from the total number of days in the month the patient was admitted and then add the total number of hospitalized days for the month in which the patient was discharged. For example, the LOS for a patient admitted on May 28 and discharged on June 6 is nine days, (May 31 − May 28) + June 6.

When a patient is admitted and discharged on the same day, the LOS is one day. A partial day's stay is never reported as a fraction of a day. The LOS for a patient discharged the day after admission also is one day. Thus, the LOS for a patient who was admitted to the ICU on May 10 at 9:00 a.m. and died at 3:00 p.m. the same day is one day. Likewise, the LOS for a patient admitted on May 12 and discharged on May 13 is one day.

When the LOS for all patients discharged for a given period of time is summed, the result is the **total length of stay**. If five patients are discharged from the pediatric unit on May 9, the total LOS is calculated as follows:

| Patient | LOS |
|---------|-----|
| 1 | 5 |
| 2 | 3 |
| 3 | 1 |
| 4 | 8 |
| 5 | 10 |
| Total Length of Stay | 27 |

In the preceding example, the total LOS is 5 + 3 + 1 + 8 + 10 = 27 days. The total LOS is also referred to as the number of days of care provided to patients discharged or died, or the **discharge days**.

The total LOS divided by the number of patients discharged is the **average length of stay** (ALOS). Using the data in the previous example, the ALOS for the five patients discharged from the pediatric unit is 27/5 = 5.4 days. The general formula for calculating ALOS is:

$$\frac{\text{Total length of stay for a given period}}{\text{Total number of discharges (including deaths) for the same period}}$$

As with the other measures already discussed, the ALOS for adults and children is reported separately from the ALOS for newborns. Table 1.5 reviews the formulae for ALOS.

Table 1.5    **Calculation of LOS Statistics**

| Indicator | Numerator | Denominator |
|---|---|---|
| Average LOS | Total length of stay (discharge days) for a given period | Total number of discharges, including deaths, for the same period |
| Average LOS for adults and children (A&C) | Total length of stay for A&C discharges (discharge days) for a given period | Total number of A&C discharges, including deaths, for the same period |
| Average LOS for newborns (NBs) | Total length of stay for all NB discharges (discharge days) for a given period | Total number of NB discharges, including deaths, for the same period |

Exhibit 1.5 displays an example of a hospital statistical summary prepared by the HIM department on the basis of census and discharge data.

## Hospital Death Rates

The **death rate** is based on the number of patients discharged—alive and dead—from the facility. Deaths are considered discharges because they are the end point of a period of hospitalization. In contrast to the rates discussed in the preceding section, newborns are not counted separately from adults and children.

Exhibit 1.5    **Statistical Summary, Critical Care Hospital for Period Ending July 20xx**

| | July 20xx | | Year-to-Date | |
|---|---|---|---|---|
| **Admissions** | **Actual** | **Budget** | **Actual** | **Budget** |
| Medical | 728 | 769 | 5,075 | 5,082 |
| Surgical | 578 | 583 | 3,964 | 3,964 |
| OB/GYN | 402 | 440 | 2,839 | 3,027 |
| Psychiatry | 113 | 99 | 818 | 711 |
| Physical Medicine & Rehab | 48 | 57 | 380 | 384 |
| Other Adult | 191 | 178 | 1,209 | 1,212 |
| Total Adult | 2,060 | 2,126 | 14,285 | 14,380 |
| Newborn | 294 | 312 | 2,143 | 2,195 |
| Total Admissions | 2,354 | 2,438 | 16,428 | 16,575 |

Exhibit 1.5 *Continued*

| Average Length of Stay | July 20xx | | Year-to-Date | |
|---|---|---|---|---|
| | **Actual** | **Budget** | **Actual** | **Budget** |
| Medical | 6.1 | 6.4 | 6.0 | 6.1 |
| Surgical | 7.0 | 7.2 | 7.7 | 7.7 |
| OB/GYN | 2.9 | 3.2 | 3.5 | 3.1 |
| Psychiatry | 10.8 | 11.6 | 10.4 | 11.6 |
| Physical Medicine & Rehab | 27.5 | 23.0 | 28.1 | 24.3 |
| Other Adult | 3.6 | 3.9 | 4.0 | 4.1 |
| Total Adult | 6.3 | 6.4 | 6.7 | 6.5 |
| Newborn | 5.6 | 5.0 | 5.6 | 5.0 |
| Total ALOS | 6.2 | 6.3 | 6.5 | 6.3 |

| Patient Days | July 20xx | | Year-to-Date | |
|---|---|---|---|---|
| | **Actual** | **Budget** | **Actual** | **Budget** |
| Medical | 4,436 | 4,915 | 30,654 | 30,762 |
| Surgical | 4,036 | 4,215 | 30,381 | 30,331 |
| OB/GYN | 1,170 | 1,417 | 10,051 | 9,442 |
| Psychiatry | 1,223 | 1,144 | 8,524 | 8,242 |
| Physical Medicine & Rehab | 1,318 | 1,310 | 10,672 | 9,338 |
| Other Adult | 688 | 699 | 4,858 | 4,921 |
| Total Adult | 12,871 | 13,700 | 95,140 | 93,036 |
| Newborn | 1,633 | 1,552 | 12,015 | 10,963 |
| Total Patient Days | 14,504 | 15,252 | 107,155 | 103,999 |

| Other Key Statistics | July 20xx | | Year-to-Date | |
|---|---|---|---|---|
| | **Actual** | **Budget** | **Actual** | **Budget** |
| Average Daily Census | 485 | 482 | 498 | 486 |
| Average Beds Available | 677 | 660 | 677 | 660 |
| Clinic Visits | 21,621 | 18,975 | 144,271 | 136,513 |
| Emergency Visits | 3,822 | 3,688 | 26,262 | 25,604 |
| Inpatient Surgery Patients | 657 | 583 | 4,546 | 4,093 |
| Outpatient Surgery Patients | 603 | 554 | 4,457 | 3,987 |

**GROSS DEATH RATE**   The **gross death rate** is the proportion of all hospital discharges that resulted in death. It is the basic indicator of mortality in a health care facility. The gross death rate is calculated by dividing the total number of deaths occurring in a given time period by the total number of discharges, including deaths, for the same time period. The formula for calculating the gross death rate is:

$$\frac{\text{Total number of inpatient deaths (including NBs) for a given period} \times 100}{\substack{\text{Total number of discharges, including A\&C and NB deaths,} \\ \text{for the same period}}}$$

For example, Critical Care Hospital experienced 21 deaths (adults, children, and newborns) during the month of May. There were 633 total discharges, including deaths. Therefore, the gross death rate is $(21/633) \times 100 = 3.3\%$.

**NET DEATH RATE**   The **net death rate** is an adjusted death rate. It is calculated in the belief that certain deaths should not "count against the hospital." It is an adjusted rate because patients who die within 48 hours of admission are not included in the net death rate. The reason for excluding them is that 48 hours is not enough time to positively affect patient outcome. In other words, the patient was not admitted to the hospital in a manner timely enough for treatment to have an effect on his or her outcome. However, in view of currently available technology, some people believe that the net death rate is no longer a meaningful indicator. The formula for calculating the net death rate is:

$$\frac{\substack{\text{Total number of inpatient deaths (including NBs) minus deaths} \\ < 48 \text{ hours for a given period} \times 100}}{\substack{\text{Total number of discharges (including A\&C and NB deaths) minus deaths} \\ < 48 \text{ hours for the same period}}}$$

Continuing with the preceding example, 3 of the 21 deaths at Critical Care Hospital occurred within 48 hours of admission. Therefore, the net death rate is $[(21 - 3)/(633 - 3)] \times 100 = 2.9\%$.

**NEWBORN DEATH RATE**   Even though newborn deaths are included in the hospital's gross and net death rates, the newborn death rate may be calculated separately. Newborns include only infants born alive in the hospital. The **newborn death rate** is the number of newborns that died in comparison to the total number of newborns discharged, alive and dead. To qualify as a newborn death, the newborn must have been delivered alive. A stillborn infant is not included in either the newborn death rate or the gross or net death rates. The formula for calculating the newborn death rate is:

$$\frac{\text{Total number of NB deaths for a given period} \times 100}{\text{Total number of NB discharges (including deaths) for the same period}}$$

**FETAL DEATH RATE**    Stillborn deaths are called fetal deaths. A **fetal death** is a death that occurs prior to the fetus' complete expulsion or extraction from the mother in a hospital facility, regardless of the length of the pregnancy. Thus, stillborns are neither admitted nor discharged from the hospital. A fetal death occurs when the fetus fails to breathe or show any other evidence of life, such as beating of the heart, pulsation of the umbilical cord, or movement of the voluntary muscles.

Fetal deaths also are classified into categories based on the fetus' length of gestation or weight:

- **Early fetal death**: Less than 20 weeks gestation, or a weight of 500 grams or less.
- **Intermediate fetal death**: At least 20 but less than 28 weeks gestation, or a weight between 501 and 1000 grams.
- **Late fetal death**: 28 weeks gestation, or a weight of more than 1000 grams.

To calculate the **fetal death rate**, the total number of intermediate and late fetal deaths for the period is divided by the total number of live births and intermediate and late fetal deaths for the same period. The formula for calculating the fetal death rate is:

$$\frac{\text{Total number of intermediate and late fetal deaths for a given period} \times 100}{\substack{\text{Total number of live births plus total number of intermediate and} \\ \text{late fetal deaths for the same period}}}$$

For example, during the month of May, Critical Care Hospital experienced 269 live births and 13 intermediate and late fetal deaths. The fetal death rate is therefore $[13/(269 + 13)] \times 100 = 4.6\%$.

**MATERNAL DEATH RATE (HOSPITAL INPATIENT)**    Hospitals also calculate the maternal death rate. A **maternal death** is the death of any woman from any cause related to, or aggravated by, pregnancy or its management, regardless of the duration or site of the pregnancy. Maternal deaths resulting from accidental or incidental causes are not included in the maternal death rate.

Maternal deaths are classified as direct or indirect. A **direct maternal death** is the death of a woman resulting from obstetrical complications of the pregnancy, labor, or puerperium (the period lasting from birth until six weeks after delivery). Direct maternal deaths are included in the maternal death rate. An **indirect**

**maternal death** is the death of a woman from a previously existing disease or a disease that developed during pregnancy, labor, or the puerperium that was not due to obstetric causes, although the physiologic effects of pregnancy were partially responsible for the death.

The **maternal death rate** may be an indicator of the availability of prenatal care in a community. The hospital also may use it to help identify conditions that could lead to a maternal death. The formula for calculating the maternal death rate is:

$$\frac{\text{Total number of direct maternal deaths for a given period} \times 100}{\begin{array}{c}\text{Total number of maternal discharges, including deaths,}\\ \text{for the same period}\end{array}}$$

For example, during the month of May, Critical Care Hospital experienced 275 maternal discharges. Two of these patients died. The maternal death rate for May is therefore (2/275) × 100 = 0.73%. Table 1.6 summarizes hospital-based mortality rates.

Table 1.6   **Calculation of Hospital-Based Mortality Rates**

| Rate | Numerator × 100 | Denominator |
|---|---|---|
| Gross death rate | Total number of inpatient deaths, including NBs, for a given time period | Total number of discharges, including A&C and NB deaths, for the same period |
| Net death rate (Institutional death rate) | Total number of inpatient deaths, including NBs, minus deaths < 48 hours for a given time period | Total number of discharges, including A&C and NB deaths, minus deaths < 48 hours for the same period |
| Newborn death rate | Total number of NB deaths for a given period | Total number of NB discharges, including deaths, for the same period |
| Fetal death rate | Total number of intermediate and late fetal deaths for a given period | Total number of live births plus total number of intermediate and fetal deaths for the same period |
| Maternal death rate | Total number of direct maternal deaths for a given period | Total number of maternal (obstetric) discharges, including deaths, for the same period |

## Autopsy Rates

An **autopsy** is an examination of a dead body to determine the cause of death. Autopsies are very useful in the education of medical students and residents. In addition, they can alert family members to conditions or diseases for which they may be at risk.

Autopsies are of two types:

- **Hospital inpatient autopsy**: An examination of the body of a patient who died while being treated in the hospital. The patient's death marks the end of his or her stay in the hospital. A pathologist or some other physician on the medical staff who has been given responsibility performs this type of autopsy in the facility.
- **Hospital autopsy**: An examination of the body of an individual who at some time in the past had been a hospital patient but was not an inpatient at the time of death. A pathologist or some other physician on the medical staff who has been given responsibility performs this type of autopsy.

The following sections describe the different types of autopsy rates.

**GROSS AUTOPSY RATE**    A **gross autopsy rate** is the proportion or percentage of deaths that are followed by the performance of an autopsy. The formula for calculating the gross autopsy rate is:

$$\frac{\text{Total inpatient autopsies for a given period} \times 100}{\text{Total number of inpatient deaths for the same period}}$$

For example, during the month of May, Critical Care Hospital experienced 21 deaths. Autopsies were performed on four of these patients. Therefore, the gross autopsy rate is $(4/21) \times 100 = 19.0\%$.

**NET AUTOPSY RATE**    The bodies of patients who have died are not always available for autopsy. For example, a coroner or medical examiner may claim a body for an autopsy for legal reasons. In these situations, the hospital calculates a **net autopsy rate**. In calculating the net autopsy rate, bodies that have been removed by the coroner or medical examiner are excluded from the denominator. The formula for calculating the net autopsy rate is:

$$\frac{\text{Total number of autopsies on inpatient deaths for a period} \times 100}{\substack{\text{Total number of inpatient deaths minus unautopsied coroners' or} \\ \text{medical examiners' cases for the same period}}}$$

Continuing with the example in the preceding section, the medical examiner claimed three of the four patients scheduled for autopsy. The numerator remains the same because four autopsies were performed. However, because three of the deaths were identified as medical examiner's cases and removed from the hospital, they are subtracted from the total of 21 deaths. Thus, the net autopsy rate is $[4/(21 - 3)] \times 100 = 22.2\%$.

**HOSPITAL AUTOPSY RATE**   A **hospital autopsy rate** is an adjusted rate that includes autopsies on anyone who once may have been a hospital patient. The formula for calculating the hospital autopsy rate is:

$$\frac{\text{Total number of hospital autopsies for a given period} \times 100}{\substack{\text{Total number of deaths of hospital patients whose bodies are available} \\ \text{for hospital autopsy for the same period}}}$$

The hospital autopsy rate can include either or both of the following:

- Inpatients who died in the hospital, except those removed by the coroner or medical examiner. When the hospital pathologist or another designated physician acts as an agent in the performance of an autopsy on an inpatient, the death and the autopsy are included in the percentage.
- Other hospital patients, including ambulatory care patients, hospital home care patients, and former hospital patients who died elsewhere but whose bodies were made available for autopsy by the hospital pathologist or other designated physician. These autopsies and deaths are included when the percentage is computed.

Generally, it is impossible to determine the number of bodies of former hospital patients who may have died during a given time period. In the formula, the phrase "available for hospital autopsy" involves several conditions, including:

- The autopsy must be performed by the hospital pathologist or a designated physician on the body of a patient treated in the hospital at some time.
- The report of the autopsy must be filed in the patient's health record and with the hospital laboratory or pathology department.
- The tissue specimens must be maintained in the hospital laboratory.

Exhibit 1.6 explains how to calculate the hospital autopsy rate.

**NEWBORN AUTOPSY RATE**   Autopsy rates usually include autopsies performed on newborn infants unless a separate rate is requested. The formula for calculating the **newborn autopsy rate** is:

$$\frac{\text{Total number of autopsies on NB deaths for a given period} \times 100}{\text{Total number of NB deaths for the same period}}$$

Exhibit 1.6 **Calculation of Hospital Autopsy Rate**

In June, 33 inpatient deaths occurred. Three of these were medical examiner's cases. Two of the bodies were removed from the hospital and so were not available for hospital autopsy. One of the medical examiner's cases was autopsied by the hospital pathologist. Fourteen other autopsies were performed on hospital inpatients who died during the month of June. In addition, autopsies were performed in the hospital on:

- A child with congenital heart disease who died in the emergency department
- A former hospital inpatient who died in an extended care facility and whose body was brought to the hospital for autopsy
- A former hospital inpatient who died at home and whose body was brought to the hospital for autopsy
- A hospital outpatient who died while receiving chemotherapy for cancer
- A hospital home care patient whose body was brought to the hospital for autopsy
- A former hospital inpatient who died in an emergency vehicle on the way to the hospital

Calculation of total hospital autopsies:

      1  autopsy on medical examiner's case
   +14  autopsies on hospital inpatients
   + 6  autopsied on hospital patients whose bodies were available for autopsy
   ———
     21  autopsies performed by the hospital pathologist

Calculation of number of deaths of hospital patients whose bodies were available for autopsy:

    33  inpatient deaths
   − 2  medical examiner's cases
   + 6  deaths of hospital patients
   ———
    37  bodies available for autopsy

Calculation of hospital autopsy rate:

$$\frac{\text{Total number of hospital autopsies for period} \times 100}{\substack{\text{Total number of deaths of hospital patients with bodies available} \\ \text{for hospital autopsy for the period}}}$$

$$(21 \times 100)/37 = 56.8\%$$

**FETAL AUTOPSY RATE**   Hospitals also sometimes calculate the **fetal autopsy rate**. Fetal autopsies are performed on stillborn infants who have been classified as either intermediate or late fetal deaths. This is the proportion or percentage of autopsies done on intermediate or late fetal deaths out of the total number of intermediate or late fetal deaths. The formula for calculating the fetal autopsy rate is:

$$\frac{\text{Total number of autopsies on intermediate and late fetal deaths for a given period} \times 100}{\text{Total number of intermediate and late fetal deaths for the same period}}$$

Table 1.7 summarizes the different autopsy rates.

## Hospital Infection Rates

The most common morbidity rates calculated for hospitals are related to **hospital-acquired** infections. The hospital must monitor the number of infections that occur in its various patient care units continuously. Infection can adversely affect the course of a patient's treatment and possibly result in death. The Joint Commission on Accreditation of Healthcare Organizations (JCAHO) requires hospi-

Table 1.7   **Calculation of Hospital Autopsy Rates**

| Rate | Numerator × 100 | Denominator |
|------|-----------------|-------------|
| Gross autopsy rate | Total number of autopsies on inpatient deaths for a given period | Total number of inpatient deaths for the same period |
| Net autopsy rate | Total number of autopsies on inpatient deaths for a given period | Total number of inpatient deaths minus unautopsied coroner or medical examiner cases for the same period |
| Hospital autopsy rate | Total number of autopsies on inpatient deaths for a given period | Total number of deaths of hospital patients whose bodies are available for hospital autopsy for the same period |
| Newborn (NB) autopsy rate | Total number of autopsies on NB deaths for a given period | Total number of NB deaths for the same period |
| Fetal autopsy rate | Total number of autopsies on intermediate and late fetal deaths for a given period | Total number of intermediate and late fetal deaths for the same period |

tals to follow written guidelines for reporting all types of infections. Examples of the different types of infections are respiratory, gastrointestinal, surgical wound, skin, urinary tract, septicemias, and infections related to intravascular catheters.

The hospital infection rate can be calculated for the entire hospital or for a specific unit in the hospital. It also can be calculated for the specific types of infections. Ideally, the hospital should strive for an infection rate of 0.0%. The formula for calculating the nosocomial infection rate is:

$$\frac{\text{Total number of hospital infections for a given period} \times 100}{\text{Total number of discharges (including deaths) for the same period}}$$

For example, Critical Care Hospital discharged 725 patients during the month of June. Thirty-two of these patients had hospital-acquired infections. The infection rate is therefore $(32/725) \times 100 = 4.4\%$.

**POSTOPERATIVE INFECTION RATE**    Hospitals often track their postoperative infection rate. The **postoperative infection rate** is the proportion or percentage of infections in clean surgical cases out of the total number of surgical operations performed. A clean surgical case is one in which no infection existed prior to surgery. The postoperative infection rate may be an indicator of a problem in the hospital environment or of some type of surgical contamination.

The person calculating the postoperative infection rate must know the difference between a surgical procedure and a surgical operation. A **surgical procedure** is any separate, systematic process on or within the body that can be complete in itself. A physician, dentist, or some other licensed practitioner performs a surgical procedure, with or without instruments, for the following reasons:

- To restore disunited or deficient parts
- To remove diseased or injured tissues
- To extract foreign matter
- To assist in obstetrical delivery
- To aid in diagnosis

A **surgical operation** involves one or more surgical procedures that are performed on one patient at one time using one approach to achieve a common purpose. An example of a surgical operation is the resection of a portion of both the intestine and the liver in a cancer patient. This involves two procedures—the removal of a portion of the liver and the removal of a portion of the colon—but it is considered only one operation because there is only one approach or incision. In contrast, an esophagoduodenoscopy (EGD) and a colonoscopy performed at the same time is an example of two procedures with two different approaches. In the former, the approach is the upper gastrointestinal tract; in the latter, the approach is the lower gastrointestinal tract. In this case, the two procedures do not have a common approach or purpose.

The formula for calculating the postoperative infection rate is:

$$\frac{\text{Number of infections in clean surgical cases for a given period} \times 100}{\text{Total number of surgical operations for the same period}}$$

## Consultation Rate

A **consultation** occurs when two or more physicians collaborate on a particular patient's diagnosis or treatment. The attending physician requests the consultation and explains his or her reason for doing so. The consultant then examines the patient and the health records and makes recommendations in a written report. The formula for calculating the consultation rate is:

$$\frac{\text{Total number of patients receiving consultations for a given period} \times 100}{\text{Total number of discharges and deaths for the same period}}$$

## CASE-MIX STATISTICAL DATA

Case mix is a method of grouping patients according to a predefined set of characteristics. Diagnosis-related groups (DRGs) are used to determine case mix in hospitals. The case-mix index (CMI) is the average DRG weight for patients discharged from the hospital. The CMI is a measure of the resources used in treating the patients in each hospital or group of hospitals. It is calculated for all patients discharged but may also be calculated and displayed as discharges by payer (Exhibit 1.7), or the discharges of a particular physician (Exhibit 1.8).

Exhibit 1.7 **Case Mix Index by Payor, Critical Care Hospital, 20xx**

| Payor | CMI | N |
|---|---|---|
| Commercial | 1.8830 | 283 |
| Gov Managed Care | 0.9880 | 470 |
| Managed Care | 1.4703 | 2,336 |
| Medicaid | 1.3400 | 962 |
| Medicare | 2.0059 | 1,776 |
| Other | 1.3251 | 148 |
| Self-Pay | 1.3462 | 528 |
| Total | 1.5671 | 6,503 |

Exhibit 1.8 **Case Mix Index by Physician, General Medicine, 20xx**

| Physician | CMI | N |
|-----------|--------|-----|
| A | 1.0235 | 71 |
| B | 1.6397 | 71 |
| C | 1.1114 | 86 |
| Total | 1.2501 | 228 |

Exhibit 1.9 provides an example of a case-mix calculation for 10 DRGs at Critical Care Hospital. The CMI is calculated by multiplying the number of cases for each DRG by the relative weight of the DRG. The results are then summed (1511.2332) and divided by the total number of cases ($n = 484$). By convention, the CMI is calculated to five decimal points and rounded to four.

The CMI can be used to indicate the average reimbursement for the hospital. From Exhibit 1.7, the CMI is 1.5670, indicating that reimbursement is approximately 56.7% greater than the hospital's base rate. If the CMI is greater than 1.0,

Exhibit 1.9 **Calculation Case Mix Index for Ten DRGs, Critical Care Hospital, 20xx**

| DRG | N | Relative Weight (RW) | N × RW |
|-------|-----|------------------------|------------|
| 24 | 84 | 1.4367 | 120.6828 |
| 125 | 41 | 1.0947 | 44.8827 |
| 127 | 61 | 1.0265 | 62.6165 |
| 174 | 41 | 1.0025 | 41.1025 |
| 182 | 43 | 0.8223 | 35.3589 |
| 202 | 45 | 1.3120 | 59.0400 |
| 320 | 26 | 0.8853 | 23.0178 |
| 416 | 31 | 1.5918 | 49.3458 |
| 475 | 61 | 3.6000 | 219.6000 |
| 483 | 51 | 16.7762 | 855.5862 |
| Total | 484 | | 1511.2332 |
| CMI | | | 3.1224 |

Exhibit 1.10    **Benchmark Data, Critical Care Hospital Versus National Average for DRG 127, Heart Failure and Shock, 20xx**

|  | ALOS | Mortality Rate | Average Charges |
|---|---|---|---|
| Critical Care Hospital | 4.6 | 0.3% | $12,042 |
| National Average | 5.4 | 5.0% | $ 9,694 |

the hospital's average payment is greater than its base rate; conversely, if the CMI is less than 1.0, the hospital's average payment is less than its base rate.

The CMI also is used as a proxy measure of the severity of illness of Medicare patients. In Exhibit 1.7, we can see that Medicare patients, as expected, have the highest CMI, 2.0059. Medicare patients are usually sicker than the population under age 65.

Other data analyzed by DRG include LOS and mortality rates. LOS and mortality data are benchmarked against the hospital's peer group and national data. The process of benchmarking is comparing the hospital's performance to an external standard or benchmark. An excellent source of information for benchmarking purposes is the Healthcare Cost Utilization Project database (HCUPnet), which is available online at *http://hcupnet.ahrq.gov*. A comparison of hospital and national data for DRG 127 appears in Exhibit 1.10.

Gross analysis of the data indicates that Critical Care Hospital's ALOS and mortality rate are better than the national average. At the same time, their average charges are somewhat higher than the national average.

## STATISTICAL DATA USED IN AMBULATORY CARE FACILITIES

Ambulatory care includes health care services provided to patients who are not hospitalized (that is, who are not considered inpatients or residents and do not stay in the health care facility overnight). Such patients are referred to as **outpatients**. Most ambulatory care services today are provided in freestanding physicians' offices, emergency care centers, and ambulatory diagnostic surgery centers that are not owned or operated by acute care organizations. However, hospitals do provide many hospital-based health care services to outpatients. Hospital outpatients receive services in one or more areas within the hospital, including clinics, same-day surgery departments, diagnostic departments, and emergency departments.

Outpatient statistics include records of the number of patient visits and the types of services provided. Many different terms are used to describe outpatients and ambulatory care services, including:

- **Hospital ambulatory care**: Hospital-directed preventive, therapeutic, and rehabilitative services provided by physicians and their surrogates to patients who are not hospital inpatients or home care patients.
- **Outpatient**: A patient who receives care without being admitted for inpatient or residential care.
- **Hospital outpatient**: A patient who receives services in one or more of the facilities owned and operated by a hospital.
- **Emergency outpatient**: A patient who is admitted to the emergency department or equivalent service of a hospital for diagnosis and treatment of a condition that requires immediate medical services, dental services, or related health care services.
- **Clinic outpatient**: A patient who is admitted to a clinical service of a clinic or hospital for diagnosis or treatment on an ambulatory basis.
- **Referred outpatient**: A patient who is provided special hospital-based diagnostic or therapeutic services on an ambulatory basis. The services are ordered by a referring physician and the responsibility for medical care remains with that physician rather than with the hospital.
- **Outpatient visit**: A provision of services to an outpatient in one or more units or facilities located in or directed by the provider maintaining the outpatient health care services.
- **Encounter**: A contact between a patient and a health care professional who has primary responsibility for assessing and treating a patient at a given contact and for exercising independent medical judgment.
- **Occasion of service**: A specified, identifiable service involved in the care of a patient or consumer that is not an encounter. Occasions of service may be the result of an encounter, for example, to fulfill physicians' orders for tests or procedures ordered as part of an encounter.
- **Ambulatory surgery centers**: Hospital-based or freestanding surgical facilities that perform elective surgical procedures on patients who are classified as outpatients and who are typically released from the facility on the same day the surgery was performed. Also referred to as short-stay surgery, one-day surgery, same-day surgery, or come-and-go surgery services.

## CONCLUSION

Rates, ratios, and proportions are commonly used to describe hospital populations. Hospital-based rates are used for a variety of purposes. First, they describe the general characteristics of the patients treated at the facility. Hospital administrators use the data to monitor the volume of patients treated monthly, weekly, or within some other specified time frame. The statistics give health care decision-makers the information they need to plan facilities and to monitor inpatient and outpatient revenue streams. With the knowledge of how clinical data are collected and analyzed, the HIM professional can become an invaluable member of the health care team.

## REFERENCES

Johns, M.L. (ed.) (2006) *Health Information Management Technology: An Applied Approach*, 2nd Edition. Chicago: American Health Information Management Association.

LaTour, Kathleen M., and S. Maki-Eichenwald (eds.) (2006) *Health Information Management: Concepts, Principles, and Practice*, 2nd Edition. Chicago: American Health Information Management Association.

Horton, Loretta A. (2004) *Calculating and Reporting Healthcare Statistics*. Chicago: American Health Information Management Association.

Osborn, Carol E. (2005) *Statistical Applications for Health Information Management*. Sudbury, MA: Jones and Bartlett Publishers.

# APPENDIX 1-A

## EXERCISES FOR SOLVING PROBLEMS

### Knowledge Questions

1. Define the key terms listed at the beginning of this chapter.
2. Describe the differences and similarities between rates, ratios, and proportions.

### Multiple Choice

1. What term would be applied to a comparison of the number of female patients to the number of male patients who were discharged from DRG YYY?
   a. Ratio
   b. Percentage
   c. Proportion
   d. Rate
2. There are 6 males in a class of 20 students. What is the best term to describe the comparison?
   a. Ratio
   b. Percentage
   c. Proportion
   d. Rate
3. Which of the following descriptive statistics is calculated by applying this equation: $\dfrac{x}{y} \times 10^n$?
   a. Ratio
   b. Proportion
   c. Rate
   d. All of the above

4. The number of inpatients present at the census-taking time each day plus the number of inpatients who were both admitted and discharged after the census-taking time the previous day is the:
   a. Inpatient census
   b. Daily inpatient census
   c. Inpatient service day
   d. Inpatient bed occupancy ratio
5. Which of the following is not a type of inpatient hospital discharge?
   a. Death
   b. Intra-hospital transfer from MICU to medicine service
   c. Discharge against medical advice
   d. Discharge transfer to a long-term care facility
6. Which of the following is a unit of measure equal to the services received by one inpatient during a 24-hour period?
   a. Inpatient census
   b. Inpatient service day
   c. Daily inpatient census
   d. Average daily inpatient census
7. What does the hospital gross death rate include?
   a. Deaths of hospital inpatients only
   b. All inpatient deaths and still-born infants

c. Deaths of all inpatients and deaths occurring in the emergency department

d. Deaths of all inpatients, DOAs, and deaths occurring in the emergency department

8. When computing the C-section rate, the denominator is the total number of _____.

a. Births

b. Deliveries

c. Obstetrical discharges

d. Newborns

9. At midnight, December 1, the inpatient census at Watson Hospital was 378. On December 2, 18 patients were discharged alive, 1 patient died, 22 patients were admitted, and 2 patients were admitted and discharged the same day. How many inpatient service days were provided on December 2?

a. 375

b. 377

c. 381

d. 383

10. At Critical Care Hospital, 238 operations were performed in January. Fifteen of these patients developed infections within 10 days of surgery. During January, 432 patients were admitted and 470 patients were discharged. What is the postoperative infection rate for the month?

a. 0.06%

b. 3.19%

c. 3.47%

d. 6.30%

11. On December 1, Critical Care Hospital had a bed capacity of 520. On December 15, 45 beds were closed. During the month of December, there were 13,050 inpatient service days, 15,450 days rendered to discharged patients, and 945 discharges and deaths. What is the inpatient bed occupancy rate for December?

a. 80.9%

b. 84.5%

c. 84.7%

d. 85.0%

12. In August, Critical Care Hospital discharged 1575 patients and admitted 1650 patients. The hospital provided 10,215 days of service to inpatients and 9763 days of service to discharged patients. What is the average daily census at Critical Care Hospital for the month of August?

a. 315

b. 323

c. 330

d. 334

13. Using the information from Question 10, what is the average length of stay at Critical Care Hospital for the month of August?

a. 5.9 days

b. 6.2 days

c. 6.5 days

d. 6.8 days

## Problems

1. For the month of August, Critical Care Hospital (a 425-bed hospital) provided 12,220 days of service to hospital inpatients. Calculate the average daily census and the inpatient bed occupancy rate for the month.

2. For the month of March, Critical Care Hospital experienced 19

deaths, 9 of which occurred within 48 hours of admission. It also experienced 522 live discharges. Calculate the gross death rate and the net death rate for the month.

3. For the month of March, Critical Care Hospital experienced 150 deliveries, 7 of which were C-sections. Calculate the C-section rate.

4. Beginning January 1, 2005, Critical Care Hospital had 175 inpatient beds. On June 15, the bed count was increased to 200. There were 67,106 inpatient service days provided to hospital inpatients, and 68,012 days of service provided to discharged patients. The hospital experienced 9601 admissions and 9488 discharges. Calculate the average daily census for the year. Also, calculate the ALOS and the bed occupancy rate for the year.

5. During 2005, Critical Care Hospital experienced 31 late and intermediate fetal deaths and 1000 live births. Calculate the fetal death rate.

6. Twenty patients were discharged from the MICU during the week of January 1. Five of these patients had a hospital-acquired infection. What is the acquired infection rate for the MICU for the week of January 1?

7. During the month of April, 822 patients were discharged from Critical Care Hospital. A total of 122 patients had consults from specialty physicians. What is the consultation rate for the month of April?

8. Dr. Green discharged 21 patients from General Medicine Service during the month of August. Table 1-A.1 presents the number of patients discharged by DRG. Calculate the CMI for Dr. Green.

9. Review the hypothetical data on deaths in the MICU in Table 1-A.2 and answer the questions below:

   a. What is the ratio of male deaths to female deaths?

   b. What proportion of the patients who died were admitted from the Emergency Department? What proportion were transfers from other hospitals?

   c. The total number of patients discharged from DRG 475 was 61. What is the gross death rate for DRG 475?

   d. The total number of patients discharged from DRG 483 was 51. What is the gross death rate for DRG 483?

Table 1-A.1   **Dr. Green's Discharges by DRG, General Medicine Service, 20xx**

| DRG | DRG Title | RW | N | N*DRG |
|-----|-----------|----|----|-------|
| 079 | Respiratory Infections & Inflammations Age > 17 w/CC | 1.5974 | 2 | |
| 085 | Pleural Effusion w/CC | 1.1927 | 1 | |
| 087 | Pulmonary Edema | 1.3430 | 3 | |
| 089 | Simple Pneumonia & Pleurisy Age > 17 w/CC | 1.0463 | 1 | |
| 121 | Circulatory Disorders w/AMI & Major Complications, Discharged Alive | 1.6169 | 1 | |
| 130 | Peripheral Vascular Disorders w/CC | .9505 | 1 | |
| 143 | Chest Pain | .5480 | 1 | |
| 174 | GI Hemorrhage w/CC | 1.0025 | 2 | |
| 182 | Esophagitis, Gastroenteritis & Miscellaneous Digestive Disorders Age > 17 w/CC | .8223 | 2 | |
| 240 | Connective Tissue Disorder w/CC | 1.3153 | 1 | |
| 243 | Medical Back Problems | .7525 | 1 | |
| 316 | Renal Failure | 1.2987 | 1 | |
| 395 | Red Blood Cell Disorders Age > 17 | .8307 | 1 | |
| 416 | Septicemia Age > 17 | 1.5918 | 1 | |
| 450 | Poisoning & Toxic Effects of Drugs Age > 17 w/o CC | .4246 | 1 | |
| 475 | Respiratory System Diagnosis w/Ventilator Support | 3.6000 | 1 | |

Table 1-A.2   **Critical Care Hospital, Deaths in the MICU by DRG**

| DRG | DRG Title | Adm Source | Gender | LOS |
|-----|-----------|-----------|--------|-----|
| 001 | Craniotomy Age >17 W Cc | SNF | Male | 2 |
| 014 | Intracranial Hemorrhage & Stroke W Infarct | Other | Male | 3 |
| 014 | Intracranial Hemorrhage & Stroke W Infarct | Emerdept | Female | 3 |
| 020 | Nervous System Infection Except Viral Meningitis | Other | Female | 15 |
| 075 | Major Chest Procedures | Hospital | Male | 6 |
| 105 | Cardiac Valve & Oth Major Cardiothoracic Proc W/O Card Cath | Hospital | Female | 23 |
| 123 | Circulatory Disorders W Ami, Expired | Hospital | Male | 7 |
| 123 | Circulatory Disorders W Ami, Expired | Other | Male | 1 |
| 123 | Circulatory Disorders W Ami, Expired | Other | Male | 4 |
| 123 | Circulatory Disorders W Ami, Expired | Emerdept | Male | 5 |
| 172 | Digestive Malignancy W Cc | Emerdept | Male | 1 |
| 172 | Digestive Malignancy W Cc | Physician | Male | 1 |

| DRG | DRG Title | Adm Source | Gender | LOS |
|---|---|---|---|---|
| 188 | Other Digestive System Diagnoses Age >17 W Cc | SNF | Female | 1 |
| 191 | Pancreas, Liver & Shunt Procedures W Cc | Hospital | Male | 9 |
| 202 | Cirrhosis & Alcoholic Hepatitis | Physician | Female | 15 |
| 202 | Cirrhosis & Alcoholic Hepatitis | Other | Male | 1 |
| 202 | Cirrhosis & Alcoholic Hepatitis | Emerdept | Male | 24 |
| 205 | Disorders Of Liver Except Malig,Cirr,Alc Hepa W Cc | Physician | Male | 20 |
| 331 | Other Kidney & Urinary Tract Diagnoses Age >17 W Cc | Physician | Male | 44 |
| 357 | Uterine & Adnexa Proc For Ovarian Or Adnexal Malignancy | Physician | Female | 24 |
| 416 | Septicemia Age >17 | Hospital | Female | 4 |
| 416 | Septicemia Age >17 | Other | Male | 2 |
| 449 | Poisoning & Toxic Effects Of Drugs Age >17 W Cc | Other | Male | 1 |
| 473 | Acute Leukemia W/O Major O.R. Procedure Age >17 | Physician | Male | 5 |
| 475 | Respiratory System Diagnosis With Ventilator Support | Physician | Male | 25 |
| 475 | Respiratory System Diagnosis With Ventilator Support | Physician | Female | 1 |
| 475 | Respiratory System Diagnosis With Ventilator Support | Hospital | Female | 1 |
| 475 | Respiratory System Diagnosis With Ventilator Support | Other | Female | 1 |
| 475 | Respiratory System Diagnosis With Ventilator Support | Hospital | Female | 21 |
| 475 | Respiratory System Diagnosis With Ventilator Support | Other | Male | 5 |
| 475 | Respiratory System Diagnosis With Ventilator Support | Hospital | Female | 8 |
| 475 | Respiratory System Diagnosis With Ventilator Support | Emerdept | Female | 10 |
| 475 | Respiratory System Diagnosis With Ventilator Support | Clinic | Male | 13 |
| 475 | Respiratory System Diagnosis With Ventilator Support | SNF | Female | 1 |
| 475 | Respiratory System Diagnosis With Ventilator Support | Emerdept | Male | 5 |
| 475 | Respiratory System Diagnosis With Ventilator Support | Clinic | Female | 4 |
| 475 | Respiratory System Diagnosis With Ventilator Support | Emerdept | Male | 3 |
| 475 | Respiratory System Diagnosis With Ventilator Support | Other | Female | 12 |
| 475 | Respiratory System Diagnosis With Ventilator Support | Other | Female | 5 |
| 483 | Trac W Mech Vent 96+Hrs Or Pdx Except Face, Mouth & Neck Dx | Hospital | Female | 30 |
| 483 | Trac W Mech Vent 96+Hrs Or Pdx Except Face, Mouth & Neck Dx | Hospital | Male | 19 |
| 483 | Trac W Mech Vent 96+Hrs Or Pdx Except Face, Mouth & Neck Dx | Hospital | Male | 22 |
| 483 | Trac W Mech Vent 96+Hrs Or Pdx Except Face, Mouth & Neck Dx | Physician | Female | 46 |
| 483 | Trac W Mech Vent 96+Hrs Or Pdx Except Face, Mouth & Neck Dx | Other | Female | 28 |

# CHAPTER 2

**POPULATION-BASED MORBIDITY AND MORTALITY MEASURES**

## KEY TERMS

Certificate of death
Certificate of live birth
Confounding variable
Epidemiology
Mortality rates
    Age-adjusted death rate
    Age-specific death rate (ASDR)
    Case fatality rate
    Cause-specific death rate
    Crude death rate
    Gender-specific death rate
    Infant mortality rate
    Maternal mortality rate

Neonatal mortality rate
Postneonatal mortality rate
Proportionate mortality ratio
    (PMR)
Race-specific death rate
Standard mortality ratio (SMR)
Morbidity rates
    Incidence rate
    Point prevalence rate
    Prevalence rate
Report of fetal death
Report of induced termination of
    pregnancy
Vital statistics

## LEARNING OBJECTIVES

At the conclusion of this chapter, you should be able to:

1. Define key terms.

2. Calculate measures of morbidity, mortality, and risk of disease for communities.

3. Identify variables that affect morbidity and mortality rates over time.

4. After adjustment, compare health care facility mortality/morbidity rates with community, state, and national rates.

5. Locate health care-related state and federal databases online.

6. Use health care data collected from online databases in comparative statistical reports.

## POPULATION-BASED MORTALITY MEASURES

As the profession of health information management moves into integrated health care delivery systems and assumes more prominence in managed care organizations, it becomes more important to be familiar with community-based mortality and morbidity data. This type of information is often used in planning health services, such as the number of inpatient facilities, type of outpatient facilities, and number or size of managed care plans for a given community, as well as for developing managed care contracts with hospitals and physicians.

Population-based statistics are based on mortality and morbidity rates from which the health of a population can be inferred. The entire defined population is used in the collection and reporting of these statistics. The size of the defined population serves as the denominator in the calculation of these rates.

## Crude Death Rate

The **crude death rate** is a measure of the actual or observed mortality in a given population. Crude rates apply to a population without regard to characteristics of the population, such as the distribution of age or gender. The crude death rate is the starting point for further development of adjusted rates. It measures the proportion of a population that has died during a specific period of time (usually one year) or the number of deaths per 1000 people in a community for a given period of time. The crude death rate is calculated as follows:

$$\frac{\text{Total deaths during a given time interval} \times 10^n = \text{deaths per } 10^n}{\text{Estimated mid-interval population}}$$

The mid-interval population is the estimated population of a given community at the midpoint of the time frame under study.

In calculating the crude death rate, the power of $n$ is usually equal to the value that will result in a value greater than 1. This allows for an easier interpretation of the rate—a death rate of less than 1 per 100 is not very meaningful. For example, the annual midyear population of Anytown, USA, may be 1,996,355, and 275 deaths occurred in that particular year. The power of $n$ that will result in a whole number is 4: $10^4 = 10 \times 10 \times 10 \times 10 = 10,000$. The crude death rate is then calculated as follows:

$$\frac{275 \times 10,000}{1,996,355} = \frac{2,750,000}{1,996,355} = 1.38 \text{ deaths per } 10,000$$

When analyzing crude death rates—or any type of rate—it is important to remember that these events do not occur in a vacuum. When analyzing any data set, we must remember that the data do not stand alone but reflect trends in the environment. Trends in death rates can be influenced by three variables: time, place, and person. Examples of time, place, and person variables are outlined in Exhibit 2.1. An example of how trended data may be affected by time, place, and person variables is presented in Figure 2.1. The line graph shows that the number of

Exhibit 2.1    **Variables Affecting Trends in Community Morbidity and Mortality**

- Time

  Transition from International Classification of Diseases, 9th Revision (ICD-9) to ICD-10 in coding of death certificates

  Improvements in medical technology

  Earlier detection and diagnosis of disease

- Place

  Changes in environments

  International and intra-national differences in medical technology and the use of medical technology

  Diagnostic practices of physicians

  Variation in physician practice patterns by region

- Person

  Age

  Sex

  Ethnicity

  Social habits (smoking, diet, alcohol)

  Genetic background

  Emotional and mental characteristics

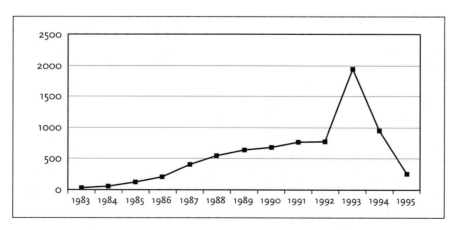

Figure 2.1    **AIDS Cases Diagnosed in Ohio by Year, 1983–1995**

*Source:* Reprinted from *Prevention Monthly,* Vol. 19, No. 3, p. 6, 1996, Ohio Department of Health.

newly diagnosed acquired immune deficiency syndrome (AIDS) cases steadily increased from 1983 to 1992, then a rather dramatic increase occurred in 1993, which was then followed by a return to previous levels in 1994 and 1995. What happened in 1993 that resulted in such a large increase in the number of newly diagnosed AIDS cases?

This is an example of how the time variable can affect the number of cases diagnosed. In 1993, the case definition of AIDS changed so that individuals who tested positive for the human immunodeficiency virus (HIV) were designated as having full-blown AIDS at an earlier point in the progression of their disease. In 1993, the case definition was expanded to include HIV-positive cases with low CD4 counts, pulmonary tuberculosis, and recurrent pneumonia as AIDS qualifying conditions. The result was that a large number of HIV-positive individuals who already had one of these conditions suddenly qualified as AIDS cases.

Now let us return to our discussion of the crude death rate. Crude rates do not allow for valid comparisons across populations because of differences in the populations, primarily age. This is because age is the most important variable that influences mortality. To illustrate, consider two hypothetical crude mortality rates for the states of Arizona (10.9 per 1000) and Alaska (4.4 per 1000). The conclusion drawn from a comparison of the crude mortality rates is that the death rate is 148% higher in Arizona than in Alaska: (10.9 − 4.4)/4.4 × 100 = 148%. However, the discrepancy is due largely to the age differences in the populations of Arizona and Alaska. In general, the population in Arizona is older than the population in Alaska. Without adjusting the rate, one might erroneously conclude that the Alaskan population was healthier than the population of Arizona. In this example, the comparison is confounded by age. **Confounding variable** is a general term used to describe the effect of a third variable on the estimate of risk of a health outcome.

Confounding occurs when a variable related to outcome is differentially distributed across the levels (or categories) of a variable of interest. When this happens, we must take measures to separate the effect of the confounding variable—in this case, age—from the effect of the variable of interest. We may accomplish this by selecting subjects to be compared so that they are matched with respect to the confounding variables or by using statistical adjustments during analysis to remove the effect of the confounding variable.

For example, review the data in Table 2.1. An analysis of the data reveals that the overall crude death rate is less for blacks than for whites, but that the age-specific death rate for blacks is higher than the rates for whites in almost every age group. Why is there such a contradiction? It is because the 2003 population of the state of Maryland consisted of old whites and young blacks—32.0% of the white population was 24 years old or younger, and 39.5% of the black population was 24 years old or younger (Table 2.2).

Table 2.1  **Age-Specific Death Rates per 1,000 Population, State of Maryland, 2003**

| Race | Crude Rate | < 1 Yr. | 1–4 Yrs. | 5–14 Yrs. | 15–24 Yrs | 25–44 Yrs. | 45–64 Yrs. | ≤ 65 Yrs. |
|---|---|---|---|---|---|---|---|---|
| White | 8.9 | 5.4 | 0.2 | 0.13 | 0.76 | 1.38 | 5.38 | 51.29 |
| Black | 7.3 | 13.8 | 0.4 | 0.23 | 1.60 | 2.82 | 9.62 | 50.27 |

*Source:* United States Department of Health and Human Services, Centers for Disease Control and Prevention (CDC), CDC On-Line Database, wonder.cdc.gov.

## Age-Specific Death Rates

In Table 2.1, we see the age-specific death rates (ASDR) for both whites and blacks. The ASDR is calculated as follows:

$$\frac{\text{Number of deaths in the age group of interest} \times 10^n}{\text{Estimated mid-period population in the age group of interest}}$$

## Age-Adjusted Death Rates

**Age-adjusted death rates** are used when there are differences in the age distribution for the populations that are being compared. In Table 2.2, you can see that the population proportions for each age group vary slightly by race. For example, the proportion of whites that are older than age 65 is 0.134 (13.4%) and the proportion of blacks that are older than 65 is 0.076 (7.6%). When we adjust the crude rate for age, we are constructing a summary rate that is free of age bias. In Table 2.2, the ASDR for each age group is expressed as a percentage. There are two methods for adjusting the crude death rate—direct and indirect. We will first discuss the direct method of standardization.

## Direct Standardization

To age-adjust the crude death rates, we compare the two groups being studied to a standard population. We then apply the ASDRs for each group to this standard population. As an example, we will use the data in Table 2.2 to standardize the crude death rates for whites and blacks in the state of Maryland. The crude death rate for whites is 0.89 per 100, and the crude death rate for blacks is 0.73 per 100. To calculate the standardized rate, we first calculate the ASDR for each age group in the two populations, and we then combine the populations for each age group. By multiplying the ASDR for each group by the combined population, we can obtain the expected number of deaths for each group as if the population for each age group were the same. For example, for the age group from 1 to 4 years, we add

Table 2.2 **Calculation of Crude Death Rate, State of Maryland, 2003**

| Age | (a) White Population | (b) Pop. Prop. | (c) Deaths | (d) ASDR (c/a) ×100 | (e) Black Population | (f) Pop. Prop. | (g) Deaths | (h) ASDR (g/f) ×100 |
|---|---|---|---|---|---|---|---|---|
| < 1 | 45,000 | 0.012 | 242 | 0.54% | 26,125 | 0.016 | 361 | 1.38% |
| 1–4 | 176,090 | 0.049 | 36 | 0.02% | 100,987 | 0.062 | 42 | 0.04% |
| 5–14 | 474,420 | 0.132 | 63 | 0.01% | 268,198 | 0.166 | 63 | 0.02% |
| 15–24 | 458,120 | 0.127 | 350 | 0.08% | 244,879 | 0.151 | 391 | 0.16% |
| 25–44 | 1,025,527 | 0.284 | 1,414 | 0.14% | 502,154 | 0.310 | 1,417 | 0.28% |
| 45–64 | 945,500 | 0.262 | 5,090 | 0.54% | 354,558 | 0.219 | 3,412 | 0.96% |
| 65+ | 483,006 | 0.134 | 24,776 | 5.13% | 122,785 | 0.076 | 6,173 | 5.03% |
| Total | 3,607,663 | 1.000 | 31,971 | 0.89% | 1,619,686 | 1.000 | 11,869 | 0.73% |
| | Crude Death Rate = 0.89/100 | | | | Crude Death Rate = 0.73/100 | | | |

*Source:* United States Department of Health and Human Services, Centers for Disease Control and Prevention (CDC), CDC On-Line Database, wonder.cdc.gov.

176,090 and 100,987 to obtain a total of 277,077. We then multiply the combined population total for each age group by the ASDR to obtain the expected number of deaths for each age group in each of the populations being compared. Thus, the groups are compared on an equal basis. The expected death rate for each population is calculated as follows:

| Group | Age Group | Total Population | ASDR | Expected Number of Deaths |
|---|---|---|---|---|
| White | 1–4 | 277,077 | 0.0002 | 55.42 |
| Black | 1–4 | 277,077 | 0.0004 | 110.83 |

After we have calculated the expected number of deaths for each age group in each population, we sum the expected number of deaths in each population group, as in Table 2.3. For whites, the total number of expected deaths is 41,254.26; for blacks, the total is 49,672.69. The expected number of deaths for each population group is then divided by the combined population. The result is that the standardized age-adjusted death rate for blacks is slightly higher (0.95%) than that for whites (0.79%).

Even though the standardized adjusted rate is not "real," it allows researchers to make better comparisons between groups. The crude death rates indicate that the mortality rate is slightly higher for whites than for blacks, but the adjusted rates indicate that mortality among blacks is 0.16% higher than that for whites. Without adjustment, we would make the assumption that mortality was slightly higher

Table 2.3    **Calculation of Adjusted Death Rate, Direct Standardization, State of Maryland, 2003**

| Age | (a) Total Population | (b) ASDR Whites | (c) Expected No. Deaths (a × b) | (d) ASDR Blacks | (e) Expected No. Deaths (a × d) |
|---|---|---|---|---|---|
| < 1 | 71,125 | 0.54% | 382.49 | 1.38% | 982.82 |
| 1–4 | 277,077 | 0.02% | 56.65 | 0.04% | 115.23 |
| 5–14 | 742,618 | 0.01% | 98.62 | 0.02% | 174.44 |
| 15–24 | 702,999 | 0.08% | 537.09 | 0.16% | 1,122.48 |
| 25–44 | 1,527,681 | 0.14% | 2,106.37 | 0.28% | 4,310.88 |
| 45–64 | 1,300,058 | 0.54% | 6,998.73 | 0.96% | 12,510.78 |
| 65+ | 605,791 | 5.13% | 31,074.31 | 5.03% | 30,456.06 |
| Total | 5,227,349 | | 41,254.26 | | 49,672.69 |

Standardized
Age-Adjusted Rate = 0.79%
(41,254.26 × 100)/5,227,349

Standardized
Age-Adjusted Rate = 0.95%
(49,672.69 × 100)/5,227,349

*Source:* United States Department of Health and Human Services, Centers for Disease Control and Prevention (CDC), CDC On-Line Database, wonder.cdc.gov.

in the white population. An adjusted rate informs us that this may not necessarily be the case.

## Indirect Standardization

The indirect method of standardization is used when the ASDRs are not available or when the population that we wish to compare is small, as when we are comparing hospital inpatients to much larger populations. When using this method, we use standard rates obtained from some population and apply them to our population of interest. The basic steps for indirect standardization appear in Exhibit 2.2. In our hypothetical example, we compare total Utah hospital discharges from 2005 that resulted in death due to pneumonia to the number of hospital discharges that resulted in death due to pneumonia in Salt Lake County, Utah.

In our calculations in Table 2.4, we see that the overall mortality rate due to pneumonia in the state of Utah is 3.41% and that the mortality rate in Salt Lake County is (56/1895) × 100 = 2.96%. Salt Lake County had 7.99 fewer deaths than what was expected on the basis of the standard rates for the state of Utah; therefore, the expected mortality rate is (63.99/1895) × 100 = 3.38%. To make the comparison to the standard rates, we calculate a **standard mortality ratio (SMR)**. The SMR compares the actual number of deaths in the group under study (Salt

---

Exhibit 2.2    **Basic Steps for Indirect Standardization**

1. Determine the standard mortality rates for pneumonia in the state of Utah for the age groups of interest.
2. Multiply the ASDR for the state of Utah (column c from Table 2.4) times the number of county discharges in each age category to obtain the expected number of deaths for each category in Salt Lake County, Utah (columns $c \times d$ = column f from Table 2.4).
3. Sum the number of expected deaths.
4. Compare the standard mortality ratio (SMR), which compares the number of actual or observed deaths to the number of expected deaths. In Table 2.4, the number of actual or observed deaths is 56, and the number of expected deaths is 63.99.
5. Multiply the SMR by 100. The SMR is interpreted as a percentage lesser or greater than that of the standard population.

---

Lake County) to the expected number of deaths based on the standard population rates that were applied to the study group. For the data in Table 2.4, the SMR is calculated as

$$\text{SMR} = \frac{\text{Observed death rate}}{\text{Expected death rate}} = \frac{0.0296}{0.0338} = 0.8757$$

$$0.8757 \times 100 = 87.57\%$$

If the calculated SMR is equal to 100%, the number of observed deaths is the same as the number of expected deaths. If the SMR is greater than 100%, the number of observed deaths is greater than the number of expected deaths. The interpretation of the SMR is that Salt Lake County's pneumonia death rate is approximately 12% less than that for the whole state of Utah. Stated another way, the death rate is 12% less than what would be expected on the basis of the mortality rates due to pneumonia for the entire state of Utah.

In summary, rates should be adjusted to remove the effect of the confounding variable for which the adjustment has been made—in this case, age. However, it is always necessary to calculate the crude death rate because this represents the actual event. An adjusted death rate is used for comparative purposes; adjusted rates do not reveal the underlying raw data that are shown by the crude rates.

## Race- and Gender-Specific Death Rates

Mortality rates may be calculated for any variable of interest, such as race or gender, using the same basic formula specified for calculating the crude death rate.

Table 2.4   **Mortality Rates Due to Pneumonia (ICD-9-CM Codes 480–486) 2005, Ages 35+, State of Utah vs. Salt Lake County, Utah**

| | State of Utah | | | Salt Lake County, Utah | | |
|---|---|---|---|---|---|---|
| Age | **(a)** Utah Discharges | **(b)** No. Deaths | **(c)** ASDR (b × 100)/a | **(d)** County Discharges | **(e)** Observed Deaths | **(f)** Expected Deaths (c × d) |
| 35–44 | 342 | 5 | 1.46% | 122 | 0 | 1.78 |
| 45–54 | 603 | 11 | 1.82% | 239 | 5 | 4.35 |
| 55–64 | 798 | 17 | 2.13% | 290 | 3 | 6.18 |
| 65–74 | 1,161 | 29 | 2.50% | 357 | 11 | 8.93 |
| 75+ | 2,636 | 127 | 4.82% | 887 | 37 | 42.75 |
| Total | 5,540 | 189 | 3.41% | 1,895 | 56 | 63.99 |

Observed Death Rate    2.96%

Expected Death Rate    3.38%

$$\text{SMR} = \frac{0.0296}{0.0338} = 0.8757$$

*Source:* Utah Inpatient Hospital Discharge Data, Public Data www.health.state.ut.us.

Historically, in the United States men have had higher mortality rates than women, but the gap may be narrowing. In 1995, the U.S. gender-specific rate was 9.2 per 1000 for men and 8.6 per 1000 for women. However, in 2003 the unadjusted gender-specific death rate for both women and men was 8.4 per 1000 (Table 2.5).

It would be misleading to review the **gender-specific death rates** without review of the individual age-specific rates. Table 2.5 indicates that the death rate for men is higher for every age group. If we want to determine why the death rate of men is higher than that for women, we can compare causes of death by gender and age group. For example, in the combined age groups from 15 to 44 years, the death rate for men is higher than that for women because accidental death is the leading cause of death for men in these age groups. Gender-specific diseases may account for the differences in the death rates for other age groups, such as prostate cancer in men and breast cancer in women. Calculating the age-specific rates and gender-specific rates can help us better understand what is taking place in the health care environment.

## Cause-Specific Death Rates

The **cause-specific death rate** is the death rate due to a specified cause. It may be stated for an entire population or for any age, gender, or race. The numerator is the number of deaths due to a specified cause and the denominator is the size of

Table 2.5    **Gender-Specific Death Rates, United States, 2003**

| Age | Women | | | Men | | |
| --- | --- | --- | --- | --- | --- | --- |
| | Population | Deaths | Rate/ 1,000 | Population | Deaths | Rate/ 1,000 |
| <1 | 1,958,070 | 12,123 | 6.2 | 2,045,536 | 15,902 | 7.8 |
| 1–4 Years | 7,705,794 | 2,139 | 0.3 | 8,059,879 | 2,826 | 0.4 |
| 5–9 years | 9,655,369 | 1,258 | 0.1 | 10,119,907 | 1,640 | 0.2 |
| 10–14 years | 10,336,612 | 1,546 | 0.1 | 10,856,749 | 2,510 | 0.2 |
| 15–19 years | 9,959,789 | 3,889 | 0.4 | 10,518,680 | 9,706 | 0.9 |
| 20–24 years | 10,063,772 | 5,009 | 0.5 | 10,663,922 | 14,964 | 1.4 |
| 25–34 Years | 19,650,112 | 12,698 | 0.6 | 20,222,486 | 28,602 | 1.4 |
| 35–44 Years | 22,236,935 | 33,026 | 1.5 | 22,133,659 | 56,435 | 2.5 |
| 45–54 Years | 20,760,943 | 66,099 | 3.2 | 20,043,656 | 110,682 | 5.5 |
| 55–64 years | 14,475,412 | 106,058 | 7.3 | 13,424,324 | 156,461 | 11.7 |
| 65–74 Years | 9,987,683 | 182,076 | 18.2 | 8,349,361 | 231,421 | 27.7 |
| 75–84 years | 7,714,465 | 360,692 | 46.8 | 5,154,207 | 342,332 | 66.4 |
| 85+ years | 3,268,543 | 459,640 | 140.6 | 1,444,924 | 228,212 | 157.9 |
| Total | 147,773,499 | 1,246,253 | 8.4 | 143,037,290 | 1,201,693 | 8.4 |

*Source:* Data from Centers for Disease Control, CDC Wonder Data Base, http://wonder.cdc.gov.

the population at midyear. It is usually expressed in terms of a rate per 100,000 ($10^n = 10^5 = 100,000$). The formula is

$$\frac{\text{Deaths assigned to a specified cause during a given interval} \times 100,000}{\text{Estimated mid-interval population}}$$

Table 2.6 presents the cause-specific death rates for men and women. The cause-specific death rate for pneumonia in the population aged 45 or older is 63.0 per 100,000 for women and 56.8 per 100,000 for men. Whereas the overall cause-specific death rate for women is higher than for men, the cause-specific rates for each age group are consistently higher for men than for women. In reviewing the rates in Table 2.6, we can also see that the death rate increases with age for both men and women.

## Case Fatality Rate

The **case fatality rate**, or killing power of a disease, measures the probability of death among the diagnosed cases of a disease. It is most often used as a measure in acute infectious disease: the higher the ratio, the more virulent the infection.

Table 2.6    **Cause-Specific Mortality Rates, by Gender, Due to Influenza and Pneumonia (ICD-10 Codes J10–J18.9), Age 45+, United States, 2003**

| Age | Women | | | Men | | |
|---|---|---|---|---|---|---|
| | Population | Deaths | Rate/1,000 | Population | Deaths | Rate/1,000 |
| 45–54 | 20,760,943 | 861 | 4.1 | 20,043,656 | 1,279 | 6.4 |
| 55–64 | 14,475,412 | 1,359 | 9.4 | 13,424,324 | 1,771 | 13.2 |
| 65–74 | 9,987,683 | 2,949 | 29.5 | 8,349,361 | 3,882 | 46.5 |
| 75–84 | 7,714,465 | 9,813 | 127.2 | 5,154,207 | 9,629 | 186.8 |
| 85+ | 3,268,543 | 20,447 | 625.6 | 1,444,924 | 10,950 | 757.8 |
| Total | 56,207,046 | 35,429 | 63.0 | 48,416,472 | 27,511 | 56.8 |

*Source:* Data from Centers for Disease Control, CDC Wonder Data Base, http://wonder.cdc.gov.

The case fatality rate is not useful in chronic disease because such diseases have a longer and more variable course.

The formula for the case fatality rate is

$$\frac{\text{Number of deaths due to a disease during a given time interval} \times 100}{\text{Number of cases of the disease in the same time interval}}$$

## Proportionate Mortality Ratio

The **proportionate mortality ratio (PMR)** describes the proportion of all deaths for a given time interval that are due to a specific cause. Each cause is expressed as a percentage of all deaths, and the sum of all the causes is 1 (100%). The PMR is not a mortality rate because the denominator is all deaths, not the population in which the deaths occurred. Its formula is

$$\frac{\text{Number of deaths due to a disease during a given time interval} \times 100}{\text{Number of deaths from all causes in the same time interval}}$$

The PMR is often used to make comparisons between and within age groups and occupational groups, as well as for the general population. The PMR for pneumonia appears in Table 2.7.

## Maternal Mortality Rate

The **maternal mortality rate** measures deaths associated with pregnancy. Pregnancy often places a woman at risk for medical problems that would not usually be encountered in the nonpregnant state, such as hemorrhage or toxemia of pregnancy.

Table 2.7  **Proportionate Mortality Ratios for Influenza and Pneumonia (ICD-10 Codes J10–J18.9), United States, 2003**

| Age Group | Influenza and Pneumonia Deaths | Total Deaths | PMR/100 |
|---|---|---|---|
| <1 year | 322 | 28,025 | 1.15 |
| 1–4 years | 163 | 4,965 | 3.28 |
| 5–9 years | 75 | 2,898 | 2.59 |
| 10–14 years | 72 | 4,056 | 1.78 |
| 15–19 years | 80 | 13,595 | 0.59 |
| 20–24 years | 144 | 19,973 | 0.72 |
| 25–34 years | 373 | 41,300 | 0.90 |
| 35–44 years | 992 | 89,461 | 1.11 |
| 45–54 years | 2,140 | 176,781 | 1.21 |
| 55–64 years | 3,130 | 262,519 | 1.19 |
| 65–74 years | 6,831 | 413,497 | 1.65 |
| 75–84 years | 19,442 | 703,024 | 2.77 |
| 85+ years | 31,397 | 687,852 | 4.56 |
| Total | 65,161 | 2,447,946 | 2.66 |

*Source:* Data from Centers for Disease Control, CDC Wonder Data Base, http://wonder.cdc.gov.

Pregnancy also complicates chronic conditions such as diabetes mellitus and heart disease. In some women, pregnancy precipitates gestational diabetes. The maternal mortality rate is calculated only for deaths that are related to pregnancy; thus, if a pregnant woman is killed in an automobile accident, the death is not considered a pregnancy-related death. The maternal mortality rate is calculated as

$$\frac{\text{Number of deaths assigned to causes related to pregnancy during a given time period}}{\text{Number of live births reported during the same period}}$$

Because the maternal mortality rate is usually very small, it is usually expressed as the number of deaths per 100,000 live births.

## Rates of Infant Mortality

There are three rates of infant mortality, all of which are based on age. Of the three, the infant mortality rate is the most commonly used measure for comparing the health status between nations. All three rates are expressed in terms of the number of deaths per 1000.

**NEONATAL MORTALITY RATE**   The neonatal period is defined as the period from birth up to but not including 28 days of age. The numerator is the number of deaths of infants under 28 days of age during a given time period, and the denominator is the total number of live births reported during the same period. The **neonatal mortality rate** may be used as an indirect measure of the quality of prenatal care or the mother's prenatal behavior (e.g., tobacco, alcohol, and drug use).

**POSTNEONATAL MORTALITY RATE**   The postneonatal period is the time period from 28 days of age up to but not including one year of age. The numerator is the number of deaths among children from age 28 days up to but not including one year of age during a given time period, and the denominator is the total number of live births reported less the number of neonatal deaths during the same period. The **postneonatal mortality rate** is often used as an indicator of the quality of the infant's home environment.

**INFANT MORTALITY RATE**   In effect, the **infant mortality rate** is a summary of the neonatal and postneonatal mortality rates. The numerator is the number of deaths among children under one year of age, and the denominator is the number of live births reported during the same period. Table 2.8 provides a summary of these rates.

## FREQUENTLY USED MEASURES OF MORBIDITY

Some commonly used measures to describe the presence of disease in a community or a specific location, such as a nursing home, are incidence and prevalence rates. Disease can be illness, injury, or disability, and measures can be further elaborated into specific measures of age, gender, race, or other characteristics of a particular population.

### Incidence Rate

The **incidence rate** is the most commonly used measure for comparing the frequency of disease in populations. Populations are compared using rates instead of raw numbers because rates adjust for differences in the size of the populations. The incidence rate expresses the probability or risk of illness in a population over a period of time. The formula for calculating the incidence rate is

$$\frac{\text{Total number of new cases of a specific disease during a given time interval} \times 10^n}{\text{Total population at risk during the same time interval}}$$

For the incidence rate, the denominator represents the population from which the case in the numerator arose, such as a nursing home, school, or company.

Table 2.8    **Frequently Used Mortality Measures**

| Measure | Numerator | Denominator | $10^n$ |
|---|---|---|---|
| Crude death rate | Total no. of deaths reported during given time interval | Estimated mid-interval population | 1,000 or 10,000 |
| Cause-specific death rate | Total no. of deaths due to a specific cause during a given time interval | Estimated mid-interval population | 100,000 |
| Proportionate mortality ratio | Total no. of deaths due to a specific cause during a given time interval | Total no. of deaths from all causes during the same time interval | 100 or 1,000 |
| Case fatality rate | Total no. of deaths assigned to a specific disease during a given time interval | Total no. of cases of the disease during the same time interval | 100 |
| Neonatal mortality rate | No. of deaths under 28 days of age during a given time interval | No. of live births during the same time interval | 1,000 |
| Postneonatal rate | No. of deaths from 28 days up to and not including one year of age, during a given time interval | No. of live births during the same time interval less neonatal deaths | 1,000 |
| Infant mortality rate | No. of deaths under one year of age during a given time interval | No. of live births during the same time interval | 1,000 |
| Maternal mortality rate | No. of deaths assigned to pregnancy-related causes during a given time interval | No. of live births during the same time interval | 100,000 |

For $10^n$, a value is selected so that the smallest rate calculated results in a whole number.

## Prevalence Rate

The **prevalence rate** is the proportion of persons in a population that have a particular disease at a specific point in time or over a specified period of time. The formula for calculating the prevalence rate is

$$\frac{\text{All new and pre-existing cases of a specific disease during a given time interval} \times 10^n}{\text{Total population during the same time period}}$$

Incidence and prevalence rates are often confused. The rates differ by which cases are included in the numerator. The numerator of the incidence rate is new cases occurring during a given time period; the numerator of the prevalence rate is all cases present during a given time period. In comparing the two, you can see that the incidence rate includes only individuals whose illness began during a specified period of time, whereas the prevalence rate includes all individuals ill from a specified cause, regardless of when the illness began. A case is counted in prevalence until the individual recovers. Exhibit 2.3 presents an example of incidence and prevalence rates in a nursing home.

At times we may be interested in tracking prevalence rates more closely—for example, tracking *Klebsiella pneumoniae* on a daily basis. We can do this by calculating the **point prevalence rate**. The point prevalence rate is the number of cases of a specific disease at a specific point in time. The point prevalence rate is narrower in its time frame than the general prevalence rate. Table 2.9 displays the point prevalence rates for each day during one week in January.

For a summary of morbidity measures, see Table 2.10.

## Exhibit 2.3  Calculation of Incidence and Prevalence Rates of *Klebsiella pneumoniae* at the Manor Nursing Home, Month of January

At Manor Nursing Home, 10 new cases of *Klebsiella pneumoniae* occurred in January. For the month of January there were a total of 17 cases of *Klebsiella pneumoniae*. The facility had 250 residents during January.

What are the incidence and prevalence rates for *Klebsiella pneumoniae* during January?

**Incidence Rate**

1. Identify the variable of interest (numerator) and population at risk (denominator).

   Numerator: Total number of new cases of *Klebsiella pneumoniae* in January

   Denominator: Total number of nursing home residents in January

2. Identify the numerator and denominator.

   Numerator: 10

   Denominator: 250

3. Set up the rate.

   $(10 \times 100)/250$

4. Divide the numerator by the denominator and multiply by 100 ($10^n = 10^2$)

   $(10 \times 100/250) = 4.0\%$

   The incidence rate for *Klebsiella pneumoniae* for the month of January is 4.0%.

(*continues*)

Exhibit 2.3   *Continued*

**Prevalence Rate**

1. Identify the variable of interest (numerator) and population at risk (denominator).

   Numerator: total number of cases of *Klebsiella pneumoniae* in January

   Denominator: total number of nursing home residents in January

2. Identify the numerator and denominator.

   Numerator: 17

   Denominator: 250

3. Set up the rate.

   $(17 \times 100)/250$

4. Divide the numerator by the denominator and multiply by 100 ($10^n = 10^2$).
   $(17 \times 100)/250 = 6.8\%$

   The prevalence rate for *Klebsiella pneumoniae* for the month of January is 6.8%

Table 2.9   **Point Prevalence Rates of *Klebsiella pneumoniae* for the Manor Nursing Home, Week of January 3**

|                      | Sun  | Mon  | Tues | Wed  | Thurs | Fri  | Sat  |
|----------------------|------|------|------|------|-------|------|------|
| No. of cases         | 10   | 12   | 14   | 13   | 15    | 16   | 16   |
| No. of residents     | 250  | 250  | 250  | 250  | 250   | 250  | 250  |
| Point prevalence rate| 4.0% | 4.8% | 5.6% | 5.2% | 6.0%  | 6.4% | 6.4% |

Table 2.10   **Frequently Used Measures of Morbidity**

| Rate | Numerator | Denominator |
|------|-----------|-------------|
| Incidence rate | Total no. of new cases of a specific disease during a given time interval | Total population at risk during the same time interval |
| Prevalence rate | All new and preexisting cases of a specific disease during a given time interval | Total population during the same time interval |

## National Notifiable Diseases Surveillance System

In 1878, Congress authorized the U.S. Marine Hospital Service to collect morbidity reports on cholera, smallpox, plague, and yellow fever from U.S. consuls overseas. This information was used to implement quarantine measures to prevent the spread of these diseases to the United States. In 1879, Congress provided for the weekly collection and publication of reports of these diseases. In 1893, Congress expanded the scope to include weekly reporting from states and municipalities. To provide for more uniformity in data collection, Congress enacted a law in 1902 that directed the Surgeon General to provide standard forms for the collection, compilation, and publication of reports at the national level. In 1912, the states and U.S. territories recommended that infectious disease be immediately reported by telegraph. By 1928, all states, the District of Columbia, Hawaii, and Puerto Rico were participating in the national reporting of 29 specified diseases. In 1961, the Centers for Disease Control and Prevention (CDC) assumed responsibility for the collection and publication of data concerning nationally notifiable diseases.

A notifiable disease is one for which regular, frequent, and timely information on individual cases is considered necessary to prevent and control the spread of this disease. The list of notifiable diseases varies over time and by state. The Council of State and Territorial Epidemiologists (CSTE) collaborate with the CDC to determine which diseases should be reported. State reporting to the CDC is voluntary; however, all states generally report the internationally quarantinable diseases in accordance with the World Health Organization's International Health Regulations. Completeness of reporting varies by state and type of disease and may be influenced by any of the following factors:

- The type and severity of the illness
- Whether treatment in a health care facility was sought
- The diagnosis of an illness
- The availability of diagnostic services
- The disease-control measures in effect
- The public's awareness of the disease
- The resources, priorities, and interests of state and local public health officials

Information that is reported includes date, county, age, gender, race/ethnicity, and disease-specific epidemiologic information; personal identifiers are not included. A strict CSTE Data Release Policy regulates the dissemination of the data. A list of nationally notifiable infectious diseases appears in Exhibit 2.4. The list is updated annually.

National morbidity data are reported weekly. Public health managers and providers use the reports to rapidly identify disease epidemics and to understand the patterns of disease occurrence. Case-specific information is included in the reports. Changes in age, gender, race/ethnicity, and geographical distributions can be monitored and investigated as necessary.

Exhibit 2.4 **Nationally Notifiable Infectious Diseases, United States, 2005**

Acquired immunodeficiency syndrome
  (AIDS)
Anthrax
Arboviral neuroinvasive and non-
  neuroinvasive diseases
  California serogroup virus disease
  Eastern equine encephalitis virus disease
  Powassan virus disease
  St. Louis encephalitis virus disease
  West Nile virus disease
  Western equine encephalitis virus disease
Botulism
Brucellosis
Charcroid
*Chlamydia trachomatis*, genital
Cholera
Coccidioidomycosis
Cryptosporidiosis
Cyclosporiasis
Diphtheria
Ehrlichiosis
Enterohemorrhagic *Escherichia coli*
Giardiasis
Gonorrhea
*Haemophilus influenzae*, invasive disease
Hansen disease
Hantavirus pulmonary syndrome
Hemolytic uremic syndrome,
  post-diarrheal
Hepatitis, viral, acute
  Hepatitis A, acute
  Hepatitis B, acute
  Hepatitis B virus, perinatal infection
  Hepatitis C, acute
Hepatitis, viral, chronic
  Chronic hepatitis B
  Hepatitis C virus infection (past or
  present)

HIV infection
Influenza-associated pediatric mortality
Legionellosis
Listeriosis
Lyme disease
Malaria
Measles
Meningococcal disease
Mumps
Pertussis
Plague
Poliomyelitis, paralytic
Psittacosis
Q fever
Rabies (animal and human)
Rocky Mountain spotted fever
Rubella
Rubella, congenital syndrome
Salmonellosis
Severe acute respiratory syndrome–
  associated Coronavirus (SARS-CoV)
  disease
Shigellosis
Smallpox
Streptococcal disease, invasive, Group A
Streptococcal toxic-shock syndrome
*Streptococcus pneumoniae*, drug resistant,
  invasive disease
*Streptococcus pneumoniae*, invasive in
  children < 5 years
Syphilis
  Syphilis, primary
  Syphilis, secondary
  Syphilis, latent
  Syphilis, late latent
  Syphilis, latent unknown duration
  Neurosyphilis
  Syphilis, late, non-neurological

| | |
|---|---|
| Syphilis, congenital | Vancomycin–intermediate *Staphylococcus* |
|   Syphilitic stillbirth |   *aureus* (VISA) |
| Tetanus | Vancomycin–resistant *Staphylococcus aureus* |
| Toxic-shock syndrome |   (VRSA) |
| Trichinellosis (Trichinosis) | Varicella (morbidity) |
| Tuberculosis | Varicella (deaths only) |
| Tularemia | Yellow fever |
| Typhoid fever | |

*Source:* Centers for Disease Control, Division of Public Health Surveillance and Informatics. Nationally Notifiable Infectious Disease, United States, 2005. Information from www.cdc.gov/epo/dphsi/infdis2005.htm.

## Public Health Statistics and Epidemiological Information

Vital statistics are collected and reported at community, regional, and national levels. The term **vital statistics** refers to the collection and analysis of data related to the crucial events in life: birth, death, marriage, divorce, fetal death, and induced terminations of pregnancy. These statistics are used to identify trends. For example, a higher-than-expected death rate among newborns may be an indication of the lack of prenatal services in a community. A number of deaths in a region due to the same cause may indicate an environmental problem.

These types of data are used as part of the effort to preserve and improve the health of a defined population—the public health. The study of factors that influence the health status of a population is called **epidemiology**.

## National Vital Statistics System

The National Vital Statistics System (NVSS) is responsible for maintaining the official vital statistics of the United States. These statistics are provided to the federal government by state-operated registration systems. The NVSS is housed in the National Center for Health Statistics (NCHS) of the CDC.

To facilitate data collection, standard forms and model procedures for the uniform registration of events are developed and recommended for state use through the cooperative activities of the individual states and the NCHS. The standard certificates represent the minimum basic data set necessary for the collection and publication of comparable national, state, and local vital statistics data. The standard forms are revised about every ten years, with the last revision completed in 2003. To effectively implement these new certificates, the NCHS is working with its state partners to improve the timeliness, quality, and sustainability of the vital statistics system, along with collection of the revised and new content of the 2003 certificates. These revisions can be viewed online at *http://www.cdc.gov/nchs/nvss.htm*.

The **certificate of live birth** (birth certificate) is used for registration purposes and is composed of two parts. The first part contains the information related to the child and the parents. The second part is used to collect data about the mother's pregnancy. This information is used for the collection of aggregate data only. No identification information appears on this portion of the certificate nor does it ever appear on the official certificate of birth. Pregnancy-related information includes complications of pregnancy, concurrent illnesses or conditions affecting pregnancy, and abnormal conditions or congenital anomalies of the newborn. Lifestyle factors, such as use of alcohol and tobacco, also are collected. Thus, the birth certificate is the major source of maternal and natality statistics. Contents of the U.S. certificate of live birth appear in Exhibit 2.5.

Data collected from death certificates are used to compile causes of death in the United States. The **certificate of death** contains decedent information, place of death information, medical certification, and disposition information. Data on causes of death are classified and coded using the International Classification of Diseases (ICD). Beginning in 1999, the United States implemented ICD-10 for the coding of causes of death. Examples of the content of death certificates appear in Exhibit 2.6.

A **report of fetal death** is completed when a pregnancy results in a stillbirth. This report contains information on the parents, the history of the pregnancy, and the cause of the fetal death. Information collected on the pregnancy is the same as that recorded on the birth certificate. To assess the effects of environmental exposures on the fetus, the parents' occupational data are collected. Data items related to the fetus include:

- The cause of fetal death, whether fetal or maternal
- Other significant conditions of the fetus or mother
- When the fetus died—before labor, during labor or delivery, or unknown
- Risk factors related to the pregnancy

The **report of induced termination of pregnancy** records information on the place of the induced termination of pregnancy, the type of termination procedure, and the patient (Exhibit 2.7.)

A tool for monitoring and exploring the interrelationships between infant death and risk factors at birth is the linked birth and infant death data set. This is a service provided by the NCHS. In this data set, the information from the death certificate (such as age and underlying or multiple causes of death) is linked to the information in the birth certificate (such as age, race, birth weight, prenatal care usage, maternal education, and so on) for each infant who dies in the United States, Puerto Rico, the Virgin Islands, and Guam. The purpose of the data set is to use the many additional variables available from the birth certificate to conduct a detailed analysis of infant mortality patterns.

Exhibit 2.5    **Content of US Certificate of Live Birth, 2003**

**Child's Information**
  Child's name
  Time of birth
  Sex
  Date of birth
  Facility (hospital) Name (if not an
    institution, give street address)
  City
  County

**Mother's Information**
  Current legal name
  Date of birth
  Mother's name prior to first marriage
  Birthplace
  Residence (state)
  County
  City
  Street Number
  Zip Code
  Inside city limits?
  Mother Married?
  If no, has paternity acknowledgment
    been signed in the hospital?'
  Social security number (SSN) requested
    for child?
  Mother's SSN
  Father's SSN
  Education
  Hispanic origin?
  Race

**Father**
  Current legal name
  Date of birth
  Birthplace
  Education
  Hispanic origin?
  Race

**Pregnancy History**
  Date of first prenatal care visit
  Date of last prenatal care visit
  Total number of prenatal visits for this
    pregnancy
  Number of previous live births
  Mother's height
  Mother's pregnancy weight
  Mother's weight at delivery
  Did mother get WIC food for herself
    during this pregnancy?
  Number of previous live births
  Number of other pregnancy outcomes
  Cigarette smoking before and during
    pregnancy
  Principal source of payment for this
    delivery
  Date of last live birth
  Date of last other pregnancy outcome
  Date last normal menses began
  Risk factors in this pregnancy
  Infections present and/or treated during
    this pregnancy
  Obstetric procedures
  Onset of labor
  Characteristics of labor and delivery
  Method of delivery
  Maternal mortality

**Newborn Information**
  Birthweight
  Obstetric estimate of gestation
  Apgar score (1 and 5 minutes)
  Plurality
  If not born first (born second, third,
    etc.)
  Abnormal conditions of newborn
  Congenital anomalies of the newborn

*(continues)*

Exhibit 2.5    *Continued*

Was infant transferred within 24 hours of
    delivery?
Is infant living at time of report?
Is infant being breastfed at discharge?

*Source:* U.S. Department of Health and Human Services. National Center for Health Statistics. National Vital Statistics
System. Information from www.cdc.gov/nchs/nvss.htm.

Exhibit 2.6    **Content of U.S. Certificate of Death, 2003**

**Decedent Information**
    Name
    Sex
    Social security number
    Age
    Date of birth
    Birthplace
    Residence (state)
    County
    City or town
    Street and number
    Zip code
    Inside city limit?
    Ever in U.S. armed forces?
    Marital status at time of death
    Surviving spouse's name (If wife, give
        name prior to first marriage)
    Father's name
    Mother's name (prior to first marriage)
    Decedent's education
    Hispanic origin?
    Race
    Informant's name
    Relationship to decedent
    Mailing address
**Disposition Information**
    Method of disposition
    Place of disposition (cemetery,
        crematory, other)
    Location
    Name and address of funeral facility

**Place of Death Information**
    Place of death
        If hospital, indicate inpatient,
            emergency room/outpatient, dead on
            arrival
        If somewhere other than hospital,
            indicate hospice, nursing home/long-
            term care facility, decedent's home,
            other
    Facility name
    City, state, zip code
    County
**Medical Certification**
    Date pronounced dead
    Time pronounced dead
    Signature of person pronouncing death
    Date signed
    Actual or presumed date of death
    Actual or presumed time of death
    Was medical examiner contacted?
    Immediate cause of death
        Due to _____
        Due to _____
        Due to _____
    Other significant conditions contributing
        to death
    Was an autopsy performed?
    Were autopsy findings available to
        complete the cause of death?
    Did tobacco use contribute to death?
    If female indicate pregnancy status

| | |
|---|---|
| Manner of death | Location of injury |
| For deaths due to injury: | Describe how injury occurred |
| Date of injury | If transportation injury, specify |
| Time of injury | if driver/operator, passenger, |
| Place of injury | pedestrian, other |
| Injury at work? | |

*Source:* U.S. Department of Health and Human Services. National Center for Health Statistics. National Vital Statistics System. Information from www.cdc.gov/nchs/nvss.htm.

Exhibit 2.7 **Content of U.S. Standard Report of Induced Termination of Pregnancy, 1997**

| | |
|---|---|
| **Place of Induced Termination** | Zip code |
| Facility name | Hispanic origin? |
| Address (city, town, state, county) | Race |
| **Patient Information** | Education |
| Patient Identification | Date last normal menses began |
| Age at last birthday | Clinical estimate of gestation |
| Marital status | Previous pregnancies |
| Date of pregnancy termination | Live births |
| Residence (city, town, state, county) | Other terminations |
| Inside city limits? | Type of termination procedure |

*Source:* U.S. Department of Health and Human Services. National Center for Health Statistics. National Vital Statistics System. Information from www.cdc.gov/nchs/nvss.htm.

Birth, death, fetal death, and termination of pregnancy certificates provide vital information for use in medical research, epidemiological studies, and other public health programs. In addition, they are the source of data for compiling morbidity, birth, and mortality rates that describe the health of a given population at the local, state, or national level. Because of their many uses, the data on these certificates must be complete and accurate.

## CONCLUSION

In this chapter, we have discussed rates, ratios, and proportions in the form of mortality and morbidity rates. Facility-based morbidity and mortality rates can be compared with community, state, or national rates after adjustment. We may adjust rates by either the direct or the indirect method. Crude rates are important for internal analysis or other noncomparative purposes.

## REFERENCES

Johns, M.L. (ed.) (2006) *Health Information Management Technology: An Applied Approach*, 2nd Edition. Chicago: American Health Information Management Association.

LaTour, Kathleen M., and S. Maki-Eichenwald. (eds.) (2006) *Health Information Management: Concepts, Principles, and Practice*, 2nd Edition. Chicago: American Health Information Management Association.

Ohio Department of Health. (1996) *Prevention Monthly* 19;3:6.

U.S. Department of Health and Human Services, Public Health Service. (1992) Principles of epidemiology: An introduction to applied epidemiology and biostatistics.

U.S. Department of Health and Human Services, Centers for Disease Control and Prevention (CDC), National Center for Health Statistics (NCHS), Office of Analysis, Epidemiology (OAE). (2006) Compressed Mortality File (CMF) compiled from CMF 1999–2003 Series 20, No. 2I 2006, on CDC WONDER online database. *http://wonder.cdc.gov*.

U.S. Department of Health and Human Services, Centers for Disease Control and Prevention (CDC), National Center for HIV, STD and TB Prevention, Division of HIV/AIDS Prevention. AIDS Public Information Data Sets, CDC WONDER online database. *http://wonder.cdc.gov*.

Utah Inpatient Hospital Discharge Data Set. *http://hlunix.hl.state.ut.us/hda*.

# APPENDIX 2-A

## EXERCISES FOR SOLVING PROBLEMS

### Knowledge Questions

1. Define the key terms listed at the beginning of this chapter.
2. Outline the procedure for age-adjusting crude mortality rates by the direct standardization method.
3. Describe the differences between the direct and indirect standardization methods of adjusting mortality and morbidity rates.
4. Describe the differences between neonatal mortality rate, post-neonatal mortality rate, and infant mortality rate.
5. Describe the difference between incidence and prevalence rates.

### Multiple Choice

1. Which of the following is a measure of the actual observed mortality in a community?
   a. Crude death rate
   b. Gender-specific death rate
   c. Cause-specific death rate
   d. Age-adjusted death rate

   For Questions 2 and 3, refer to the following table:

   | Age Group | Population | Number of Deaths |
   |---|---|---|
   | < 30 | 15,000 | 20 |
   | 30–65 | 17,000 | 55 |
   | > 65 | 6,000 | 155 |

2. What is the crude mortality rate?
   a. 230
   b. 6.1 per 1000
   c. 8.6 per 1000
   d. 6.1 per 10,000
3. The age-specific death rate for the over-65 age group is:
   a. 155
   b. 25.8 per 1000
   c. 1.55 per 10,000
   d. 25.8 per 10,000
4. The number of deaths under 28 days of age during a given time period is termed the:
   a. Infant morality rate
   b. Neonatal mortality rate
   c. Newborn mortality rate
   d. Postneonatal mortality rate
5. The total number of deaths due to a specific cause during a given time interval is termed the:
   a. Case fatality rate
   b. Cause-specific death rate
   c. Proportionate mortality rate
   d. Standard mortality ratio
6. Which entity creates model procedures for the preparation of vital records such as birth and death certificates?
   a. The registrar for each state
   b. National Centers for Health Statistics
   c. County departments of health
   d. Hospital departments of health information management

7. Which entity is responsible for the weekly collection and publication of notifiable diseases in the United States?
   a. Public Health Service
   b. Centers for Disease Control and Prevention
   c. National Centers for Health Statistics
   d. World Health Organization

8. A nursing home has 75 residents. During an influenza outbreak, the nursing home reports 25 new cases of influenza during the week of January 8th. What is the incidence rate?
   a. 0.03%
   b. 3.0%
   c. 33.3%
   d. Not enough information provided

9. Which of the following conditions would be the most likely to fall into the category of notifiable diseases as defined by the National Notifiable Diseases Surveillance System?
   a. Diabetes mellitus
   b. Coronary artery disease
   c. Fracture of major bones
   d. HIV infection

10. All new and pre-existing cases of a specific disease during a given time interval is termed the:
    a. Incidence rate
    b. Prevalence rate
    c. Community disease rate
    d. Point prevalence rate

## Problems

1. Review the hypothetical data on deaths in the MICU in Table 2-A.1 and answer the questions below.

   a. What is the ratio of male deaths to female deaths?
   b. What proportion of the patients who died were admitted from the Emergency Department? What proportion were transfers from other hospitals?
   c. The total number of patients discharged from DRG 475 was 61. What is the case fatality rate for DRG 475?
   d. The total number of patients discharged from DRG 483 was 51. What is the case fatality rate for DRG 483?

2. Review the data in Table 2-A.2 and answer the questions below.
   a. What is the case fatality rate for AIDS for the years 1981 through 1995?
   b. The midyear population for the state of Ohio in 1994 was 11,140,950. What is the incidence rate for AIDS for 1994?

3. Complete the columns in Table 2-A.3.
   a. Compute the age-specific death rates for whites and blacks.
   b. Compute the 2003 overall crude death rate for the state of California and the crude death rates for whites and blacks.
   c. Compute the 2003 age-adjusted death rates for whites and blacks in the state of California using the standardized method.
   d. Is there a difference between the age-adjusted mortality rates for whites and blacks? If so, explain the reason for the discrepancy.

**Table 2-A.1** **Critical Care Hospital, Deaths in the MICU by DRG**

| DRG | DRG Title | Adm Source | Gender | LOS |
|---|---|---|---|---|
| 001 | Craniotomy Age >17 W Cc | SNF | Male | 2 |
| 014 | Intracranial Hemorrhage & Stroke W Infarct | Other | Male | 3 |
| 014 | Intracranial Hemorrhage & Stroke W Infarct | Emerdept | Female | 3 |
| 020 | Nervous System Infection Except Viral Meningitis | Other | Female | 15 |
| 075 | Major Chest Procedures | Hospital | Male | 6 |
| 105 | Cardiac Valve & Oth Major Cardiothoracic Proc W/O Card Cath | Hospital | Female | 23 |
| 123 | Circulatory Disorders W AMI, Expired | Hospital | Male | 7 |
| 123 | Circulatory Disorders W AMI, Expired | Other | Male | 1 |
| 123 | Circulatory Disorders W AMI, Expired | Other | Male | 4 |
| 123 | Circulatory Disorders W AMI, Expired | Emerdept | Male | 5 |
| 172 | Digestive Malignancy W Cc | Emerdept | Male | 1 |
| 172 | Digestive Malignancy W Cc | Physician | Male | 1 |
| 188 | Other Digestive System Diagnoses Age >17 W Cc | SNF | Female | 1 |
| 191 | Pancreas, Liver & Shunt Procedures W Cc | Hospital | Male | 9 |
| 202 | Cirrhosis & Alcoholic Hepatitis | Physician | Female | 15 |
| 202 | Cirrhosis & Alcoholic Hepatitis | Other | Male | 1 |
| 202 | Cirrhosis & Alcoholic Hepatitis | Emerdept | Male | 24 |
| 205 | Disorders Of Liver Except Malig,Cirr,Alc Hepa W Cc | Physician | Male | 20 |
| 331 | Other Kidney & Urinary Tract Diagnoses Age >17 W Cc | Physician | Male | 44 |
| 357 | Uterine & Adnexa Proc For Ovarian Or Adnexal Malignancy | Physician | Female | 24 |
| 416 | Septicemia Age >17 | Hospital | Female | 4 |
| 416 | Septicemia Age >17 | Other | Male | 2 |
| 449 | Poisoning & Toxic Effects Of Drugs Age >17 W Cc | Other | Male | 1 |
| 473 | Acute Leukemia W/O Major O.R. Procedure Age >17 | Physician | Male | 5 |
| 475 | Respiratory System Diagnosis With Ventilator Support | Physician | Male | 25 |
| 475 | Respiratory System Diagnosis With Ventilator Support | Physician | Female | 1 |
| 475 | Respiratory System Diagnosis With Ventilator Support | Hospital | Female | 1 |
| 475 | Respiratory System Diagnosis With Ventilator Support | Other | Female | 1 |
| 475 | Respiratory System Diagnosis With Ventilator Support | Hospital | Female | 21 |
| 475 | Respiratory System Diagnosis With Ventilator Support | Other | Male | 5 |
| 475 | Respiratory System Diagnosis With Ventilator Support | Hospital | Female | 8 |
| 475 | Respiratory System Diagnosis With Ventilator Support | Emerdept | Female | 10 |
| 475 | Respiratory System Diagnosis With Ventilator Support | Clinic | Male | 13 |

(*continues*)

Table 2-A.1   *Continued*

| DRG | DRG Title | Adm Source | Gender | LOS |
|-----|-----------|------------|--------|-----|
| 475 | Respiratory System Diagnosis With Ventilator Support | SNF | Female | 1 |
| 475 | Respiratory System Diagnosis With Ventilator Support | Emerdept | Male | 5 |
| 475 | Respiratory System Diagnosis With Ventilator Support | Clinic | Female | 4 |
| 475 | Respiratory System Diagnosis With Ventilator Support | Emerdept | Male | 3 |
| 475 | Respiratory System Diagnosis With Ventilator Support | Other | Female | 12 |
| 475 | Respiratory System Diagnosis With Ventilator Support | Other | Female | 5 |
| 483 | Trac W Mech Vent 96+Hrs Or Pdx Except Face, Mouth & Neck Dx | Hospital | Female | 30 |
| 483 | Trac W Mech Vent 96+Hrs Or Pdx Except Face, Mouth & Neck Dx | Hospital | Male | 19 |
| 483 | Trac W Mech Vent 96+Hrs Or Pdx Except Face, Mouth & Neck Dx | Hospital | Male | 22 |
| 483 | Trac W Mech Vent 96+Hrs Or Pdx Except Face, Mouth & Neck Dx | Physician | Female | 46 |
| 483 | Trac W Mech Vent 96+Hrs Or Pdx Except Face, Mouth & Neck Dx | Other | Female | 28 |

Table 2-A.2   **AIDS Cases in Ohio 1981–1995**

| | | |
|------|------|-----|
| 1981 | 2 | 2 |
| 1982 | 7 | 7 |
| 1983 | 27 | 25 |
| 1984 | 58 | 56 |
| 1985 | 120 | 113 |
| 1986 | 211 | 198 |
| 1987 | 401 | 374 |
| 1988 | 540 | 482 |
| 1989 | 631 | 537 |
| 1990 | 682 | 577 |
| 1991 | 763 | 644 |
| 1992 | 775 | 587 |
| 1993 | 1935 | 908 |
| 1994 | 947 | 259 |
| 1995 | 259 | 63 |

*Source:* US DHHS, Public Health Service, CDC, National Center for HIV, STD, and TB Prevention, AIDS Public Information Data Set, CDC WONDER On-line Database, wonder.cdc.gov.

Table 2-A.3   **Age Specific Mortality Rates, State of California, 2003**

| Age | (a)<br>White<br>Pop | (b)<br>Deaths<br>per<br>1,000 | (c)<br>White<br>ASDR | (d)<br>Black<br>Pop | (e)<br>Deaths<br>per<br>1,000 | (f)<br>Black<br>ASDR | (g)<br>Comb Pop<br>Tot | (h)<br>Expected<br>No. of<br>Deaths,<br>Whites<br>(g × c) | (I)<br>Expected<br>No. of<br>Deaths,<br>Blacks<br>(g × f) |
|---|---|---|---|---|---|---|---|---|---|
| <1 | 429,511 | 2,130 | | 37,591 | 408 | | 467,102 | | |
| 1–4 | 1,627,070 | 439 | | 157,710 | 70 | | 1,784,780 | | |
| 5–9 | 2,046,063 | 282 | | 223,448 | 35 | | 2,269,511 | | |
| 10–14 | 2,157,618 | 373 | | 249,464 | 53 | | 2,407,082 | | |
| 15–19 | 1,958,101 | 1,201 | | 217,838 | 206 | | 2,175,939 | | |
| 20–24 | 1,984,041 | 1,640 | | 189,934 | 305 | | 2,173,975 | | |
| 25–34 | 4,059,559 | 3,398 | | 366,264 | 614 | | 4,425,823 | | |
| 35–44 | 4,301,525 | 7,415 | | 414,771 | 1,263 | | 4,716,296 | | |
| 45–54 | 3,723,683 | 14,523 | | 327,883 | 2,542 | | 4,051,566 | | |
| 55–64 | 2,462,805 | 20,348 | | 192,067 | 2,819 | | 2,654,872 | | |
| 65–74 | 1,535,605 | 31,716 | | 116,784 | 3,326 | | 1,652,389 | | |
| 75–84 | 1,127,540 | 58,993 | | 63,582 | 4,197 | | 1,191,122 | | |
| 85+ | 428,395 | 59,904 | | 22,337 | 3,047 | | 450,732 | | |
| Total | 27,841,516 | 202,362 | | 2,579,673 | 18,885 | | 30,421,189 | | |

*Source:* Data from Centers for Disease Control and Prevention, CDC Wonder Data Base, http://wonder.cdc.gov.

4. At Critical Care Hospital, the complication rate for hip replacement surgery is 8.96%. The relevant statistics appear in Table 2-A.4. The administrative staff at the hospital is concerned that the hospital complication rate does not compare favorably with the overall complication rate of all patients with hip replacement surgery in the county. The complication rate for the county is 5.5%. The county complication rate for patients age 65 or older is 8.0%; for those under age 65, the complication rate is 3.0%. Using the indirect method of standard-ization, calculate the complication rate for the hospital that has been adjusted for age.

5. The overall mortality rate for patients who have had a cerebrovascular accident (CVA) is 15.8%. You have been asked to compare the hospital's mortality rate to that of the state. Using the data provided in Table 2-A.5, calculate:
   a. the observed mortality rate
   b. the expected mortality rate
   c. the standard mortality ratio (SMR) for the hospital, using the indirect method of standardization

Explain the results.

Table 2-A.4  **Critical Care Hospital, Hip Replacement Surgery**

| Age Group | No. of Patients | No. of Patients with Complications | Complication Rate |
|-----------|-----------------|-------------------------------------|-------------------|
| ≥ 65 | 170 | 17 | 10.00% |
| < 65 | 42 | 2 | 4.76% |
| Total | 212 | 19 | 8.96% |

Table 2-A.5  **Mortality Rates for CVAs, State versus City General Hospital**

| Severity of Illness | State Mortality Rate | Hospital Discharges for CVA | Observed Deaths | Expected Deaths |
|---------------------|----------------------|-----------------------------|-----------------|-----------------|
| 1 | 4.2 | 55 | 2 | |
| 2 | 5.9 | 116 | 8 | |
| 3 | 7.8 | 195 | 20 | |
| 4 | 20.9 | 147 | 29 | |
| 5 | 34.6 | 62 | 32 | |
| | | 575 | 91 | |

## Online Activities

An important skill for the health information management professional is the ability to search online for information. This can be particularly useful when one is searching for comparative information. This activity is designed to provide experience working with an online interactive database and to provide experience analyzing and summarizing the results of data queries.

**THE HEALTHCARE COST AND UTILIZATION PROJECT (HCUP)**  The Healthcare Cost and Utilization Project (HCUP), a database supported by the Agency for Healthcare Research and Quality (AHRQ), can provide a wealth of information for benchmarking purposes. This interactive database allows researchers to identify, track, analyze, and compare hospital statistics at the regional, state, and national levels. Table 2-A.6 displays a sample report.

The website address for the HCUP database is *http://www.ahrq.gov/hcupnet*. Read the description of the information available at the website. Locate "Quick Statistics," which contains data from the National Inpatient Sample (NIS). Select "2003," then select "Overall Statistics for Hospital Stays."

Table 2-A.6  HCUP Query, Outcomes by Patient Characteristics for DRG 416, Septicemia, Age > 17, 2002

| Age Group | Total Number of Discharges | ALOS | Average Charges | In-Hospital Deaths | Routine Discharges | Short Term Hospital | Other Institution | Home Health Care | Against Medical Advice | Missing Discharge Status |
|---|---|---|---|---|---|---|---|---|---|---|
| Total | 299,479 | 7.3 | $25,996 | 55,657 (18.6%) | 107,531 (35.9%) | 9,442 (3.2%) | 93,435 (31.2%) | 30,650 (10.2%) | 1,658 (0.6%) | 849 (0.3%) |
| 18–44 | 26,210 | 6.9 | $26,610 | 2,019 (7.7%) | 15,731 (60.0%) | 1,282 (4.9%) | 3,341 (12.7%) | 2,961 (11.3%) | 802 (3.1%) | |
| 45–64 | 63,372 | 7.4 | $29,356 | 8,803 (13.9%) | 31,905 (50.3%) | 2,906 (4.6%) | 11,898 (18.8%) | 7,109 (11.2%) | 571 (0.9%) | |
| 65–84 | 148,087 | 7.5 | $26,322 | 28,334 (19.1%) | 48,879 (33.0%) | 4,413 (3.0%) | 50,139 (33.9%) | 15,502 (10.5%) | 220 (0.1%) | 460 (0.3%) |
| 85+ | 61,801 | 6.9 | $21,556 | 16,501 (26.7%) | 11,006 (17.8%) | 841 (1.4%) | 28,057 (45.4%) | 5,078 (8.2%) | * | 173 (0.3%) |

Source: Agency for Healthcare Research and Quality http://www.ahrq.gov/hcupnet.

1. What is the total number of inpatient discharges for 2003?
2. What are the mean charges for 2003?
3. What is the average length of stay for 2003?
4. What percentage of hospital inpatients died in 2003?
5. What age group had the greatest proportion of discharges for 2003?
6. What was the total national health bill for 2003?

# CHAPTER 3    GRAPHIC DISPLAY OF DATA

## KEY TERMS

Bar charts
  Grouped bar chart
  One-variable bar chart
  Stacked bar chart
  100% component bar chart
Bubble chart
Line graph
Pie chart
Scatter diagram

Stem-and-leaf plot
Tables
  Box head
  Cell
  Note
  Source
  Stub
  Table shell
Two-by-two contingency

## LEARNING OBJECTIVES

At the conclusion of this chapter, you should be able to:

1. Define key terms.

2. Determine which graphic technique is appropriate for the type of information to be conveyed.

3. Outline the essential components of tables.

4. Correctly prepare tables for one, two, three, or four variables.

5. Outline the principles for the construction of bar charts and pie charts.

6. Differentiate between one-variable bar charts, grouped bar charts, stacked bar charts, and 100% component bar charts.

7. Correctly prepare bar charts, pie charts, and bubble charts.

8. Correctly prepare line graphs, scatter diagrams, and stem-and-leaf plots.

The purpose of tables, charts, and graphs is to summarize and display data clearly and effectively. They are all means of summarizing quantities of information to the reader. Tables, charts, and graphs offer the opportunity to analyze data sets and to explore, understand, and present distributions, trends, and relationships in the data. The primary purpose of tables, charts, and graphs is to communicate information about the data to the user.

Whether the graphic technique used is a table, chart, or graph, it should:

- Display the data
- Allow the viewer to think about what the data convey
- Avoid distortion of the data
- Encourage the reader to make comparisons
- Reveal data at several levels, from a broad overview to the fine detail
- Serve a reasonably clear purpose: description, exploration, tabulation, or decoration
- Be closely related to the statistical and verbal descriptions of the data set

## CONSTRUCTION OF TABLES

A **table** is an orderly arrangement of values that groups data into rows and columns. Almost any type of quantitative information can be grouped into tables. For example, we can use tables to display frequencies for such vital statistics as morbidity rates or hospital admission and discharge data. Tables are useful for demonstrating patterns and other types of relationships. They also serve as a basis for more visual displays of data, such as graphs and charts, where some of the detail may be lost. Because tables generally do not capture the interest of the reader, they should be used sparingly.

A table should be self-explanatory, even if it is taken out of its original context. A table should convey all the information necessary for the reader to understand the data. Check the table to be sure that:

- It is a logical unit.
- It is self-explanatory. Ask yourself if the table can stand on its own if photo-copied and removed from its context.
- All sources are specified.
- Headings are specific and understandable for every column and row.
- Row and column totals are checked for accuracy.
- Cells are not left blank; enter "0" or "—" (em dash).
- Categories are mutually exclusive and exhaustive.

Consideration should also be given to the alignment of data in tables. Guidelines for aligning text include the following:

- Align text in a table to the left.
- Text that serves as a column label may be centered.
- Numeric values should be aligned to the right.
- If the numeric values contain decimals, they should be decimal aligned.

Exhibit 3.1    **Table Shell**

| TITLE **Box Head** | | Sex | | | | | |
|---|---|---|---|---|---|---|---|
| | | **Male** | | **Female** | | **Total** | |
| | **Age** | **No** | **%** | **No.** | **%** | **No.** | **%** |
| Stub | | Row Variable | | → → → → | | → → → → | |
| | | → → → → | | | | | |
| | <45 | | | Column Variable | | | |
| | 45–54 | | | ↓ | | | |
| | 55–64 | | | ↓ | | | |
| | 65–74 | | | ↓ | | | |
| | 75+ | | | ↓ | | | |

Note:

*Source:* Adapted from Self-Instructional Manual for Cancer Registries, Book 7: Statistics and Epidemiology for Cancer Registries, p. 23, U.S. Department of Health and Human Services, Public Health Service, National Institutes of Health, National Cancer Institute.

Some word-processing and statistical software programs have features that assist in the formatting of tables. The essential components of a table are outlined in Exhibit 3.2.

## Table Shells

Although data cannot be analyzed until they have been collected, it is useful to prepare a **table shell** that shows how the data will be organized and displayed. It also helps one work through the data collection process in advance to ensure that once the data have been collected, they can be analyzed in the manner desired. The basic shell for construction of tables appears in Exhibit 3.1. Table shells are tables that are complete except for the data.

## One-Variable Tables

The most basic table is a frequency distribution with just one variable. The first column shows the values or categories of the variable represented by the data, such as age or gender. The second column shows the number of persons or events

Exhibit 3.2    **Essential Components of Tables**

TITLE

The title should be as complete as possible and should clearly relate the content of the table. It should answer the following questions:

- What are the data? (e.g., counts, percentages)
- Who? (e.g., white females with breast cancer; black males with lung cancer)
- Where are the data from? (e.g., hospital, state, community)
- When? (e.g., year, month)

For example: Site distribution by Age and Sex of Cancer Patients upon First Admission to General Hospital

BOX HEAD

The box head contains the captions or column headings. The heading of each column should contain as few words as possible but should explain briefly exactly what the data in the column represent.

STUB

The row captions are known as the stub. Items in the stub should be grouped to facilitate interpretation of data. For example, group ages into five-year intervals.

CELL

The box formed by the intersection of a column and a row.

Optional Items:

NOTE

Anything in the table that cannot be understood by reader from the title, box head, or stub should be explained by notes. Notes contain numbers, preliminary or revised numbers, or explanations for any unusual numbers. Definitions, abbreviations, and/or qualifications for captions or cell names should be footnoted. A note usually applies to a specific cell(s) within the table, and a symbol, such as ** or #, may be used to key the cell to the note. If several notes are required, it is better to use small letters than to use symbols for numbers. Note numbers may be confused with the numbers within the table.

SOURCE

If data from a source outside your research are used, the exact reference to the source should be given. Indicating the source lends authenticity to the data and allows the reader to locate the original source if more information is needed.

*Source:* Adapted from Self-Instructional Manual for Cancer Registries, Book 7: Statistics and Epidemiology for Cancer Registries, p. 24, U.S. Department of Health and Human Services, Public Health Service, National Institutes of Health, National Cancer Institute.

Table 3.1 **XYZ Hospital Admissions by Gender, 20xx**

| Sex | Admissions | % |
| --- | --- | --- |
| Male | 30 | 60.0% |
| Female | 20 | 40.0% |
| Total | 50 | 100.0% |

that fall into each category. A third column may be added to show the percentage of persons or events in each category. Because of rounding, column totals for percentages often add up to 99.9% or 100.1%. Even when this occurs, the total given should be 100.0% with a footnote explaining that the difference is due to rounding. An example of a one-variable table is presented in Table 3.1, which displays some hypothetical admissions data. The variable is gender, which is divided into two mutually exclusive categories, male and female.

## Two- and Three-Variable Tables

We can use tables to display data that have more than one variable. Data can be tabulated to show counts by two or three variables, such as age and gender. A two-variable table that is cross-tabulated is usually called a **two-by-two contingency table**. In Table 3.2, "lung cancer patients" is classified on two variables, race and gender; race is the row variable and gender is the column variable. Contingency tables (which will be discussed in greater detail in Chapter 8) are often used in calculating measures of association such as chi square.

Table 3.3 and Table 3.4 are examples of data classified on three and four variables. Because tables classifying data on more than two variables can be quite confusing to the reader, they should be avoided if at all possible.

In a three-variable classification table, it sometimes becomes quite challenging to arrange the data in a readable format. A multidimensional relationship must be shown in a two-dimensional space. In Table 3.3, we have expanded the classification of the lung cancer data to include not only race/ethnicity and gender but also

Table 3.2 **XYZ Hospital, Lung Cancer Patients by Race and Gender, 20xx**

| Race | Sex | | Total |
| --- | --- | --- | --- |
| | Male | Female | |
| White | 316 | 204 | 520 |
| Black | 35 | 15 | 50 |
| Total | 351 | 219 | 570 |

Table 3.3    **Age-Adjusted Rates by Geographical Location, Race/Ethnicity, and Gender, Cancer of the Colon and Rectum, SEER Registries for 2000–2003, Age–Adjusted to the 2000 US Standard Population**

| Geographical Region | Race/Ethnicity | Gender | | Total |
| --- | --- | --- | --- | --- |
| | | Male | Female | |
| San Francisco/Oakland | White | 56.2 | 41.2 | 48.0 |
| | Black | 57.6 | 43.9 | 49.5 |
| | Asian or Pacific Islander | 50.6 | 38.0 | 43.5 |
| | Hispanic | 50.4 | 31.9 | 39.8 |
| | *Total* | *56.3* | *41.4* | *48.0* |
| Connecticut | White | 67.9 | 48.8 | 57.1 |
| | Black | 63.0 | 54.0 | 57.6 |
| | American Indian/ Alaskan Native | 5.6 | 16.4 | 12.8 |
| | Asian or Pacific Islander | 46.3 | 17.9 | 29.7 |
| | Hispanic | 65.1 | 45.1 | 53.5 |
| | *Total* | *67.8* | *49.4* | *57.3* |
| Detroit | White | 63.4 | 46.7 | 53.8 |
| | Black | 82.3 | 61.2 | 69.5 |
| | American Indian/ Alaskan Native | 41.7 | 13.0 | 26.7 |
| | Asian or Pacific Islander | 44.7 | 26.5 | 34.2 |
| | Hispanic | 47.1 | 28.7 | 37.6 |
| | *Total* | *66.9* | *49.5* | *56.8* |

*Source:* Surveillance, Epidemiology, and End Results (SEER) Program (*www.seer.cancer.gov*).

geographical region. The row categories are first divided by geographical region and then by race/ethnicity. In Table 3.4 (a three-variable table), types of cancer are first divided by primary site and then classified by race and gender.

## CHARTS AND GRAPHS

**Graphs** and **charts** of various types are the best means for presenting data for quick visualization of relationships. Graphs and charts emphasize the main points and analyze and clarify relationships between variables that might otherwise remain elusive.

Regardless of the type of graph or chart that is being prepared, several principles of construction should be followed. First, it is important to avoid any distortion of the data. To avoid distortion, the representation of numbers on the graph

Table 3.4    **Age-Adjusted Invasive Cancer Incidence Rates per 100,000, by Selected Primary Sites, Race, and Gender, 2002**

| Site | Whites | | | Blacks | | | All Races | | |
|------|--------|--------|-------|--------|--------|-------|--------|--------|-------|
| | Male | Female | Total | Male | Female | Total | Male | Female | Total |
| Colon | 42.5 | 33.2 | 37.2 | 51.9 | 41.2 | 45.3 | 43.3 | 34.1 | 38.0 |
| Liver | 7.0 | 2.6 | 4.6 | 10.9 | 3.6 | 6.8 | 7.9 | 2.8 | 5.2 |
| Pancreas | 12.1 | 9.2 | 10.5 | 15.1 | 12.9 | 13.9 | 12.3 | 9.5 | 10.8 |
| Lung & Bronchus | 85.6 | 54.9 | 67.9 | 105.7 | 50.3 | 72.3 | 86.4 | 53.7 | 67.5 |
| Melanoma of Skin | 22.8 | 15.2 | 18.3 | 0.9 | 0.9 | 0.9 | 20.9 | 13.6 | 16.6 |
| Kidney | 18.1 | 9.2 | 13.2 | 18.8 | 10.0 | 13.7 | 18.0 | 9.2 | 13.1 |
| *All Sites* | *536.8* | *408.9* | *460.8* | *615.1* | *377.5* | *471.0* | *545.5* | *405.0* | *462.2* |

*Source:* US Cancer Statistics Working Group. United States Cancer Statistics: 1999–2002 Incidence and Mortality Web-based report. Available at www.cdc.gov/cancer/cpcr/uscs.

should be directly proportional to the numerical quantities that are being represented on the graph. It is also important to consider proportion and scale. Graphs should accommodate the eye in that they should emphasize the horizontal; that is, graphs should be greater in length than they are in height. The "three-quarter high" rule is a useful guide: the height (*y*-axis) of the graph should be three-fourths the length (*x*-axis) of the graph. A longer horizontal axis helps to point out the causal variable in more detail. Other helpful hints in preparing graphs or charts include spelling out abbreviations in a note so that misunderstandings are avoided; using colors to help understand groupings that may appear in the graph; and using both upper- and lowercase letters in titles, as the use of all capital letters can be unfriendly to the eyes.

There are many types of charts. We will first discuss the construction of charts for variables that all into categories. Examples of variables that fall into categories are gender (male and female) and third-party payer (Medicare, Medicaid, Commercial, Managed Care, and so on).

## Bar Charts

**ONE-VARIABLE BAR CHART** We can use **bar charts** to display data for one or more variables. Bar charts are appropriate for displaying data that are categorical. The simplest bar chart is the **one-variable bar chart**, where each category of the variable is represented by a bar. In Figure 3.1, the bar represents one variable—the crude death rate for cancer of the trachea, bronchus, and lung—which is placed in categories by years, 1994 through 2003. There is one bar representing the crude

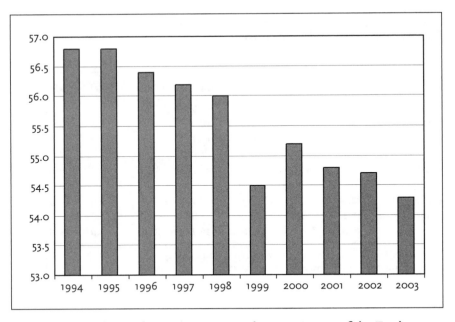

Figure 3.1    **Crude Death Rate per 100,000 by Year, Cancer of the Trachea, Bronchus, and Lung, ICD-9-CM Codes 162.0–162.9, 1994–1998; and ICD-10 Codes C34.0–C34.9, 1999–2003**

*Source:* CDC Wonder On-Line Database wonder.cdc.gov.

death rate for each of the ten years in the bar chart. Guidelines for construction of a bar chart are summarized in Exhibit 3.3.

The length or height of each bar is proportional to the number of persons or events in the category. The presentation of the information in this bar chart makes it easy to see at a glance that the crude death rate was the greatest in 1995, and then steadily declined until 1999. There was a slight increase in the crude death rate in 2000, and then began another steady decline until 2003.

Bar charts may be drawn either horizontally or vertically. Figure 3.2 presents the same information that appears in Figure 3.1 but in a horizontal format. Personal preference determines the format used.

Computer software makes it easy to present bar charts in either two-dimensional or three-dimensional form. When bars are presented in three-dimensional form, it is sometimes difficult for the reader to estimate the true height of the bar. In a three-dimensional bar chart, the back edges of the bar are higher than the front edge, as in Figure 3.3. To make sure that the reader correctly interprets the bar, label the data points at a point on the bars, as shown in Figure 3.3.

Exhibit 3.3   **Guidelines for Constructing a Bar Chart**

When constructing a bar chart, keep the following points in mind:

- Arrange the bar categories in a natural order, such as alphabetical order, order by increasing age, or an order that will produce increasing or decreasing bar lengths.
- The bars may be positioned vertically or horizontally.
- The bars should be of the same width.
- The length of the bars should be in proportion to the frequency of the event.
- Avoid using more than three bars (categories) within a group of bars.
- Leave a space between adjacent groups of bars but not between bars within a group.
- Code different variables by differences in bar color, shading, cross-hatching, etc. Include a legend that interprets your code.

*Source:* Adapted from Self-Instructional Manual for Cancer Registries, Book 7: Statistics and Epidemiology for Cancer Registries, p. 251, U.S. Department of Health and Human Services, Public Health Service, National Institutes of Health, National Cancer Institute.

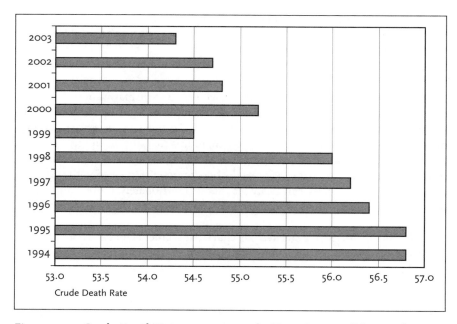

Figure 3.2   **Crude Death Rate per 100,000 by Year, Cancer of the Trachea, Bronchus, and Lung, ICD-9-CM Codes 162.0–162.9, 1994–1998; and ICD-10 Codes C34.0–C34.9, 1999–2003**

*Source:* CDC Wonder On-Line Database wonder.cdc.gov.

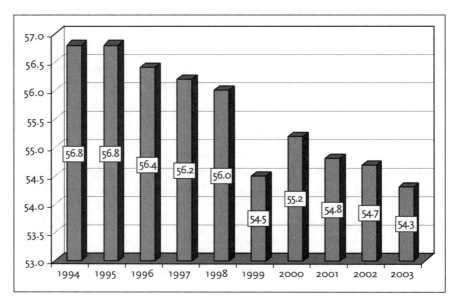

Figure 3.3 **Crude Death Rate per 100,000 by Year, Cancer of the Trachea, Bronchus, and Lung, ICD-9-CM Codes 162.0–162.9, 1994–1998; and ICD-10 Codes C34.0–C34.9, 1999–2003**

*Source:* CDC Wonder On-Line Database wonder.cdc.gov.

**GROUPED BAR CHARTS** A **grouped bar chart** is used to display information from tables containing two or three variables. An example of a grouped bar chart can be demonstrated by the variable "gender," which has two categories: male and female. Bars within a group are usually joined; in this case, the grouping is by year. The number of bars within a grouping should be limited to three. There must also be a legend to indicate what categories the bars represent. In viewing the grouped bar chart in Figure 3.4, we can easily see that proportionately, more women than men were admitted to the hospital for the years 2005 and 2006.

**STACKED BAR CHARTS** In a **stacked bar chart**, bar segments for each data category are stacked like building blocks on top of one another to form a single bar. In a stacked bar chart, the bar represents the total number of cases that occurred in a category; the segments of the bar represent the frequency of cases within the category. As an example, the data that appear in Table 3.4 are presented as a stacked bar chart in Figure 3.5. Each bar in the stacked bar chart represents the total number of cancer cases for a specific primary site. The bar segments represent the number of men and the number of women affected within the total number of cases.

Stacked bar charts should be used with caution because they are very difficult to interpret. These bar charts can be difficult to interpret because except for the

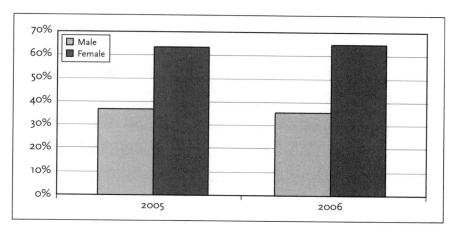

Figure 3.4   **Percentage of Hospital Admissions by Gender, 2005 and 2006**

bottom category, the categories do not rest on a flat baseline. What this means is that where one category of the variable ends, the next begins. Each category rides the bumps of those below it. From the stacked bar graph in Figure 3.5, it can be readily seen that incidence rates are higher for men than for women, but the exact number of cases for women in each category is difficult to determine. Stacked bar charts are deceptive, so they are often used to exaggerate or hide information.

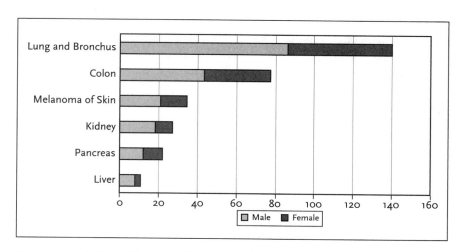

Figure 3.5   **Adjusted Invasive Cancer Incidence Rates per 100,000 by Gender, by Selected Primary Site, 2002**

*Source:* US Cancer Statistics Working Group. United States Cancer Statistics: 1999–2002 Incidence and Mortality Web-based Report. Available at www.cdc.gov/cancer/cpcr/uscs.

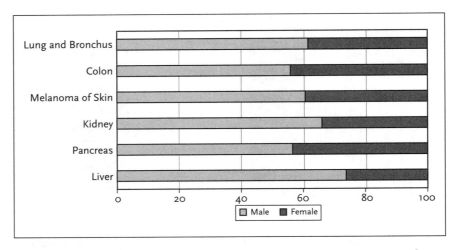

Figure 3.6 **Age Adjusted Invasive Cancer Incidence Rates per 100,000 by Gender, by Selected Primary Site, 2002**

**100% COMPONENT BAR CHARTS** The **100% component bar chart** is a variant of the stacked bar chart. In a 100% bar chart, all of the bars are of the same height and show the variable categories as percentages of the total rather than the actual values. Each bar is much like its own pie chart. A set of 100% bar charts can be used instead of multiple pie charts. This is more advantageous because it is easier to make comparisons between bars than between pies. Figure 3.6 presents the same information that appears in Figure 3.5. The stacked bars for each year represent 100% of the various types of cancer cases by gender. Each category of the gender variable is represented in terms of a percentage, in one bar.

## Pie Charts

A **pie chart** is an easily understood chart in which the sizes of the slices show the proportional contribution of each part of the pie. We can use pie charts to show the component parts of a single group or variable. To calculate the size of each slice of the pie, first determine the proportion of the pie to be represented by each slice. Multiply the proportion by 360—the total number of degrees in a circle. The result will be the size of each slice in degrees.

In the pie chart in Figure 3.7, one slice of the pie (acute myeloid leukemia) represents 34% of the cases, or 34% of the pie. Within the pie chart, this slice of the pie equals $360° \times 0.34 = 122.4°$. All other leukemia types represent 30% of the cases, and the size of its respective slice is $360° \times 0.30 = 108°$; one category of the pie (chronic lymphoid leukemia) represents 20% of the cases, which is equivalent to $360° \times 0.20 = 72°$. The remaining slices of the pie represent chronic myeloid

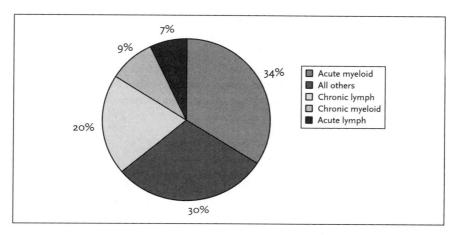

Figure 3.7    **Leukemia Cancer Deaths, by Type, 1997–2001, Ordering by Magnitude of Groupings**
*Source:* SEER Cancer Statistics Review, 1975–2001 National Cancer Institute.

leukemia, 9% and 32.4° of the pie, and acute lymphoid leukemia, 7% and 25.2° of the pie. The sum of the degrees for each slice of the pie is 122.4° + 108° + 72° + 32.4° + 25.2° = 360°.

The pie chart in Figure 3.7 demonstrates how the whole pie is divided into segments. By convention, the largest slices of the pie begin at 12 o'clock, as in Figure 3.7. The slices of the pie should be arranged in some logical order. In Figure 3.8,

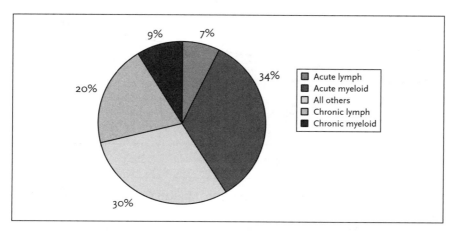

Figure 3.8    **Leukemia Cancer Deaths, by Type, 1997–2001, Alphabetical Order**
*Source:* SEER Cancer Statistics Review, 1975–2001 National Cancer Institute.

acute lymphoid leukemia appears in the 12 o'clock position. This is an example where pie slices are arranged in alphabetical order rather than according to descending magnitude.

It is not recommended to use pie charts to compare multiple distributions because they are not optimal for comparing components for more than one group. When components of more than one group are to be compared, a 100% component bar chart should be used.

## Line Graphs

A **line graph** is often used to display time trends and survival curves. The *x*-axis shows the unit of time from left to right, and the *y*-axis measures the values of the variable being plotted.

A line graph does not represent a frequency distribution. A line graph consists of a line connecting a series of points on an arithmetic scale. Like all graphs, it should be designed so that it is easy to read. The selection of proper scales, complete and accurate titles, and informative legends is important. If a graph is too long and narrow—either vertically or horizontally—it has an awkward appearance and might exaggerate one aspect of the data. The upward trend for median charges for septicemia patients in the United States is displayed Figure 3.9. The line graph is especially useful when there are a large number of values to be plot-

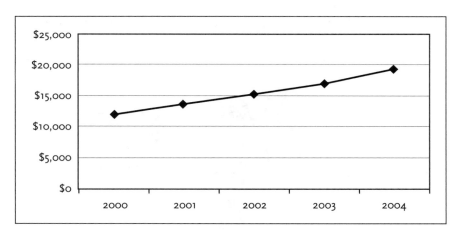

Figure 3.9    **DRG 416, Septicemia Age ≥ 17, Median Charges, United States, 2000–2004**

*Source:* H*CUPnet, Agency for Healthcare Research and Quality, United States Department of Health and Human Services. Available at http://hcupnet.ahrq.gov/HCUPnet.jsp.

ted, that is, when you have a continuous variable with an unlimited number of possible points. It also allows the presentation of several sets of data on one graph.

Either actual numbers or percentages may be used on the *y*-axis of the line graph. Use percentages on the *y*-axis when more than one distribution is to be shown on one graph. A percentage distribution allows comparisons between groups where the actual totals are different.

If more than one set of data is plotted on the same graph, different types of lines (solid or broken) should be used to distinguish between the lines. The number of lines should be kept to a minimum—a line graph can soon become too cluttered. Each line should be identified in a legend or on the graph itself.

There are two types of time-trend data: point data, which reflect an instant in time, and period data, which cover an average or total over a specified period of time, such as a one-year or five-year time frame. In point data, the scale marker on the *x*-axis indicates a particular point in time, such as one, two, or three years of survival. Alternatively, in the plotting of period data, the horizontal scale lines are used to indicate the interval limits and the values are plotted at the midpoint at each interval. For example:

| Year of Diagnosis | Midpoint of Interval |
|---|---|
| 1986–1988 | 1987 |
| 1989–1991 | 1990 |
| 1992–1994 | 1993 |
| 1995–2000 | 1997.5 |

Table 3.5 presents an example of point data that are graphed in Figure 3.10. Other examples are presented in Table 3.6 and Figure 3.11.

## Scatter Diagrams

A **scatter diagram**, or scatter plot, is a graphic technique used to display the relationship between two variables that fall on an arithmetic scale. One variable is plotted on the *x*-axis and the other is plotted on the *y*-axis. To create a scatter diagram, there must be a pair of values for every person, group, or other entity in the data set, one value for each variable. Each pair of values is plotted by placing a point on the graph where the two values intersect. To interpret a scatter diagram, analyze the overall pattern of the plotted points. Plotted points that appear to fall in a straight line indicate a linear relationship between *x* and *y*, whereas widely scattered points indicate no relationship between *x* and *y*. Table 3.7 presents hypothetical data of test scores and the grade point averages of ten students. Figure 3.12 is a scatter plot that depicts the relationship between the two variables, test scores (*x*) and grade point average (*y*).

Table 3.5 **Five-Year Survival Rates for Kidney and Renal Pelvis Cancer for Patients Diagnosed 1986–1988, 1989–1991, 1992–1994, 1995–2000**

| Year of Diagnosis | Midpoint of Interval | Race | | |
|---|---|---|---|---|
| | | Total | Whites | Blacks |
| 1986–1988 | 1987 | 57.0 | 57.6 | 53.6 |
| 1989–1991 | 1990 | 60.1 | 60.8 | 58.1 |
| 1992–1994 | 1993 | 62.5 | 63.1 | 60.0 |
| 1995–2000 | 1997.5 | 63.9 | 63.9 | 63.5 |

*Source:* SEER Cancer Statistics Review, 1975–2001. National Cancer Institute.

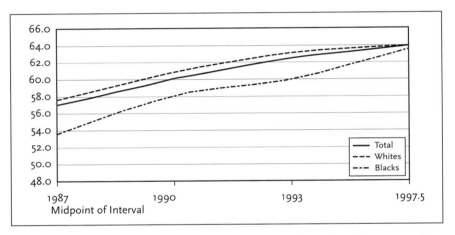

Figure 3.10 **Five Year Survival Rates for Kidney and Renal Pelvis Cancer for Patients Diagnosed 1986–1988, 1989–1991, 1992–1994, 1995–2000**
*Source:* SEER Cancer Statistics Review, 1975–2001 National Cancer Institute.

The scatter diagram in Figure 3.12 indicates a strong linear relationship between the variables test score and grade point average. Scatter diagrams are used to assist in the interpretation of inferential statistics, such as correlation and linear regression. We will discuss these topics in Chapter 7.

## Bubble Charts

**Bubble charts** are a type of scatter diagram with circular symbols used to compare three variables; the size of the symbol indicates the value of a third variable.

Table 3.6    **Survival Rates by Year of Diagnosis, Lung and Bronchus Cancer, 1994–1998**

| Years of Survival | 1994 | 1995 | 1996 | 1997 | 1998 |
|---|---|---|---|---|---|
| 1 | 41.0 | 41.6 | 41.2 | 41.7 | 41.3 |
| 2 | 24.6 | 25.5 | 25.5 | 25.4 | 25.9 |
| 3 | 19.2 | 19.6 | 19.9 | 19.9 | 20.3 |
| 4 | 16.4 | 17.1 | 16.9 | 17.2 | 17.5 |
| 5 | 14.9 | 15.2 | 15.4 | 15.5 | 15.3 |

*Source:* SEER Cancer Statistics Review, 1975–2003. National Cancer Institute.

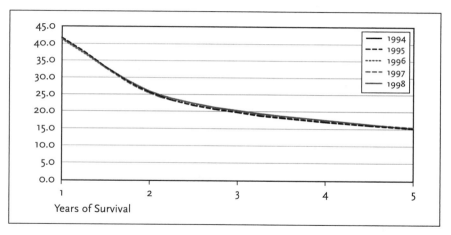

Figure 3.11    **Relative Survival Rates by Year of Diagnosis for Lung and Bronchus Cancer, 1994–1998**

*Source:* SEER Cancer Statistics Review, 1975–2003 National Cancer Institute.

In developing the chart, one variable is displayed on the vertical or *y*-axis, and two variables are displayed on the horizontal or *x*-axis.

As an example, an investigator is interested in displaying the average charges for the five highest volume DRGs in our organization. The number of discharges will be displayed on the *x*-axis and average charges will be displayed on the *y*-axis. The size of the bubble indicates the percentage of total discharges for each DRG. The data are displayed in Table 3.8 and the corresponding bubble chart is displayed in Figure 3.13. It can easily be seen that DRG 391, "Normal Newborn,"

Table 3.7 **Test Scores and Grade Point Averages of 10 Students**

| Student | Test Score (X) | GPA (Y) |
|---------|----------------|---------|
| 1 | 24 | 1.5 |
| 2 | 61 | 3.5 |
| 3 | 30 | 1.7 |
| 4 | 48 | 2.7 |
| 5 | 60 | 3.4 |
| 6 | 32 | 1.6 |
| 7 | 19 | 1.2 |
| 8 | 22 | 1.3 |
| 9 | 41 | 2.2 |
| 10 | 46 | 2.7 |

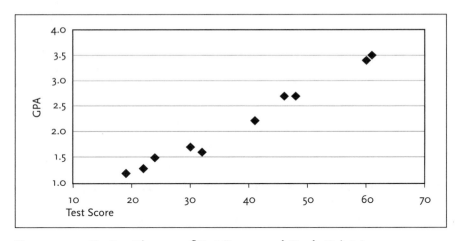

Figure 3.12 **Scatter Diagram of Test Scores and Grade Point Average**

has the highest proportion of overall discharges and the lowest average charges among the top volume DRGs.

## Stem-and-Leaf Plots

In a **stem-and-leaf plot** data can be organized so that the shape of a frequency distribution is revealed. As an example, a stem-and-leaf plot will be constructed

Table 3.8  **Top Five High Volume Discharges, Average Charges, and Percent of Total Discharges, Critical Care Hospital, 20xx**

| DRG | Number of Discharges | Average Charges | Percent of Total Discharges |
|---|---|---|---|
| 391 – Normal Newborn | 637 | $ 1,239 | 9.8% |
| 462 – Rehabilitation | 542 | $21,517 | 8.4% |
| 373 – Vaginal Delivery w/o CC | 505 | $ 5,576 | 7.8% |
| 127 – Heart Failure and Shock | 287 | $12,043 | 4.4% |
| 371 – Cesarean Section w/o CC | 189 | $ 7,626 | 2.9% |

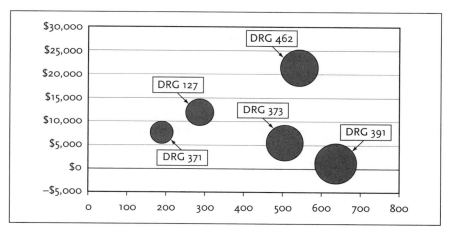

Figure 3.13  **Bubble Chart, Top Five High Volume Discharges, Average Charges, and Percent of Total Discharges, Critical Care Hospital, 20xx**

on the age of 12 patients discharged from DRG 15, "Nonspecific Cerebrovascular and Precerebral Occlusion without Infarction." The ages are ranked in order from highest to lowest:

44, 51, 52, 52, 62, 65, 65, 66, 68, 72, 76, 82

To develop the plot, break each number into two parts. The last number is called the "leaf" and the rest of the number is called the "stem." So for the number 51, 1 is the leaf and 5 is the stem, and for the number 125, 5 is the leaf and 12 is the stem. The data are then arranged in a table that looks somewhat like a "T," with the stem portion in the first column and the leaf portion in the second column.

For our data set, the stems are 4, 5, 6, 7, and 8. The leaf portion is then filled in with the last digits that correspond to each stem as shown:

| Stem | Leaf |
|------|-------|
| 4 | 4 |
| 5 | 122 |
| 6 | 25568 |
| 7 | 26 |
| 8 | 2 |

The completed plot reveals the distribution of the data set. It can immediately be seen that the lowest value in the distribution is 44 and the highest is 82, and there are five observations in the 60s age group. If we turn the table on its side, we can see that we have a fairly normal bell-shaped distribution.

## Electronic Spreadsheets

Electronic spreadsheets, such as Microsoft Excel, can be used to facilitate the data collection and analysis processes. The advantage of using one of these tools is that charts and graphs can be formulated at the time the data are being analyzed. Because instruction in the use of these tools is beyond the scope of this chapter, it is

|   |   |   | 8 |   |   |
|------|---|---|---|---|---|
| L |   |   | 8 |   |   |
| e |   |   | 6 |   |   |
| a |   | 2 |   |   |   |
| f |   | 2 | 5 | 6 |   |
|   | 4 | 1 | 2 | 2 | 2 |
| Stem | 4 | 5 | 6 | 7 | 8 |

strongly recommended that the reader become well versed in the use of available commercial software.

## Conclusion

Tables, charts, and graphs are effective methods of summarizing and displaying data in a clear, concise format. Tables are often used to display data, and they may be used to display data about one or more variables. An advantage of tables is that large amounts of data may be displayed and summarized, as in a four-way table. However, if too much information is included in a table, it can be confusing to the reader.

Bar charts or graphs are often used for displaying data that fall into categories such as gender and third-party payer. Bar charts allow for the quick visualization of the variable of interest. Relationships between two variables are also easily seen in a bar chart. Bar charts may take the form of a simple bar chart, a grouped bar chart, a stacked bar chart, or a 100% component bar chart. The form selected should be appropriate to the data and easily interpreted by the reader.

Pie charts are useful for displaying the parts of a whole. For example, we could display the proportion of patients admitted by third-party payer, or the proportion of burn patients admitted by severity of burn. Pie charts should be used to display proportions of a variable that has only one category; pie charts are not appropriate for comparing distributions of variables that have more than one category.

Line graphs are used to display trends in data. A line graph consists of a line connecting a series of points on an arithmetic scale. To avoid distortion in the data, the graph should not be too long or too narrow. When constructing bar graphs and line graphs, the "three-quarters-high" rule should be used as a guide to avoid data distortion. Either actual numbers or percentages may be displayed in a line graph.

Scatter diagrams are used to display the relationship between two variables that are arithmetic rather than categorical. One variable is plotted on the $x$-axis and the other on the $y$-axis. Bubble charts are similar to scatter diagrams but compare three variables rather than only two. Finally, stem-and-leaf plots are used to organize data so that the shape of a frequency distribution is revealed.

## REFERENCES

Agency for Healthcare Research and Quality, U.S. Department of Health and Human Services, HCUPnet. National and regional estimates of hospital use for all patients from the HCUP Nationwide Inpatient Sample (NIS), *http://hcupnet.ahrq.gov/HCUPnet.jsp*.

Ries L.A.G., Eisner, M.P., Kosary, C.L., Hankey, B.F., Clegg, L., Mariotto, A., Feuer, E.J., and Edwards, B.K. (eds.) SEER Cancer Statistics Review, 1975–2001. Bethesda, MD: National Cancer Institute. *http://seer.cancer.gov/csr*.

National Cancer Institute, DCCPS, Surveillance Research Program, Cancer Statistics Branch, Surveillance, Epidemiology, and End Results (SEER) Program, SEER Stat Database: Incidence. SEER 17 Regs Public-Use, Nov 2005 Sub (2000–2003), released April 2006, based on the November 2005 submission. *http://www.seer.cancer.gov*.

U.S. Cancer Statistics Working Group. (2005) United States Cancer Statistics: 1999–2002, *Incidence and Mortality Web-based Report*. Atlanta: U.S. Department of Health and Human Services, Centers for Disease Control and Prevention (CDC), and National Cancer Institute. *http://www.cdc.gov/cancer/cpcr/uscs*.

U.S. Department of Health and Human Services, Centers for Disease Control and Prevention (CDC), National Center for Health Statistics (NCHS). Compressed Mortality File

(CMF). Compiled from CMF 1968–1988, Series 20, No. 2A 2000, CMF 1989–1998, Series 20, No. 2E 2003 and CMF 1999–2002, Series 20, No. 2H 2004 on CDC Wonder Online Database.

U.S. Department of Health and Human Services, Public Health Service. (1992) *Principles of Epidemiology: An Introduction to Applied Epidemiology and Biostatistics.* Atlanta, GA: USDHHS.

U.S. Department of Health and Human Services, Public Health Service, National Institutes of Health. (1994) Self instructional manual for cancer registries, Book 7: Statistics and epidemiology for cancer registries. NIH Publication No. 94-3766.

Utah Hospital Discharge Data, Public Dataset. *http://www.health.state.ut.us.*

# Appendix 3-A

## Exercises for Solving Problems

### Knowledge Questions

1. Define the key terms listed at the beginning of this chapter.
2. The purpose of a table, chart, or graph is to communicate information to the data user. What questions should be considered to accomplish this objective?
3. What questions should be answered in the title of a table, chart, or graph?
4. What points should be considered when constructing a bar chart?
5. Describe the differences between a stacked bar chart and a 100% component bar chart.
6. Describe the differences between a scatter diagram and a bubble chart.

### Multiple Choice

1. You want to graph the average length of stay by gender and service for the month of April. The best choice is a:
   a. Bar graph
   b. Bubble chart
   c. Line graph
   d. Pie chart

2. You want to graph the number of deaths by year due to prostate cancer. The best choice is a:
   a. Pie chart
   b. Scatter plot
   c. Line graph
   d. Stacked bar chart

3. A pie chart may be used to display the:
   a. Average length of stay by year
   b. Percentage of discharges by religion
   c. Number of discharges per year and third-party payer
   d. Number of patients discharged by gender and service

4. You want to display the number of discharges by gender and service for the last fiscal year. The best choice is a:
   a. Single-variable bar chart
   b. Two-variable bar chart
   c. Pie chart
   d. Line graph

5. You want to compare average charges and length of stay. The best choice is a:
   a. Table
   b. Pie chart
   c. Line graph
   d. Scatter diagram

## Problems

Prepare the appropriate charts and graphs for the following problems. Include a title for each and identify the data source when indicated.

1. The admissions data in Table 3-A.1 compare actual admissions by hospital service with the budgeted number of hospital admissions for the month of January for Critical Care Hospital. Using computer graphic software, construct a bar chart that compares budgeted admissions with actual admissions. Write a short summary of the results.

2. Using the data in Table 3-A.2, prepare a pie chart for January patient days by service for Critical Care Hospital.

3. Table 3-A.3 contains age-adjusted cancer incidence rates per 100,000 by Selected Primary Sites for white males and females. Construct a stacked bar chart that compares actual average length of stay with the budgeted average length of stay.

4. Organize the following statistics for the month of January into a table.

Critical Care Cancer Research Institute Statistics for January

Discharges

| | |
|---|---|
| Medicine | 198 |
| Surgery | 152 |
| Gynecology | 74 |
| Otolaryngology | 48 |

Average Length of Stay

| | |
|---|---|
| Medicine | 6.6 |
| Surgery | 6.2 |
| Gynecology | 4.4 |
| Otolaryngology | 6.0 |

Discharge Service Days

| | |
|---|---|
| Medicine | 1313 |
| Surgery | 947 |
| Gynecology | 328 |
| Otolaryngology | 290 |

5. The average charges for malignant neoplasms of the large intestine and colon and average charges for malignant neoplasms of the trachea, bronchus, and lung appear in Table 3-A.4. Prepare a line graph that compares average charges for both malignancies.

6. Review the data in Table 3-A.5. Construct a grouped bar graph to display the number of cancer cases for each site by gender and race.

Table 3-A.1 **Admissions Report for January**

| Hospital Service | Budgeted Admissions | Actual Admissions |
|---|---|---|
| Medicine | 769 | 728 |
| Surgery | 583 | 578 |
| OB/GYN | 440 | 402 |
| Psychiatry | 99 | 113 |
| Physical Medicine and Rehab | 57 | 48 |
| Other Adult | 178 | 191 |
| Newborn | 312 | 294 |

Table 3-A.2 **Patient Days by Service**

| Hospital Service | Patient Days |
|---|---|
| Medicine | 4,436 |
| Surgery | 4,036 |
| OB/GYN | 1,170 |
| Psychiatry | 1,223 |
| Physical Medicine and Rehab | 1,318 |
| Other Adult | 688 |
| Newborn | 1,633 |

Table 3-A.3 **Age Adjusted Cancer Incidence Rates by Gender per 100,000 by Selected Primary Sites**

| Site | White Males | White Females |
|---|---|---|
| Colon | 42.5 | 33.2 |
| Liver | 7.0 | 2.6 |
| Pancreas | 12.1 | 9.2 |
| Lung & Bronchus | 85.6 | 54.9 |
| Melanoma of Skin | 22.8 | 15.2 |
| Kidney | 18.1 | 9.2 |

Table 3-A.4   **Average Total Charges, Cancers of the Colon and Lung, State of Utah, 1995–2002**

| Year | Cancer of the Trachea, Bronchus, and Lung | Cancer of the Colon and Rectum |
|------|-------------------------------------------|--------------------------------|
| 1995 | $13,364 | $15,275 |
| 1996 | $15,403 | $14,622 |
| 1997 | $14,958 | $16,511 |
| 1998 | $15,232 | $16,659 |
| 1999 | $16,331 | $19,633 |
| 2000 | $19,618 | $20,424 |
| 2001 | $21,216 | $21,646 |
| 2002 | $22,256 | $22,362 |

*Source:* Utah Inpatient Hospital Discharge Dataset, Utah Office of Health Care Statistics, www.health.state.ut.us.

Table 3-A.5   **Age-Adjusted Invasive Cancer Incidence Rates per 100,000, by Selected Primary Sites, Race, and Gender, 2002**

| Site | Whites | | Blacks | |
|------|--------|---------|--------|---------|
| | Males | Females | Males | Females |
| Colon | 42.5 | 33.2 | 51.9 | 41.2 |
| Liver | 7.0 | 2.6 | 10.9 | 3.6 |
| Pancreas | 12.1 | 9.2 | 15.1 | 12.9 |
| Lung & Bronchus | 85.6 | 54.9 | 105.7 | 50.3 |
| Melanoma of Skin | 22.8 | 15.2 | 0.9 | 0.9 |
| Kidney | 18.1 | 9.2 | 18.8 | 10.0 |

*Source:* US Cancer Statistics Working Group. United States Cancer Statistics: 1999–2002 Incidence and Mortality Web-based report. Available at www.cdc.gov/cancer/cpcr/uscs.

# CHAPTER 4

**INTRODUCTION TO MEASUREMENT**

**LEARNING OBJECTIVES**

At the conclusion of this chapter, you should be able to:

1. Define key terms.
2. Relate the importance of validity and reliability to the measurement process.
3. Compare and contrast the following scales of measurement: nominal, ordinal, ratio, and interval.
4. Classify variables to the scales of measurement.
5. Identify variables as either discrete or continuous.

## WHAT IS MEASUREMENT?

In the daily operations of any organization, whether in business, manufacturing, or health care, data are collected for decision making. To be effective, decision makers must have confidence in the data collected. Confidence requires that the data collected be accurate, timely, and reliable. Assurance of these aspects of data quality is what the **measurement** process is about. Our discussion of the analysis of clinical data in health care begins with the topic of measurement. We cannot accurately collect, analyze, and make conclusions regarding clinical data without an understanding of the measurement process.

In measurement, we are concerned with measuring an attribute or property of a person, object, or event according to a particular set of rules. In some cases, measurement may be direct, as when we are using a yardstick to measure the property "width of a desk" (object). However, in health care we do not always have the ability to measure persons, objects, or events directly. For example, "quality of care" cannot be measured directly with a yardstick or any other measuring device. Consequently, an indirect measure must be developed.

Whether we are dealing with direct or indirect measures, the result of the measurement process is numbers, and there must be a set of rules for assigning numbers to the objects being measured. The measurement process requires a rigorous definition of what will be collected and the method by which it will be collected so that the resulting numbers will be meaningful, accurate, and informative. The advantage of standardizing the process is that the results are the same regardless of who is doing the data collection. The resulting uniformity also allows for comparisons between and within institutions. Through measurement, one creates data that can be analyzed using statistical techniques and that can be presented as meaningful information. Through the measurement process, we can transform data into information.

To illustrate, consider the process by which the data for the Caesarean section (C-section) rate is collected. The C-section rate is often used as a performance indicator for hospital obstetric services, especially by managed care plans. A low C-section rate is desirable because C-sections are more expensive than vaginal deliveries and there is a longer recovery time for the patient. The first step in the process is to define C-section rate, the event to be measured. Now we must consider the properties that characterize this event—in other words, what data will be collected? The procedure for measuring this event is presented in Exhibit 4.1. As you can see, calculation of the C-section rate is a straightforward process.

Exhibit 4.1    **Measurement of Caesarean Section Rate**

Caesarean Section Rate (event): The ratio during any given time period of surgical deliveries (Caesarean sections) to the total number of deliveries.

**Data to Be Collected (Properties):**
  1. Total number of Caesarean sections performed for a given period
  2. Total number of deliveries for the period

**Data Sources:**
  1. Medical records of discharged obstetrical patients for the period
  2. Daily discharge reports for the period
  3. Disease and operations indexes of the International Classification of Disease, 9th Revision, Clinical Modification (ICD-9-CM)
  4. Labor and delivery room logs

**Calculation:**    $$\frac{\text{Total no. of Caesarean sections for period} \times 100}{\text{Total no. of deliveries for same period}}$$

However, quantifying some of the performance indicators developed by the Joint Commission on Accreditation of Healthcare Organizations (Joint Commission) and the Agency for Healthcare Research and Quality (AHRQ) is not always so easily accomplished. Because some performance indicators cannot be directly measured, we must use some attribute that is considered to represent the presence or absence of the attribute of interest—an indirect measure. As an analogy, consider the personal attribute of intelligence. Intelligence is a personal attribute that cannot be directly measured with a yardstick or with any type of device; instead, it is indirectly measured through a standardized IQ test that consists of questions that are assumed to be representative of intelligence.

Exhibit 4.2 outlines the procedure for collecting data on the performance indicator, "esophageal resection mortality rate." This is a performance indicator that measures outcome. The occurrence of this event is considered an indicator of an undesirable outcome and should be avoided. But in calculating the mortality rate, we must first decide who will be counted. Do we count everyone who had an esophageal resection? Do we count only those admitted for esophageal cancer? Do we count those who were diagnosed with esophageal cancer after admission? Standardization of the process helps ensure that everyone is counting the same types of cases. As you can see in Exhibit 4.2, we are interested in counting patients who have a principal or secondary diagnosis of esophageal cancer with resection of the esophagus. This occurrence must be rigorously defined, and procedures for data collection must be strictly followed.

## VALIDITY

Accuracy in measurement cannot happen without **validity**. The measuring instrument—whether a ruler, an IQ test, or a survey instrument—is considered valid if it measures what it is intended to measure and for the intended purpose. A ruler or scale is a direct measure. In health care, because we cannot measure quality with yardsticks and scales, quality is often assessed through indirect measures.

As an example, the quality measure, "Diabetes Mellitus: Hospital Admission Rate for Long-term Complications," developed by AHRQ is displayed in Exhibit 4.3. This is a community measure that focuses on the prevention of "hospital admissions for ambulatory care-sensitive conditions." Effective management of these patients in an ambulatory setting may prevent hospitalization for diabetes mellitus, a chronic condition. Thus, this performance measure is serving as an indirect measure for access to a certain type of ambulatory care in a given community. Inpatient admissions are serving as the proxy measure.

To implement this performance measure, we must ask what qualifies as a long-term diabetic complication. Is each health care facility free to define what qualifies as a diabetic complication? Are both Type I and Type II diabetics to be

Exhibit 4.2 **Example of Measurement of an Inpatient Quality Indicator**

| | |
|---|---|
| **Measure:** | Esophageal Resection Mortality Rate |
| **Type of Measure:** | Provider level, Mortality indicator for Inpatient Procedures (outcome) |
| **Rationale:** | Esophageal cancer surgery is a rare procedure that requires technical proficiency, and errors in surgical technique or management may lead to clinically significant complications such as sepsis, pneumonia, anastomotic breakdown, and death. |
| **Relationship to Quality:** | Better processes of care may reduce mortality for esophageal resection, which represents better quality care. |
| **Definition:** | Number of deaths per 100 patients with discharge procedure code of esophageal resection. |
| **Numerator:** | Number of deaths with a code of esophageal resection in any procedure field. |
| **Denominator:** | Discharges with ICD-9-CM codes of 42.40 through 42.42 in any procedure field and a diagnosis code of esophageal cancer in any field. |
| | Exclude patients transferring to another short-term hospital, MDC 14 (pregnancy, childbirth, and puerperium), and MDC 15 (newborns and neonates). |
| **Face Validity:** | Does the indicator capture an aspect of quality that is widely regarded as important and subject to provider or public health system control? |

The primary evidence for esophageal resection mortality as an indicator arises from the volume-outcome literature. The causal relationship between hospital volume and mortality is unclear, and the differing processes that may lead to better outcomes have not been identified.

*Patti MG, Corvera CU, Glasgow RE, et al. A hospital's annual rate of esophagectomy influences the operative mortality rate. J Gastrointestinal Surg 1998, 2(2): 186–92.

*Source:* AHRQ Guide to Inpatient Quality Indicators: Quality of Care in Hospitals—Volume, Mortality, and Utilization. Department of HHS, Agency for Healthcare Research and Quality, June 2002, Revision 2, September 4, 2003. www.ahrq.gov.

included? What about complications of gestational diabetes? It should become obvious that if we are to have valid data, qualifying complications must be rigorously defined. Without rigorous definition of the measure, consistent, comparable data will not result from the data collection process, and confidence in the information will be lost.

**Exhibit 4.3    AHRQ Quality Indicator—Diabetes Mellitus: Hospital Admission Rate for Long-Term Complications**

| | |
|---|---|
| **Measure:** | Diabetes Mellitus: Hospital Admission for Long-Term Complications |
| **Source:** | AHRQ quality indicators. Guide prevention quality indicators: hospital admission for ambulatory care sensitive conditions. |
| **Description:** | This indicator assesses the number of admissions for long-term diabetes per 100,000 population. |
| **Rationale:** | Long-term complications of diabetes mellitus include renal, eye, neurological, and circulatory disorders. Long-term complications occur at some time in the majority of patients with diabetes to some degree. Proper outpatient treatment and adherence to care may reduce this incidence of long-term complications, and lower rates represent better quality of care. |
| **Numerator:** | Discharges, age 18 years and older, with ICD-9-CM principal diagnosis code for long-term complications of diabetes (renal, eye, neurological, circulatory, or complications not otherwise specified). Patients transferring from another institution, MDC14 (pregnancy, childbirth, and puerperium) and MDC 15 (newborns and neonates) are excluded. |
| **Denominator:** | Population in Metropolitan Statistical Area (MSA) or county, age 18 years and older. |

*Source:* Agency for Healthcare Research and Quality. www.qualitymeasures.ahrq.gov.

## RELIABILITY

Error is integral to the measurement process, whether it is the measurement of weight, height, or blood pressure. Even when the measurement is made as accurately as the instrument allows and all procedures are followed, repeated measures do not always give exactly the same results. This is because error is a component of all measurement. But an instrument that is reliable will tend to have results that are consistent with each other over repeated trials. A measurement process is said to be reliable if repeated measurements over time on the same property or attribute give the same or approximately the same results. A yardstick is reliable because it will provide approximately the same result every time an object is measured, regardless of who is doing the measuring. An example of an unreliable measuring device is a scale that gives widely different weights each time the same object is measured.

Measures should also be **unbiased**. A measurement process is unbiased if it does not systematically overstate or understate the true value of the attribute/property being measured. An example of a biased but reliable measure is a scale that consistently measures weight 10 pounds less than the actual weight. An unbiased measure is, on average, correct.

There are three aspects of **reliability** that we will discuss: stability, internal consistency, and inter-rater agreement. **Stability**, or test-retest reliability, is the extent to which the same results are obtained on repeated applications. Stability is evaluated by administering the instrument to the same group on two separate occasions—hence the name, test-retest reliability. A reliability coefficient is calculated from the two sets of scores. The reliability coefficient ranges from 0.0 (no reliability) to 1.0 (perfect reliability).

**Internal consistency** measures the extent to which the items on the measurement instrument are homogeneous, or consistent with one another. Internal consistency is measured by Cronbach's alpha, which is often referred to as coefficient alpha. Coefficient alpha also has a range of 0.0 to 1.0; an instrument should have a minimum coefficient alpha of 0.70 for acceptability.

**Inter-rater agreement** is the extent to which results are in agreement when different individuals administer the same instrument to the same individuals or groups. This is an important concept in coding. If we have four coders assigning codes to peripheral vascular disease due to insulin-dependent diabetes mellitus, we want all four coders to come up with the same codes. Inter-rater agreement should be 100%. The **kappa coefficient** ($\kappa$) is used to assess inter-rater agreement. However, this statistic is limited because it requires that the responses be dichotomous. In the coding example, the codes would be evaluated as either right or wrong.

In using kappa, we are interested in determining the extent of agreement, not disagreement, between raters. Kappa is obtained by the following formula:

$$\kappa = \frac{A_O - A_E}{N - A_E}$$

where $A_O$ is the number of observations that are in agreement and $A_E$ is the number of observations in agreement expected by chance alone.

The value $A_O$ is obtained by summing the table diagonals ($A_O = a + d$), and the percentage of agreement is obtained by $A_O/N$. The value $A_E$ is obtained by multiplying the row total by the column total and dividing by the grand total, as follows:

$$A_E = \sum_{i=1}^{k} \frac{row\ marginal \times column\ marginal}{N}$$

The range for the kappa coefficient is −1.0 to +1.0. A negative value indicates that the proportion of agreement that resulted from chance is greater than the pro-

Table 4.1    **Results of Coding Assessments by Two Raters**

|  | Rater 2 | | |
|---|---|---|---|
| **Rater 1** | **Right** | **Wrong** | **Total** |
| Right | 80 | 20 | 100 |
| Wrong | 25 | 75 | 100 |
| Total | 105 | 95 | 200 |

portion of observed agreement. High positive values of kappa indicate strong inter-rater agreement. Let us now consider an example where two raters have been asked to evaluate the accuracy of a simple random sample of 200 medical records that have been coded. The coded charts were evaluated as right or wrong. The results appear in Table 4.1.

To obtain the number of observations that are in agreement between the two raters, $A_O$, the diagonals are summed: $80 + 75 = 155$. The percent agreement between the two raters is $(155/200) \times 100 = 77.5\%$. The number of observations in agreement that is expected by chance, $A_E$, is obtained by

$$A_E = \frac{100 \times 105}{200} + \frac{100 \times 95}{200} = 52.5 + 47.5 = 100$$

$$\kappa = \frac{A_O - A_E}{N - A} = \frac{155 - 100}{200 - 100} = 0.55$$

The interpretation of kappa is that the obtained agreement of 77.5% is approximately 55% greater than what would be achieved by chance alone. Interpretation of the kappa statistic is as follows:

| | |
|---|---|
| $\kappa < 0.20$ | negligible |
| $0.20 \leq \kappa < 0.40$ | minimal |
| $0.40 \leq \kappa < 0.60$ | fair |
| $0.60 \leq \kappa < 0.80$ | good |
| $\kappa \geq 0.80$ | excellent |

In our example, the obtained kappa coefficient, 0.55, indicates that the raters obtained fair agreement in their assessment of the sample of coded records.

In summary, a measure is reliable if the same individual measures the same attribute at another time and achieves the same result; the individual applies the measure consistently on all attributes; and several individuals reach the same result when measuring the same attribute.

## Timeliness

A critical aspect of data quality is **timeliness**. One must consider whether the data are collected and available within a useful time frame. Does the collected information represent the current condition of the patient or state of the organization? Data collected today are more critical and useful to the decision maker than data collected yesterday or two weeks ago. The value of collected data decreases with time.

For data to be accurate, the measure creating the data must be rigorously defined. A common failure in the measurement process is to undertake the measurement process without a clear definition of what is to be measured, who will use the resulting information, and how the information will be used for making decisions. The measurement process must begin with a strong commitment to identifying the information needs of those who will be using the information.

## Scales of Measurement

As stated previously, all measurement results in a number. To properly assign numbers to the measurement results, one must understand the **scales of measurement**. Understanding the differences in the scales of measurement is also critical to make appropriate use of graphic displays of data, to correctly select statistical techniques for data analysis, and to facilitate data entry.

### Nominal Scale

The **nominal** scale is the lowest level of measurement. In the nominal scale, measures are organized into categories; there is no recognition of order within these categories. Examples of categories on the nominal scale of measurement are gender, religion, and third-party payer. To facilitate computer analysis, numbers are assigned to nominal variables—for example, male = 1, female = 2. The numbers assigned to the various categories carry no numerical weight; the numbers merely serve as labels for the categories.

Statistical summaries of variables on the nominal scale can be prepared through the use of a frequency distribution. On the nominal scale, a frequency distribution would indicate the number of cases falling into each category. Using statistical notation, the frequency distribution would be represented as follows:

$$N = \sum_k f_k$$

where $N$ is the total number of cases, $f_k$ is the frequency within category, and $\sum_k$ is a summation over all categories of $k$.

Table 4.2 **Number of Patients Admitted by Method of Payment**

| Commercial Insurance | Managed Care | Medicare | Medicaid | Self-Pay | Other | Total |
|---|---|---|---|---|---|---|
| 75 | 43 | 62 | 55 | 6 | 15 | 256 |

As a hypothetical example, consider the nominal variable, "method of payment." For initial patient data collection, options may be commercial insurance ($k = 1$), managed care ($k = 2$), Medicare ($k = 3$), Medicaid ($k = 4$), self-pay ($k = 5$), or other ($k = 6$); thus, there are six categories. A frequency distribution for patients admitted by method of payment is presented in Table 4.2. In our example, the total number of patients admitted during the week of July 23rd is 256 ($N = 256$), and the number of Medicare patients (frequency) who were admitted is 62 ($f_3 = 62$).

It is sometimes useful to show the proportion of cases falling into a category $k$. This proportion is designated $p_k$. A proportion is the number of cases that fall within a particular category divided by the total number of cases, and it is represented as

$$p_k = \frac{f_k}{N}$$

The proportion of cases falling into each category will always sum to 1.0. Using the same data from Table 4.2, Table 4.3 represents the proportions and cumulative proportions for each category.

The distribution of a variable into the various categories can also be represented by percentages, which are proportions multiplied by 100. For data that fall on the nominal scale of measurement, frequencies can be represented in tables,

Table 4.3 **Proportion of Patients Admitted by Method of Payment, Week of July 23**

| Category | Frequency (f) | Proportion (p) | Cum. Proportion |
|---|---|---|---|
| Commercial Insurance | 75 | 0.293 | 0.293 |
| Managed Care | 43 | 0.168 | 0.461 |
| Medicare | 62 | 0.242 | 0.703 |
| Medicaid | 55 | 0.215 | 0.918 |
| Self-pay | 6 | 0.023 | 0.941 |
| Other | 15 | 0.059 | 1.000 |
| Total ($N$) | 256 | 1.000 | |

charts, and graphs. The most appropriate measure of central tendency for nominal-level data is the mode. For nominal data, the mode tells us the category that has the most observations. (The mode is discussed in more detail in Chapter 5.)

When designing a system of data collection for nominal variables, remember that the categories must be mutually exclusive and exhaustive. That is, each data element can fall into only one category, and all possible categories must be represented. As in the previous example, it may be appropriate to assign an "other" category when the number of data elements falling into some possible categories may be too small for data analysis, or when the category is not important to the purpose of the data collection.

## Ordinal Scale

Some non-numeric scales have an order to their categories; these are called **ordinal** variables. On the ordinal scale, the order of the numbers is meaningful, not the number itself, so the usual arithmetic operations are not meaningful. This is because the intervals or distance between categories are not necessarily equal. It is not appropriate to perform arithmetic operations, such as calculating averages, on ordinal variables.

Examples of ordinal variables are the numbers assigned to indicate class rank, the ordering of adjectives that describe patient condition, and a Likert-type scale that may be used to describe patient satisfaction. A Likert scale is a response scale often used in questionnaires and is the most widely used scale in survey research. Survey respondents are usually asked to indicate their extent of agreement with a statement, most often on a five-point scale. The range of agreement is usually from strongly disagree (5) to strongly agree (1).

Examples of ordered variables are displayed in Table 4.4. A number is assigned to represent the ordering of the variables. In the case of class rank, we know that an individual classified as a senior has completed more credit hours than a sophomore, but we cannot say that a senior has completed twice as many credit hours as a sophomore. The same is true regarding patient condition. A patient that is in critical condition is not necessarily twice as sick as an individual who is in stable condition. Only the order of the value is meaningful. On this scale, a patient in

Table 4.4 **Examples of Ordinal Variables**

| **Class Rank** | **Patient Condition** | **Patient Satisfaction** |
|---|---|---|
| 1—Freshman | 1—Resting and Comfortable | 1—Strongly agree |
| 2—Sophomore | 2—Stable | 2—Agree |
| 3—Junior | 3—Guarded | 3—No opinion |
| 4—Senior | 4—Critical | 4—Disagree |
| | | 5—Strongly disagree |

critical condition is sicker than a patient in guarded condition. The frequency distributions of ordinal variables can be portrayed in the same way as for nominal variables.

Nominal and ordinal variables are considered discrete variables. Discrete variables have gaps between successive values. DRGs are examples of discrete nominal variables.

## Scales for Metric Variables

**Metric variables** are numeric variables that answer questions of how much or how many. Metric variables fall on one of two scales of measurement: ratio or interval. Arithmetic operations may be performed on ratio- and interval-scale measures.

The **ratio** scale is the highest level of measurement. On the ratio scale, there is a defined unit of measure—a real zero point—and the intervals between successive values are equal. For example, consider the variable of length. Length has defined units of measurement, such as inches, and a true zero point, 0 inches. With a real zero point, statements such as, "Mary is twice as tall as Jill," can be made. Multiplication on the ratio scale by a constant does not change its ratio character, but the addition of a constant to a ratio measure does. For example, if an older sibling is twice as tall as a younger sibling and both grow 2 inches, the ratio of their heights is no longer 2:1. But if we multiply their respective heights by 2 (e.g., 60″ × 2 and 30″ × 2), the ratio between the two heights remains 2:1.

Measures that fall on the **interval** scale have a defined unit of measurement but do not have a true zero point. The most important characteristic of the interval scale is that the intervals between successive values are equal. On the Fahrenheit scale, the interval between 20°F and 21°F is the same as the interval between 21°F and 22°F. But because there is not a true zero on this scale, we cannot say that 40°F is twice as warm as 20°F.

An advantage of metric data is that they can be grouped. Interval and ratio variables are continuous. If a variable is continuous, it may take on fractional values, such as 85.3235°F. With continuous variables, there are no gaps between values because the values progress fractionally. Graphic techniques that may be used to display interval and ratio data include scatter diagrams, bubble charts, and stem-and-leaf diagrams. Measures of central tendency that may be reported for interval and ratio data are the mean, median, and mode.

The scale of measurement depends on the method of measurement, not on the attribute being measured. For example, if we score a test by summing the total number of correct answers, the resulting measures fall on the ratio scale. However, if each question is tallied according to the total number who answered the question correctly and the total number who answered the question incorrectly, the measures fall on the nominal scale because the measure falls into one of two categories—"correct" or "incorrect." When developing measures for any purpose, one must consider on what scale of measurement the collected data will fall so that the appropriate statistical procedures can be selected.

## CONCLUSION

Measurement is a process that requires the rigorous definition of what is being measured, the data sources, and how the variable measured will be calculated. We have discussed two major aspects of measurement: validity and reliability.

The validity of a measure is the extent to which an instrument measures what it is intended to measure. Because we cannot always measure quality with instruments such as yardsticks and scales, quality is often assessed through indirect measures.

Reliability is the extent to which an instrument gives the same results over time or over repeated measures. Several aspects of reliability exist: test-retest reliability, internal consistency, and inter-rater agreement. Test-retest reliability is the extent to which repeated administrations of an instrument provide the same results. Internal consistency is the extent to which the items on an instrument are related to one another. And inter-rater agreement is the extent to which different individuals who administer the same instrument achieve similar results.

Finally, to understand the measurement process, we must understand the differences in the scales of measurement: nominal, ordinal, interval, and ratio. In the nominal scale of measurement, measures are organized into categories; the nominal scale is the lowest level of measurement. In the ordinal scale of measurement, there is an "order" to the categories; the numbers themselves are not meaningful but the order is. On the interval and ratio scales of measurement, the intervals between successive values are equal. Arithmetic calculations may be performed on interval and ratio measures. The interval scale differs from the ratio scale in that the interval scale does not have a true zero.

## REFERENCES

Agency for Healthcare Research and Quality (AHRQ). Guide to Inpatient Quality Indicators: Quality of Care in Hospitals—Volume, Mortality, and Utilization. Department of Health and Human Services. June 2002, AHRQ Pub. No. 02-RO204, Revision 2, September 4, 2003. *http://www.ahrq.gov.*

Federal Register. Volume 68, No. 229, Friday, November 28, 2003, 66,975–66,978.

# APPENDIX 4-A

## EXERCISES FOR SOLVING PROBLEMS

### Knowledge Questions

1. Define the key terms listed at the beginning of this chapter.
2. Describe the measurement process.
3. Why are validity and reliability requirements of accuracy in the measurement process?
4. You weighed your dog this morning on your bathroom scale. His weight was 15 lb. You decided to weigh him again in the evening, and his weight had increased to 20 lb. This is most likely what type of measurement error? Explain your answer.
5. Compare and contrast the following measures of reliability: stability, internal consistency, and inter-rater agreement.
6. Define the nominal, ordinal, interval, and ratio scales of measurement.
7. What is the difference between a discrete variable and a continuous variable?

### Multiple Choice

1. You are conducting a study in which "gender" is the property of interest. The variable "gender" falls upon which of the following scales of measurement?
   a. Nominal
   b. Ordinal
   c. Ratio
   d. Interval
2. You are interested in the lengths of stay for patients of Dr. Wells for a quality improvement study. The variable "length of stay" falls upon which of the following scales of measurement?
   a. Nominal
   b. Ordinal
   c. Ratio
   d. Interval
3. You are assisting Dr. Smith in his study of burn patients. He wants to classify the number of burn patients by severity of burn: first degree, second degree, or third degree. The variable "severity of burn" falls upon which of the following scales of measurement?
   a. Nominal
   b. Ordinal
   c. Ratio
   d. Interval
4. "Severity of burn" is an example of which of the following types of variables?
   a. Continuous
   b. Discrete
   c. Interval
   d. Ratio

For Questions 5 through 8, refer to the following case:

You have designed a survey instrument with a five-point Likert-type scale consisting of statements that measure physician satisfaction with health information management services. On the scale, 1 = strongly disagree (SD) and 5 = strongly agree (SA).

5. You decide to take an average of the scores for each statement. In this case, you would be treating the data as falling upon which of the following scales of measurement?
   a. Nominal
   b. Ordinal
   c. Ratio
   d. Interval

6. After reviewing the results, you decide that the mode might be the more appropriate measure of central tendency for these data. In reporting the mode, you are treating the data as falling upon which of the following scales of measurement?
   a. Nominal
   b. Ordinal
   c. Ratio
   d. Interval

7. Which of the following variables would be considered "continuous"?
   a. Age
   b. Gender
   c. Religion
   d. Principal diagnosis code

8. Which of the following variables would be considered "discrete"?
   a. Age upon admission
   b. Patient length of stay
   c. DRG assignment upon discharge
   d. Time spent in operating room

## Problems

1. Exhibit 4-A.1 displays selected data elements from the proposed Case Mix Assessment Tool for psychiatric inpatients. Identify the scale of measurement for each element, determine if the measure is discrete or continuous, and determine what measure(s) of central tendency may be used for each—mean, median, or mode.

2. At City Hospital, 34 C-sections were performed during January; at County Hospital, 54 C-sections were performed during the month of January. During January, City Hospital had 200 deliveries, and County Hospital had 1100 deliveries. The national benchmark for the C-section rate is 15%. The head of obstetrics at City Hospital claims that their OB service provides better care than that provided at the rival hospital. Do you agree with this assessment?

3. Develop measures for the following obstetric performance indicators proposed by the Joint Commission. Your measure should include a definition, identification of data sources, and procedures for calculation (formula).
   a. Maternal readmissions within 14 days of delivery
   b. Intra-hospital maternal deaths occurring within 42 days postpartum
   c. Patients with excessive maternal blood loss

Exhibit 4.A.1  **Selected Data Elements from Case Mix Assessment Tool for Behavioral Health Care**

| Data Element | Measurement Scale Discrete/Continuous Variable | Measure of Central Tendency |
|---|---|---|
| Gender: | | |
| 1—Male | | |
| 2—Female | | |
| Number of Psychiatric Admissions | | |
| Number of Medications | | |
| Legal Status | | |
| 1—Voluntary | | |
| 2—Involuntary | | |
| 3—Criminal court hold | | |
| Unable to control substance abuse within past 30 days | | |
| 0—no | | |
| 1—yes | | |
| Activities of daily living | | |
| 0—Independent | | |
| 1—Setup help only | | |
| 2—Supervision | | |
| 3—Limited assistance | | |
| 4—Extensive assistance | | |
| 5—Maximal assistance | | |
| 6—Total dependence | | |
| White Blood Count: criteria— range 3.8–10.8 | | |
| Number of falls in last 30 days | | |

*Source:* Federal Register, Volume 68, No. 229, Friday, November 28, 2003, p. 66975.

# CHAPTER 5

# MEASURES OF CENTRAL TENDENCY AND VARIABILITY

## KEY TERMS

Apparent limits
Class interval
Degrees of freedom
Individuality
Interquartile range
Measures of central tendency
   Mean
      Trimmed mean
      Weighted mean
      Winsorized mean
   Median
   Mode
Measures of variability
   Range

Standard deviation
Variance
Parameters
Percentile rank
Percentiles
Polarization
Population
Population parameter
Quartiles
Real limits
Sample
Sample statistic
Statistics
Uniformity

## LEARNING OBJECTIVES

At the conclusion of this chapter, you should be able to:

1. Define key terms.
2. Calculate measures of central tendency—mean, median, and mode—for grouped and ungrouped frequency distributions.
3. Calculate measures of variability—range, variance, and standard deviation—for grouped and ungrouped frequency distributions.
4. Use electronic spreadsheets to calculate measures of central tendency and variation for grouped and ungrouped frequency distributions.
5. Explain why measures of central tendency and variability differ in grouped and ungrouped frequency distributions.

Two main types of measures are used to describe frequency distributions: measures of central tendency and measures of variability. Measures of central tendency measure location and focus on the typical value of a data set. Variation emphasizes differences. Measures of variability measure distance or dispersion around the typical value of a data set. Generalizations about populations from samples are based on the variation of the variables in the data set.

Descriptive measures can be computed from both populations and samples. A **population** is a group of persons or objects about which a researcher or investigator wishes to draw conclusions. A **sample** is a subset of the population. Measures that result from the compilation of data from populations are called **parameters**. Measures that result from the analysis of data from samples are called **statistics**. For example, if we were interested in determining the average age of all members of the American Health Information Management Association (AHIMA), all members of the association would make up the population; the average age would be a **population parameter**. But if we were to draw a sample from the membership list and then calculate the average age, the average would be a **sample statistic**.

## Measures of Central Tendency

As previously stated, **measures of central tendency** summarize the typical value of a variable. When we think of measures of central tendency, we usually think of averages; however, averages or the arithmetic mean may not always be the most appropriate way of summarizing the most typical value of a data set. There are three major measures of central tendency, and the selection of the relevant measure of central tendency is related to the scale of measurement used in data collection.

- The **mode** ($M_O$) is defined as the most frequently occurring observation in a frequency distribution. It is the only measure of central tendency that is appropriate for nominal data.
- The **median** ($M_D$) is the midpoint of a frequency distribution. It is appropriate for both ordinal and metric data.
- The **mean** ($\overline{X}$, pronounced "x-bar") is the arithmetic average. It is appropriate for metric data.

### Mode

The mode is the simplest measure of central tendency. With the mode, we are indicating the most frequently occurring observation for metric data or the most frequently occurring category for nominal data. The mode is an important measure of central tendency for nominal-level data because an average cannot be taken from data that are placed in categories. Averages work only when a variable has a unit of measurement. The mode is an important measure of central tendency in the sense that it shows what the typical category on a variable is. For example, if we group the membership of AHIMA by gender, on average, the typical health information management (HIM) professional is female. We can say this because approximately 92% of the membership of AHIMA is female.

Another interpretation of the mode is that if the goal is to be as accurate as possible, the mode provides the best "guess" as to the category an observation may take on a variable. That is, no other guess for a random case will be correct as often as the mode. Continuing with our example, if we were to guess the gender of a typical HIM professional, the best "guess" would be that the gender of the practitioner was female. In making this guess, we would be correct approximately 92% of the time.

The mode offers several advantages: It is easy to obtain and to interpret, it is not sensitive to extreme values, and it is easy to communicate and explain to others. However, there are inherent disadvantages in using the mode. First, the mode may not be descriptive of the data because the most common category may not occur very often, especially when there are a large number of categories. Second, the mode may not be unique. That is, two categories or metric measures can be equally likely and more common than any other category or metric measure. When this occurs, we have a bimodal or multimodal distribution. If each category occurs with equal frequency, there is no mode. Third, the mode does not provide information about the entire frequency distribution—it only tells us the most frequently occurring value or category in the frequency distribution.

Also, the mode can be overly affected by sampling variation in cases where there is a bimodal distribution. If several samples are taken from the same population, the mode may fluctuate widely from sample to sample. For nominal-level data, the mode is also sensitive to how categories are combined. The classification scheme should be at the same level of generality for all categories rather than having broad categories for some and more specific categories for others. The mode can be manipulated by making the level of generality of different categories unequal. When reading a statistical analysis that reports the mode, we should always examine the categories to make sure that the modal categories were not manipulated by the use of categories at different levels of generality. For example, compare the following hypothetical data on hospital admissions:

| Hospital Admissions by Race (A) | | Hospital Admissions by Race (B) | |
|---|---|---|---|
| White | 60% | White | 60% |
| African-American | 15% | African-American | 15% |
| Hispanic | 12% | Other | 25% |
| Asian | 8% | | |
| Other | 5% | | |

In Example A, hospital admissions by race are distributed in a way that might be expected in an urban population. However, in Example B, a biased view of admissions is presented by lumping together three of the categories, grouping Hispanic and Asian into the "Other" category. In this example, the individual presenting the data may be interested in emphasizing the low percentage in the African-American category. Combining two racial categories into the "Other" category creates a biased view of the racial makeup of hospital admissions.

For nominal or categorical data, the mode can be depicted in a bar chart (Figure 5.1).

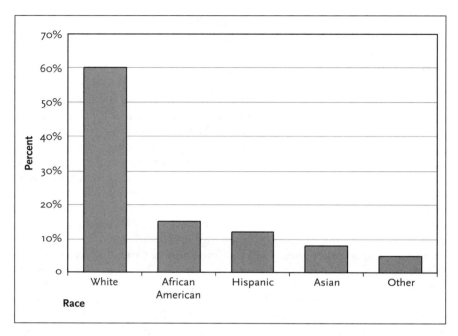

Figure 5.1  **Bar Graph for Hospital Administration by Race**

## Median

When categories of a variable are ordered, the measure of central tendency should take order into account. The median does so by finding the value of the variable that corresponds to the middle case. It is a positional measure that indicates the point at which 50% of the cases fall above and 50% of the cases fall below.

If there are an odd number of observations in the frequency distribution, the median is the middle number. In the following frequency distribution, the median is 5—there are four cases above and four cases below the value 5.

| 1 | 2 | 3 | 4 | 5 | 6 | 7 | 8 | 9 |

If there are an even number of observations, the median is the midpoint between the two middle observations. It is found by averaging the two middle scores. In the following frequency distribution, the median is (5 + 6)/2 = 5.5.

| 1 | 2 | 3 | 4 | 5 | 6 | 7 | 8 | 9 | 10 |

If the two middle observations take on the same value, the mode is that value. When determining the mode, it does not matter if there are duplicate observations in the frequency distribution. Consider the following frequency distribution:

| 1 | 2 | 2 | 3 | 4 | 4 | 4 | 5 | 6 | 7 |
|---|---|---|---|---|---|---|---|---|---|

In this distribution there are ten observations, so the median falls between the fifth and sixth observation. Therefore, the median is $(4 + 4)/2 = 4$.

The median is an important measure for data that fall on the ordinal scale of measurement. This is due to the limitations of other measures for ordered data. The mode can be used for ordinal data but it does not take "order" into account, which is the characteristic that makes the measure more than just a nominal classification. The mode can also be unrepresentative for an ordinal measure. It is also not meaningful to take an average of ordered variables because the distance between the intervals is not necessarily equal. This concept is illustrated in Table 5.1, "Hospital Ranking by Severity of Illness." Hospitals with adjacent ranks differ by as little as 0.001 (1.826 to 1.825) on their severity of illness scores or by as much as 0.127 (1.753 to 1.626).

Averages are often calculated on ordered variables, but the results may be misleading. Therefore, when choosing a measure of central tendency, you should consider not only the scale of measurement upon which the variable falls but also the purpose of the measure. There are several advantages of using the median. First, it is relatively easy to obtain. Second, it is based on the whole distribution rather than just a small portion of the distribution, as is the case with the mode. Third, the median is not influenced by extreme values or unusual outliers (outliers are

Table 5.1   **Hospital Ranking by Severity of Illness**

| Hospital Ranking | Severity Of Illness | Distance between Severity of Illness Scores |
|:---:|:---:|:---:|
| 1 | 2.152 | — |
| 2 | 2.027 | 0.125 (2.152 − 2.027) |
| 3 | 1.965 | 0.062 |
| 4 | 1.876 | 0.089 |
| 5 | 1.826 | 0.050 |
| 6 | 1.825 | 0.001 |
| 7 | 1.753 | 0.072 |
| 8 | 1.626 | 0.127 |
| 9 | 1.594 | 0.032 |

observations that are numerically distant from the rest of the data), so it is considered a resistant statistic.

The median has another advantage in that it can be computed when a distribution is open-ended at the extremes. For example, consider the median length of stay for a group of five patients who were admitted to the hospital on the same day. If two patients are discharged on Day 2 and one patient is discharged on Day 4, the median length of stay is four days. The median can be determined without waiting to see how long the remaining two patients stay in the hospital. While we can determine the median in this example, we cannot determine either the mode or the mean until the two remaining patients are discharged.

## Mean

The most effective way of summarizing the center of metric data is to average the values on the variable. The mode and median can be computed on metric data, but they do not take full advantage of the numeric information inherent in the data in the frequency distribution. The formula for calculating the mean is

$$\overline{X} = \frac{\sum_{i=1}^{n} X_i}{N}$$

where $X_i$ is each successive observation in the frequency distribution (from the first observation, $i = 1$, to the last observation, $i = n$), and $N$ is the total number of observations in the distribution.

To calculate the average daily census for the data in Table 5.2, we substitute into the above formula as follows:

$$\overline{X} = \frac{\sum_{i=1}^{n} X_i}{N} = \frac{167+185+173+182+179+173+170}{7} = \frac{1229}{7} = 175.6$$

The properties of the mean are presented in Exhibit 5.1.

There are two disadvantages associated with the mean. First, the mean can take on a fractional value even when the variable itself can take on only integer values. Consider the example in Table 5.2, which gives the daily inpatient census for one week. The average daily census results in a fractional number even though we do not have fractional patients. However, fractional values are considered more as a problem of interpretation than as a non-meaningful result. For the data in Table 5.2, we could interpret the average daily census as, "On average, the number of inpatients per day was between 175 and 176."

Table 5.2  **Daily Census, Critical Care Hospital, Week of July 1, 20xx**

| Day of Week | Daily Census |
|---|---|
| Sunday | 167 |
| Monday | 185 |
| Tuesday | 173 |
| Wednesday | 182 |
| Thursday | 179 |
| Friday | 173 |
| Saturday | 170 |
| Average Daily Census | 175.6 |

A second disadvantage is that the mean is sensitive to extreme measures. That is, the mean is strongly influenced by outliers; therefore, it is considered a nonresistant measure. For example, if in Table 5.2, the daily census for Sunday was 225 instead of 167, the average daily census would increase to 183.9.

## Weighted Mean

Often in the health care setting, we are involved in analyzing several data sets that contain the same information but for different time intervals. That is, we have several samples with separate means for each, and each sample may be of a different size. Review the data presented in Table 5.3.

What is the overall mean for the three months? One might be tempted to sum the means and divide by three, which would result in an "average of the means." This would be inappropriate because it would not take into account the difference

Exhibit 5.1  **Properties of the Arithmetic Mean**

1. The total sum of the deviations around the mean is zero.
2. The total sum of the negative deviations from the mean is always equal to the sum of the positive deviations from the mean—therefore, the mean is the balance point for the distribution.
3. The sum of the squared deviations around the mean is smaller than the sum of the squared deviations around any other value.
4. The mean is more stable over repeated measures than any other measure of center.
5. Other important statistics, namely, standard deviation and standard error of the mean, are based on deviations from the mean.

Table 5.3   **Calculation of Arithmetic and Weighted Means for Average Length of Stay (ALOS)**

| Month | Discharges (n) | Discharge Days | ALOS |
|-------|---------------|----------------|------|
| Jan | 947 | 4,228 | 4.46 |
| Feb | 763 | 3,965 | 5.20 |
| Mar | 574 | 1,842 | 3.21 |

Average of Means: (4.46 + 5.20 + 3.21)/3 = 4.29
Weighted Mean: [4.46(947) + [5.20(763)] + [3.21(574)]/2,284 = 4.39

in the sample sizes for each month. We must calculate the **weighted mean**, which takes into account the difference in the size of each sample. We calculate the weighted mean by

$$Weighted\,\overline{X} = \frac{\sum N_i \overline{X}_i}{N}$$

where $N_i$ is the number of observations in each frequency distribution, $N$ is the total number of observations in combined frequency distributions, and $X_i$ is the mean of each distribution.

To calculate the weighted mean for the data in Table 5.3, we have

$$Weighted\,\overline{X} = \frac{\sum N_i \overline{X}_i}{N} = \frac{(4.46)(947)+(5.20)(763)+(3.21)(574)}{2284} = 4.39$$

Compare the calculations in Table 5.3. The weighted mean takes into account the difference in the number of discharges for each month and is therefore more precise.

As we have already discussed, one of the disadvantages of using the mean is that it is sensitive to extreme measures. To eliminate the effects of extreme measures, the outliers may be "trimmed" from the frequency distribution before the mean is calculated. An example of a **trimmed mean** occurs in some competitive sports where the top and bottom scores are discarded before the mean score is computed.

Another method for improving the calculated mean's resistance to extreme measures is to "Winsorize" the mean. In "Winsorizing," the most extreme values are changed to equal the next less extreme values rather than being dropped totally from the data set, as in trimming. For example, the 5% trimmed mean drops the highest 5% of the observations and lowest 5% of the observations before the means are computed. The 5% **Winsorized mean** with 20 observations changes the highest value (highest 5%) to the second highest value and changes the lowest value (lowest 5%) to the second lowest. Exhibit 5.2 compares these methods.

In Exhibit 5.2, we can see that the arithmetic mean is 1257.7, which is vastly different from the trimmed mean, 1217.5, and the Winsorized mean, 1216.6. The latter two adjusted means are actually similar to the median, 1220. Which measure of central tendency best represents the distribution? This is where judgment is

Exhibit 5.2   **Calculation for Arithmetic Mean, Trimmed Mean, Winsorized Mean**

Data Set:

| | | | |
|---|---|---|---|
| 660 | 1,070 | 1,220 | 1,430 |
| 740 | 1,100 | 1,250 | 1,475 |
| 800 | 1,100 | 1,250 | 1,550 |
| 820 | 1,140 | 1,250 | 1,600 |
| 880 | 1,150 | 1,300 | 1,700 |
| 930 | 1,150 | 1,300 | 1,850 |
| 1,000 | 1,200 | 1,400 | 2,900 |

Before calculations are made, arrange the data in order from lowest to highest.

Arithmetic Mean: Sum the observations and divide by the total number of observations:
660 + 740 + ... + 2900 = 35,215/28 = 1257.7

Trimmed Mean: Eliminate the lowest number, which is 660.
Eliminate the highest number, which is 2900.
Subtract these values from the previous sum:
35,215 − (660 + 2900) = 31,655
Divide by the remaining number of observations:
31,655/26 = 1217.5

Winsorized Mean: Identify the lowest 5%, 660 and 740, which are each replaced by 800.
Identify the highest 5%, 1850 and 2900, which are replaced by 1700.
32,215 − 600 − 740 − 1850 + 2900 = 29,065
29,065 + 800 + 800 + 1700 + 1700 = 34,065
Divide by the total number of observations:
34,065/28 = 1216.6

Median: 1220

Summary:
| Arithmetic Mean: | 1257.7 |
|---|---|
| Trimmed Mean: | 1217.5 |
| Winsorized Mean: | 1216.6 |

important. The statistical analyst must "eyeball" the raw data to make this decision. It appears that the highest score, 2900, strongly influences the arithmetic mean. Therefore, the trimmed mean, the Winsorized mean, or the median better represent this data set. The data analyst should select the measure of central tendency that best describes the typical value in the frequency distribution. The analyst should include an explanation of why an alternative to the more traditional measure of central tendency—the mean—was used to describe the frequency distribution.

We can use electronic spreadsheets such as Microsoft Excel to calculate the mean, median, and mode. The data in Exhibit 5.2 should be arranged in a single column as shown in the Excel spreadsheet in Figure 5.2. To perform the statistical calculation, from the "Tools" menu, select "Data Analysis," then "Descriptive Statistics" from the dialog box. A second dialog appears in Figure 5.3. In the "Input Range," highlight the range of values to be included in the calculations, then check "Summary Statistics," "kth largest," and "kth smallest." Displayed in Exhibit 5.3, the output includes both measures of central tendency, which we have just reviewed, and measures of variability, which we will discuss in the next section. The terms "kurtosis" and "skewness" refer to the shape of the distribution, which we will discuss in Chapter 6.

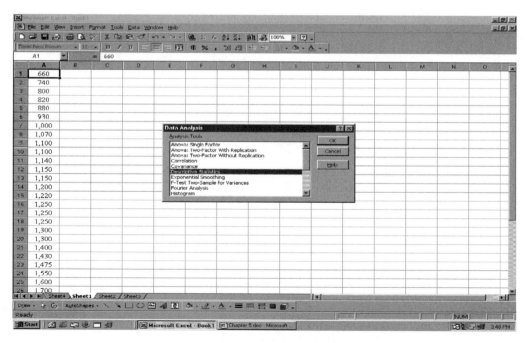

Figure 5.2   **Excel Spreadsheet—Arrangement of Data and Descriptive Statistics**

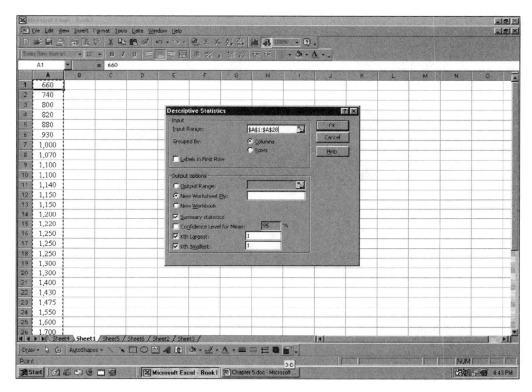

Figure 5.3   **Excel Descriptives Dialog Box**

# Measures of Variability

Measures of central tendency are not the only statistics used to summarize a frequency distribution. We also want to consider the spread of the distribution, which tells us how widely the observations are spread out around the measure of central tendency. The most commonly used **measures of variability** are the variance and the standard deviation. The scales of measurement appropriate for the use of the variance and standard deviation are the interval and ratio scales.

Measures of spread increase in value with greater variation on the variable. Measures of spread equal zero when there is no variation. Maximum spread for metric and ordinal variables occurs when cases are evenly split between two extreme groups—this is called **polarization**. Maximum dispersion for nominal variables is defined as when there is an even distribution of cases across the categories regardless of the number of categories, which is called **uniformity**. When each category of a nominal variable occurs just once, it is called **individuality**.

Exhibit 5.3    **Excel Output for "Descriptives"**

| Data Set | |
|---|---:|
| Mean | 1,257.68 |
| Standard Error | 81.46 |
| Median | 1,210.00 |
| Mode | 1,250 |
| Standard Deviation | 431.05 |
| Sample Variance | 185,802.74 |
| Kurtosis | 7.06 |
| Skewness | 2.07 |
| Range | 2,240 |
| Minimum | 660 |
| Maximum | 2,900 |
| Sum | 35,215 |
| Count | 28 |
| Largest (1) | 2,900 |
| Smallest (1) | 660 |

## Range

The simplest measure of spread is the **range**. It is simply the difference between the smallest and largest values in a frequency distribution:

$$Range = X_{max} - X_{min}$$

The range is easy to calculate but is affected by extreme measures. Therefore, it is a nonresistant measure of spread. The range varies widely from sample to sample. Only the two most extreme scores affect its value, so it is not sensitive to other values in the distribution. Also, the range is dependent upon sample size: in general, the larger the sample size, the greater the range.

Two frequency distributions may have the same range but the observations can differ greatly in variability. For example, consider the following two frequency distributions:

Distribution 1

| 1 | 2 | 3 | 4 | 5 | 6 | 7 | 8 | 9 | 10 |
|---|---|---|---|---|---|---|---|---|---|

Distribution 2

| 1 | 1.5 | 3 | 3.5 | 3.7 | 7 | 8 | 8.26 | 10 | 10 |
|---|---|---|---|---|---|---|---|---|---|

The range for both distributions is 10 − 1 = 9. But if we compare the two distributions, we see that there is more variation in Distribution 2 than in Distribution

1. This is confirmed when the variance for each distribution is calculated—the variance for Distribution 1 is 3.03, and the variance for Distribution 2 is 3.44.

## Variance and Standard Deviation

The **variance** ($s^2$) is the average of the squared deviations from the mean. The variance of a frequency distribution will be larger when the observations within the distribution are widely spread. The variance (and, as we shall see, the standard deviation) is maximized when the data are polarized. The formula for calculating the variance is

$$s^2 = \frac{\sum_{i=1}^{n}(X_i - \overline{X})^2}{N-1}$$

The squared deviations of the mean are calculated by subtracting the mean of a frequency distribution from each value in the distribution, $(X - \overline{X})$. The difference between the two values is then squared, $(X - \overline{X})^2$. The squared differences are summed and divided by $(N - 1)$.

The term $(N - 1)$ is a concept referred to as the number of **degrees of freedom**. If the mean of a frequency distribution is known, then only $(N - 1)$ observations are free to vary. Stated another way, if we know the mean and $(N - 1)$ scores, we can determine the $n$th score. The effect of dividing by $(N - 1)$ increases the value of $s^2$ slightly and is considered to be a less biased estimate of the population variance. However, when $N$ is large, the effect of using $(N - 1)$ instead of $N$ is negligible. We will encounter this concept again in Chapter 7.

As an example, we will calculate the variance for the census data that appear in Table 5.2. The average daily census is 175.6. To calculate the variance, we set up the problem as follows:

Table 5.4   **Calculating the Variance for Census Data (Table 5.2)**

| Day | Census | Census − Mean $(X - \overline{X})$ | (Census − Mean)$^2$ $(X - \overline{X})^2$ |
|---|---|---|---|
| Sunday | 167 | −8.6 | 73.96 |
| Monday | 185 | 9.4 | 88.36 |
| Tuesday | 173 | −2.6 | 6.76 |
| Wednesday | 182 | 6.4 | 40.96 |
| Thursday | 179 | 3.4 | 11.56 |
| Friday | 173 | −2.6 | 6.76 |
| Saturday | 170 | −5.6 | 31.36 |
| Total | 1,229 | ≈0* | 259.72 |

*due to rounding

Note that the property of the mean that is described in Exhibit 5.1, the sum of the deviations from the mean is equal to 0, is displayed in the above calculations. (In the above example, the sum is approximately equal to 0.0 because the mean is rounded.) Substituting into the formula, we calculate the variance as:

$$s^2 = \frac{\sum_{i=1}^{n}(X_i - \overline{X})^2}{N-1} = \frac{259.72}{6} = 43.28$$

The variance is equal to 43.28, but what does this mean? The interpretation of the variance is not easy at the descriptive level because the original units of measure are squared to arrive at the variance. However, if we take the square root of the variance, we return to the original units of measurement. The square root of variance is the **standard deviation** (*s*):

$$s = \sqrt{\frac{\sum_{i=1}^{n}(X_i - \overline{X})^2}{N-1}}$$

Continuing with the census example, the standard deviation is calculated as

$$s = \sqrt{\frac{\sum_{i=1}^{n}(X_i - \overline{X})^2}{N-1}} = \sqrt{43.28} = 6.58$$

The standard deviation is the most widely used measure of variation used in descriptive statistics. The standard deviation measures variability in the same units of measurement as the sample (i.e., height, age, length of stay, and so on). Because the standard deviation is easier to interpret, it is the preferred measure of dispersion for a frequency distribution. The standard deviation is interpreted in relation to the normal distribution, which we will discuss in Chapter 6.

As already noted, the variance is of little use in descriptive statistics, but it is important in procedures related to statistical inference. The standard deviation, which is the square root of the variance, is defined in terms of deviations from the mean. It is an important measure at the descriptive level. Procedures for calculating the mean, variance, and standard deviation of a frequency distribution are outlined in Exhibit 5.4.

## Calculating Measures of Central Tendency and Variability Using Excel

Thus far, we have reviewed the formulae for calculating the mean, range, variance, and standard deviation. We have seen that we can use Microsoft Excel to perform these calculations. In this example, we see that we must always check the output

Exhibit 5.4    **Calculation of Mean, Variance, and Standard Deviation for Ages of Nursing Home Residents**

| Patient No. | Age | $(X-\bar{X})$ | $(X-\bar{X})^2$ | Patient No. | Age | $(X-\bar{X})$ | $(X \pm 1s)$ |
|---|---|---|---|---|---|---|---|
| 1 | 76 | −6 | 36 | 11 | 82 | 0 | 0 |
| 2 | 76 | −6 | 36 | 12 | 82 | 0 | 0 |
| 3 | 78 | −4 | 16 | 13 | 82 | 0 | 0 |
| 4 | 78 | −4 | 16 | 14 | 84 | +2 | 4 |
| 5 | 78 | −4 | 16 | 15 | 84 | +2 | 4 |
| 6 | 78 | −4 | 16 | 16 | 86 | +4 | 16 |
| 7 | 80 | −2 | 4 | 17 | 88 | +6 | 36 |
| 8 | 80 | −2 | 4 | 18 | 88 | +6 | 36 |
| 9 | 80 | −2 | 4 | 19 | 90 | +8 | 64 |
| 10 | 80 | −2 | 4 | 20 | 90 | +8 | 64 |
| | | | | $\Sigma$ | 1,640 | 0 | 376 |

Using a random sample of 20 nursing home residents, calculate the average age of nursing home residents.

**Mean:**

1. Sum the observations ($\Sigma$): 1640
2. Divide by the number of observations ($N$): 20 = 1640/20 = 82

Interpretation: The average age or typical age of any nursing home resident is 82.

**Variance:**

1. Subtract the mean from each observation: $(X-\bar{X})$
2. Square each deviation from the mean: $(X-\bar{X})^2$
3. Sum the squared deviations from the mean: $\sum(X-\bar{X})^2$
4. Divide the sum of the squared deviations from the mean by $N-1$ (19).

$$s^2 = \sum(X-\bar{X})^2/N-1$$
$$= 376/19$$
$$= 19.8$$

The standard deviation is the square root of the variance:

$$s = \sqrt{\sum(X-\bar{X})^2/N-1}$$
$$= 4.45$$

Interpretation: Approximately 68% of the nursing home residents are between the ages of 77.55 and 86.45 ($X + 1s$).

Exhibit 5.5 **Excel Output of Age of Nursing Home Residents**

| Age of Nursing Home Residents | |
|---|---|
| Mean | 82 |
| Standard Error | 0.99 |
| Median | 81 |
| Mode | 78 |
| Standard Deviation | 4.45 |
| Sample Variance | 19.79 |
| Kurtosis | −0.82 |
| Skewness | 0.54 |
| Range | 14 |
| Minimum | 76 |
| Maximum | 90 |
| Sum | 1,640 |
| Count | 20 |
| Largest (1) | 90 |
| Smallest (1) | 76 |

against the original data set. In Exhibit 5.5, the output indicates that the mode is 78, but a review of the frequency distribution indicates that there are two modes, 78 and 80. Thus, the reported mode may not be a fair representation of the distribution.

In reviewing the data, you can see that the results are similar to the results that were calculated with the assistance of a hand-held calculator. Notice that the results indicate the number of observations that were included in the calculation ($n = 20$). This should always be reviewed to verify that the correct number of observations was entered into the Excel spreadsheet.

## GROUPED FREQUENCY DISTRIBUTIONS

Because it is inconvenient to work with large data sets, sometimes data are grouped into class intervals for analysis. Table 5.5 presents an example of an ungrouped frequency distribution. There are 58 patients with varying LOSs. In this format, the data are difficult to interpret, so we will group the LOSs into **class intervals**. Class intervals are ways of classifying or summarizing raw data into categories.

Table 5.5    **Patient Length of Stay (LOS)**

| LOS (X) | Frequency (f) | fX |
|---|---|---|
| 1 | 0 | 0 |
| 2 | 2 | 4 |
| 3 | 6 | 18 |
| 4 | 6 | 24 |
| 5 | 6 | 30 |
| 6 | 11 | 66 |
| 7 | 6 | 42 |
| 8 | 8 | 64 |
| 9 | 5 | 45 |
| 10 | 3 | 30 |
| 11 | 1 | 11 |
| 12 | 2 | 24 |
| 13 | 1 | 13 |
| 14 | 1 | 14 |
| Total | 58 | 385 |

## Grouping Data

The first step in grouping data is to determine the number of class intervals (categories) to use. There is no fixed rule as to how many intervals are appropriate; some recommend 5 to 15 class intervals, whereas others recommend 10 to 20. However, all agree that there should not be more than 20. As an example, we will group the LOS frequency distribution that appears in Table 5.5.

To construct the grouped frequency distribution, we will arbitrarily select five class intervals for grouping the LOS data. Next, we must determine the width of each of these intervals. This is accomplished by dividing the range of the distribution by the number of class intervals: $(14 - 2)/5 = 2.4$. The nearest odd integer value is used to select the width of the class interval; thus, the width will be 3. To construct the class interval, determine what the highest and lowest class intervals should be. These class intervals will contain the highest and lowest values in the frequency distribution.

In the LOS data in Table 5.5, the number 14 is the highest observation, and the number 2 is the lowest observation; thus, the highest and lowest class intervals must contain these values. The class interval containing the highest value should be placed at the top of the grouped frequency distribution, and the lowest class interval should be placed at the bottom of the grouped frequency distribution. Intervals should be continuous throughout the distribution; that is, there should not be any gaps in values in the distribution. Using the ungrouped data, tally the frequencies that occur in each interval. The LOS data in Table 5.5 are presented as a grouped frequency distribution in Table 5.6.

Table 5.6 groups the LOS data into seven class intervals, each having a width of 2. Also notice that there are two columns—one indicating the **apparent limits** of the class interval and the other indicating the **real limits** of the class interval. The real limits depict the continuous nature of the distribution. The interval width is the difference between the upper and lower real limits of the class interval—for example, $2.5 - 0.5 = 2$. The highest value, 14, is contained in the class interval "13–14," and the lowest value, 2, is contained in the class interval "1–2." Keep in mind that the distribution should not contain any gaps; even if there are no values that fall within a given interval, it should be included in the distribution. The midpoint ($M$) of the intervals is obtained by adding the apparent limits of the class intervals and dividing by two—for example, $(1 + 2)/2 = 1.5$, and $(3 + 4)/2 = 3.5$. The midpoint will be used in calculating the mean, median, and mode of the grouped distribution. As an alternative to the above procedure for constructing class intervals, we can use Sturges' rule as a guide:

$$k = 1 + 3.3\log_n(n)$$

where $\log_{10}$ is the usual base-10 logarithm, $k$ is the number of class intervals, and $n$ is the number of data items to be grouped into class intervals.

Using the LOS data from Table 5.5, the number of class intervals ($k$) required for the grouped frequency distribution would be calculated as follows:

$$k = 1 + 3.3\log_n(n) = 1 + 3.3\log_{10}(58) = 1 + (3.3)(1.7653) = 6.83$$

Because our result is a fraction, we will round to the nearest whole number. Thus, seven class intervals are needed for grouping the frequency distribution in Table 5.5.

After the number of class intervals has been determined, the next step is to determine the width of the intervals:

$$width = \frac{max - min}{k} = \frac{range}{k}$$

Table 5.6    **Class Intervals for Length-of-Stay Data**

| Apparent Limits | Real Limits | Tally | *f* | *M* |
|---|---|---|---|---|
| 13–14 | 12.5–14.5 | // | 2 | 13.5 |
| 11–12 | 10.5–12.5 | /// | 3 | 11.5 |
| 9–10 | 8.5–10.5 | ### /// | 8 | 9.5 |
| 7–8 | 6.5–8.5 | ### ### //// | 14 | 7.5 |
| 5–6 | 4.5–6.5 | ### ### ### // | 17 | 5.5 |
| 3–4 | 2.5–4.5 | ### ### // | 12 | 3.5 |
| 1–2 | 0.5–2.5 | // | 2 | 1.5 |
| | | | 58 | |

Table 5.7    **Grouped Frequency Distribution of Length-of-Stay Data**

| Class Interval | *f* | Cum *f* | Rel *f* | |
|---|---|---|---|---|
| 13–14 | 2 | 58 (56 + 2) | .034 (2/58) | 100.0 (96.5 + 3.4) |
| 11–12 | 3 | 56 (53 + 3) | .052 | 96.5 (91.3 + 5.2) |
| 9–10 | 8 | 53 (45+8) | .138 | 91.3 (77.5 + 13.8) |
| 7–8 | 14 | 45 (31 + 14) | .241 | 77.5 (53.4 + 24.1) |
| 5–6 | 17 | 31 (14 + 17) | .293 | 53.4 (24.1 + 29.3) |
| 3–4 | 12 | 14 (2 + 12) | .207 | 24.1 (3.4 + 20.7) |
| 1–2 | 2 | 2 | .034 | 3.4 |
| | 58 | | | |

where *max* is the largest value in the data set, *min* is the smallest value in the data set, and *k* is the number of class intervals.

$$width = \frac{14-2}{7} = \frac{12}{7} = 1.7 \approx 2$$

The results appear in Table 5.6. The data in Table 5.6 are usually summarized as presented in Table 5.7. The proportion of the total in each class interval is called the relative frequency (rel *f*) and is obtained by dividing the frequency (*f*), or number of observations in a given interval, by the total number of observations (*N*). The cumulative frequency (cum *f*) is obtained by summing the observations in each interval with the number of observations (frequencies) in the next interval, beginning with the lowest class interval and proceeding upward. The first class interval ("1–2") contains two observations; thus, the cumulative frequency is 2. The next class interval contains 12 observations; thus, the cumulative frequency is $2 + 12 = 14$. Proceed in this manner until the last class interval is reached. Exhibit 5.6 outlines the steps for constructing a grouped frequency distribution.

There are several disadvantages associated with grouped frequency distributions. First, precision in the resulting statistical calculations is lost. When values are grouped into an interval, the values might be spread evenly throughout the interval or the values might be concentrated at either end of the interval. When data are grouped, the assumption is that the observations are spread evenly across the class intervals. Second, as we have seen, different groupings can result from the same frequency distribution. Grouping a set of values does not result in a unique set of grouped scores. That is, if the same frequency distribution were grouped into slightly different class intervals, the sample statistics would not be exactly the same.

## Calculating the Mean from a Grouped Frequency Distribution

The first step in calculating the mean from a grouped frequency distribution is to determine the midpoint of each interval. Table 5.8 presents the grouped LOS with the corresponding midpoint ($X$) for each interval. The midpoint represents all ob-

---

Exhibit 5.6    **Steps in Constructing a Grouped Frequency Distribution**

1. Determine the number of class intervals needed by the Sturges rule. It is suggested that the number of intervals be limited to 20.

2. Determine the width of the class intervals by dividing the range of the frequency distribution by the number of class intervals obtained in step 1. Intervals should be set up so that one score cannot belong to more than one class interval.

3. Determine the point at which the lowest class interval should begin.

4. Record the limits of all class intervals, placing the interval containing the highest score value at the top. Intervals should be continuous and of the same width. Do not leave out class intervals in which no observations occur; to do so would create a misleading impression.

5. Using the tally system, place a tally for each observation in the corresponding class intervals.

6. Summarize the tallies for each class interval in a frequency ($f$) column.

7. Record the total ($f$) at the bottom of the frequency column.

---

servations that fall into that interval. For example, the observations 13 and 14 (from Table 5.4) fall into the class interval "13–14"; the midpoint, 13.5, represents both of these observations. The mean is obtained by multiplying the midpoint ($X$) of each class interval by its corresponding frequency ($f$); these observations are summed and then divided by the total number of observations ($N$):

$$\overline{X} = \frac{\sum fX}{N}$$

where $X$ is the midpoint of each interval.

Therefore, for the grouped LOS data, the mean is

$$\overline{X} = \frac{381}{58} = 6.57$$

The mean for the grouped data, 6.57 (Table 5.8), does not equal the mean for the ungrouped data, 385/58 = 6.64. This discrepancy illustrates the loss of precision that occurs when grouping frequency distributions.

## Calculating the Median from Grouped Data

Recall that the median is the point in a distribution at which 50% of the observations fall above and 50% of the observations fall below. To determine the median in a grouped distribution, we first must determine which observation meets this

Table 5.8    **Grouped LOS Data for Calculating the Mean**

| Class Interval | Midpoint ($X$) | $f$ | $f(X)$ |
|---|---|---|---|
| 13–14 | 13.5 | 2 | 27 |
| 11–12 | 11.5 | 3 | 34.5 |
| 9–10 | 9.5 | 8 | 76 |
| 7–8 | 7.5 | 14 | 105 |
| 5–6 | 5.5 | 17 | 93.5 |
| 3–4 | 3.5 | 12 | 42 |
| 1–2 | 41.5 | 2 | 3 |
| | | $\Sigma = 58$ | $\Sigma = 381$ |

$$\overline{X} = \Sigma fX/N$$
$$= 381/58$$
$$= 6.57$$

definition. For the LOS data in Table 5.8, the median would be the 29th value, as calculated below:

$$50\% \text{ of } N = 0.5 \times 58 = 29$$

Thus, the 29th value will be the median for the grouped distribution. Inspection of the data in Table 5.8 shows that the 29th observation falls in the interval, "5–6." How is this determined? Begin counting the frequencies ($f$) in the lowest class interval, "1–2," until the interval containing the 29th observation is located ($2 + 12 + 17 = 31$). The interval "5–6" contains the 15th, 16th, 17th, 18th, 19th, and so on up to the 31st observation. Thus, the 29th observation occurs in this interval. The cumulative frequency column provides this information for us. The median is obtained by

$$M_D = L + \frac{w(\frac{1}{2}n - c)}{f_{M_D}}$$

where $L$ is the real lower limit of the class interval containing the median, $w$ is the width of the interval, $c$ is the total number of values falling below the interval containing the median (cumulative frequency), and $f_{M_D}$ is the frequency of the values in the interval containing the median value.

Substituting into our formula, with $L = 4.5$, $w = 2$, $c = 14$, and $f_{M_D} = 17$, we have

$$M_D = 4.5 + \frac{2\left[\frac{1}{2}(58) - 14\right]}{17} = 4.5 + \frac{2(29 - 14)}{17} = 4.5 + \frac{30}{17} = 4.5 + 1.76 = 6.26$$

The median for the grouped frequency distribution is 6.26 days; the median for the ungrouped distribution is 6 days.

## Calculating the Mode from Grouped Data

There are several ways to determine the mode from grouped data. The simplest is to take the midpoint of the most frequently occurring class interval. For the LOS data in Table 5.8, the mode is 5.5 because 17 observations fall in this interval. This is referred to as the crude mode.

The second way to determine the mode from a grouped distribution adjusts the modal value in relation to the relative frequencies in the class intervals adjacent to the class interval containing the modal value. It pulls the modal value toward the adjacent class interval that has greater frequency. This mode is referred to as the refined mode and is calculated as follows:

$$Refined\ mode = L + \frac{w(f_{mo} - f_b)}{(f_{mo} - f_b) + (f_{mo} - f_a)}$$

where $L$ is the real lower limit of the class interval containing the modal value, $w$ is the width of the class interval, $f_{mo}$ is the number of values in the class interval containing the mode, $f_b$ is the number of values in the adjacent class interval below the class interval containing the mode, and $f_a$ is the number of values in the adjacent class interval above the class interval containing the mode.

For the grouped LOS data in Table 5.8, $L = 4.5$, $w = 2$, $f_{mo} = 17$, $f_b = 12$, and $f_a = 14$, so the refined mode is calculated as follows:

$$Refined\, mode = 4.5 + \frac{2(17-12)}{(17-12)+(17-14)} = 4.5 + \frac{2(5)}{5+3} = 4.5 + \frac{10}{8} = 4.5 + 1.25 = 5.75$$

Thus, the refined mode is 5.75 and the crude mode is 5.5. You can see from the calculations for the refined mode that the number of observations in the class interval that is immediately above ($f_a = 14$) the interval containing the mode is pulling the modal value in that direction. Compare the refined mode to the mode in the ungrouped frequency distribution for the LOS data in Table 5.5, where the mode is 6. The length of stay—six days—occurred 11 times.

## Calculating the Variance and Standard Deviation from Grouped Data

To compute the variance and standard deviation from grouped data, we will use what is called the raw score formula. The data from Table 5.8 are reproduced in Table 5.9, but we need to add another column—$f(X^2)$—which is the midpoint ($X^2$) multiplied by the frequency ($f$). The raw score formula for calculating the variance is

$$s^2 = \frac{\sum x^2}{N-1}$$

**Table 5.9  Grouped LOS Data for Calculating the Standard Deviation**

| Class Interval | Midpoint ($X$) | $f$ | $fX$ | $F(X^2)$ |
|---|---|---|---|---|
| 13–14 | 13.5 | 2 | 27 | 364.5 |
| 11–12 | 11.5 | 3 | 34.5 | 396.75 |
| 9–10 | 9.5 | 8 | 76 | 722.0 |
| 7–8 | 7.5 | 14 | 105 | 787.5 |
| 5–6 | 5.5 | 17 | 93.5 | 514.25 |
| 3–4 | 3.5 | 12 | 42 | 147.0 |
| 1–2 | 1.5 | 2 | 3 | 4.5 |
| | | $\Sigma = 58$ | $\Sigma = 381$ | $\Sigma = 2{,}936.5$ |

and the standard deviation is

$$s = \sqrt{\frac{\sum x^2}{N-1}}$$

where the $\sum x^2$ term is

$$\sum x^2 = \sum f(X^2) - \frac{\sum (X)^2}{N}$$

To calculate the variance and standard deviation, we have

$$\sum x^2 = 2936.5 - \frac{(381)^2}{58} = 2936.5 - 2502.78 = 433.7$$

$$s^2 = \frac{\sum x^2}{N-1} = \frac{433.7}{57} = 7.61$$

and

$$s = \sqrt{\frac{\sum x^2}{N-1}} = \sqrt{7.61} = 2.76$$

The variance and standard deviation for our LOS data are 7.61 and 2.76, respectively. Measures of central tendency and variation for the ungrouped and grouped frequency distributions are compared in Table 5.10. Note that the grouped distribution results in a greater variation than the ungrouped distribution because only the midpoint of each interval is considered in the calculations rather than the entire data set.

Table 5.10 **Measures of Central Tendency and Variation, Ungrouped Data versus Grouped Data**

|  | **Ungrouped Distribution** | **Grouped Distribution** |
| --- | --- | --- |
| Mean | 6.64 | 6.57 |
| Median | 6 | 6.26 |
| Mode | 6 | 5.75 |
| Variance | 2.76 | 7.61 |
| S.D. | 1.66 | 2.76 |

## Percentiles

Health information management professionals are often asked to "benchmark" characteristics of the organization within which they work to the performance of peer organizations. An example of a benchmark report is the quarterly Program for Evaluation Payment Patterns Electronic Report, abbreviated as the PEPPER report (Exhibit 5.7). These reports are prepared by the states' Medicare Quality Improvement Organizations (QIOs), formerly Peer Review Organizations (PROs). This report compares the performance of one hospital against all others in the state on certain DRG pairs. National DRG data indicated that certain DRGs are subject to "upcoding," that is, assigning codes that would move an inpatient discharge from a lower weighted DRG to a higher weighted DRG. Peer data are used to identify "outliers" that might indicate a health care organization is "under-coding" or "over-coding" certain types of Medicare cases. The data are reported in the form of percentiles. So, if a hospital's performance is at the 10th percentile or below, there may be opportunity to improve the quality of the codes assigned for a certain DRG pair. Alternatively, if the hospital's performance is at the 90th percentile, it could be interpreted that the hospital was "upcoding" cases to the higher weighted DRG.

**Percentiles** are measures of spread and location. Percentiles divide data into 100 equal parts. They represent the proportion of scores in a distribution that a specific score is greater than or equal to, or less than or equal to. For example, if an individual ranks 37th in a graduating class of 250, it means that 213 individuals were ranked below. Thus, 213/250 = 85.2, which, rounded, is the 85th percentile. The interpretation is that this individual ranked higher than 85% of his classmates; his percentile rank is 85. If the individual ranked first in the graduating class, the percentile rank would be 249/250 = 99.6, and the percentile rank for an individual graduating last would be 0 because there are no classmates ranked below.

Consider an example of scores on a statistics test. A total of 14 students completed the examination with the following scores:

$$25, 34, 68, 76, 80, 80, 82, 83, 85, 88, 90, 92, 97, 99$$

What is the percentile rank for the score 88? There are 14 scores, and there are 10 scores at or below 88. Dividing 10 by 14, we obtain a percentile of 71.4; that is, 71.4% of the scores were at or below a score of 88. Conversely, 28.6% of the scores fall above 88 (1.000 – 0.714).

Special types of percentiles are referred to as quartiles. **Quartiles** divide the frequency distribution into four equal parts: 25%, 50%, 75%, and 100%. The second quartile (Q2) is the median of a distribution, or the 50th percentile. The first quartile (Q1) is equal to the 25th percentile, and the third quartile (Q3) is equal to the 75th percentile. The first quartile is equal to the median of the lower half of the frequency distribution, and the third quartile is equal to the median of the upper half of the distribution.

Another measure of spread is the **interquartile range** (IQR), which is defined as the difference between the Q3 and Q1, or, IQR = Q3 – Q1. The interquartile range includes 50% of the data set and removes the influence of outliers because the highest and lowest quarters of the distribution are removed.

By direct observation, we can determine the first, second, and third quartiles as well as the interquartile range from the above data set:

| | |
|---|---|
| Q2 or median: | (82 + 83)/2 = 82.5 |
| Q1 | 76: median of the lower half of the distribution |
| Q3 | 90: median of the upper half of the distribution |
| Interquartile range: | 90 – 76 = 14 |

The percentiles and quartiles also may be calculated by ("round" means rounding to the nearest integer):

$$
\begin{aligned}
\text{88th Percentile} &= round(0.88)(N+1) \\
&= round(0.88)(14+1) \\
&= 13.2, \text{ or the 13th observation in the distribution, which} \\
&\quad \text{equals 97} \\
\text{Q1} &= round(0.25)(N+1) \\
&= round(0.25)(14+1) \\
&= 3.75, \text{ or the 4th observation in the distribution, which} \\
&\quad \text{equals 76} \\
\text{Q2} &= round(0.75)(N+1) \\
&= round(0.75)(14+1) \\
&= 11.25, \text{ or the 11th observation in the distribution, which} \\
&\quad \text{equals 90}
\end{aligned}
$$

The data in Exhibit 5.7 compares hospital-specific data for selected DRGs with state data. The report indicates that for the DRG pair 014, "Intracranial Hemorrhage and Stroke with Infarction," and 015, "Non-Specific Cardiovascular and Precerebral Occlusion without Infarction," 76% of the cases fell into the higher-weighted DRG: 14/(14 + 12) = 53.8%. This percentage falls exactly at the 10th percentile when compared to all hospitals within the state.

The general interpretation of the PEPPER report for this DRG pair in this state is that for 90% of the hospitals, up to 82.6% of their cases fall into the higher-weighted DRG, and 10% of the hospitals have up to 53.8% of their cases fall into the higher-weighted DRG. Fifty percent of the hospitals have up to 69.7% of their cases fall into the higher-weighted DRGs. For this hospital, the ranking for the

Exhibit 5.7    **Example PEPPER Paired DRG Report**

| Indicator | Hospital Performance | | | State Performance | | | |
|---|---|---|---|---|---|---|---|
| | 1st DRG | 2nd DRG | % Higher | 10th %tile | 50th %tile | 75th %tile | 90th %tile |
| 14*/15 | 14 | 12 | 53.8% | 53.8% | 69.7% | 75.8% | 82.6% |
| 79*/89 | 13 | 66 | 16.5% | 6.6% | 17.5% | 25.2% | 32.8% |
| 416*/320 | 53 | 25 | 67.9% | 25.0% | 48.4% | 65.0% | 72.3% |

*Denotes Higher Weighted DRG.

DRG pair is exactly at the 10th percentile. The conclusion is that there may be an opportunity to improve documentation and coding for this particular DRG pair. For DRGs, 416/320 = 67.9% of the hospital's cases fall into DRG 416, which is slightly above the 75th percentile for the state. The conclusion is that the coding for this pair falls within acceptable limits; that is, it does not appear that upcoding is occurring.

## CONCLUSION

The mean, median, and mode are measures of central tendency that are commonly used to describe frequency distributions. Measures of central tendency describe the "most typical" value or observation in a frequency distribution. The measure used to describe the distribution should be based on both the scale of measurement and the determination of which measure best describes the most typical observation in the frequency distribution.

Measures of spread are the variance, the standard deviation, and the range. The range tells us the distance between the lowest value in a distribution and the highest value, so in general, it does not provide much information about the frequency distribution. The standard deviation is the most common descriptive statistic used to describe the spread of a frequency distribution for metric variables. Percentiles are measures of spread and location often used in benchmarking. Percentiles are used to provide comparative information between health care organizations.

## REFERENCES

U.S. Department of Health and Human Services, Public Health Service. (1992) *Principles of Epidemiology: An Introduction to Applied Epidemiology and Biostatistics*. Atlanta, GA: USDHHS.

U.S. Department of Health and Human Services, Centers for Disease Control and Prevention (CDC), National Center for Health Statistics (NCHS), Office of Analysis, Epidemiology, and Health Promotion (OAEHP). Compressed Mortality File (CMF), compiled form CMF 1968–1988, Series 20, No. SQ 2000, CMF 1989–1998, Series 20, No. 2E 2003 and CMF 1999–2001, Series 20, No. 2G 2004 on CDC WONDER Online Database. http://wonder.cdc.gov.

# APPENDIX 5-A

## EXERCISES FOR SOLVING PROBLEMS

### Knowledge Questions

1. Define the key terms listed at the beginning of this chapter.
2. What is the difference between a population parameter and a sample statistic?
3. Compare and contrast the following measures of central tendency: mean, median, and mode.
4. Define polarization, individuality, and uniformity in relation to variability in a frequency distribution.
5. Why do measures of central tendency and the variation of ungrouped frequency distributions differ from those of grouped frequency distributions?

### Multiple Choice

1. There are 40 students in Section I of a medical terminology class and 20 students in Section II. The mean score on a midterm exam for Section I is 60, and the mean score for Section II is 70. What is the mean score for the two classes combined?
   a. 63.3
   b. 65.0
   c. 67.0
   d. Not enough information provided to answer this question
2. For the two scores 8 and 12, $\sum(X - \overline{X})^2$ is:

   a. 2           c. 8
   b. 4           d. 12
3. In a frequency distribution, the lowest score is 25, the highest score is 50, and the mean is 37.5. The range is:
   a. 11          c. 24
   b. 12.5        d. 25
4. In grouping a set of scores from a frequency distribution, the width of the class intervals should:
   a. Be equal
   b. Be at least one
   c. Vary according to the frequency within the interval
   d. Be no more than 10
5. The first class interval in the grouped frequency distribution is "5–10." The width of the interval is:
   a. 5.0         c. 6.0
   b. 5.5         d. 6.5
6. The midpoint of the class interval "5–10" is:
   a. 7.0         c. 8.0
   b. 7.5         d. 8.5
7. The width of a class interval is 3, and the midpoint is 9. The apparent lower limit of the interval is:
   a. 7.0         c. 8.0
   b. 7.5         d. 8.5
8. The "real limits" of the class interval "1–3" are:
   a. 0.5–3.5     c. 0.0–4.0
   b. 1.0–3.0     d. 1.5–2.5

The following table displays a cumulative frequency distribution of the length of stay of patients discharged from Community Be-havior Health Care during the week of April 1. Use the table below to answer Questions 9 through 14.

Table 5-A.1    **Length of Stay Cumulative Frequency Distribution**

| Class Interval for Length of Stay | f | Cum f | Cum. % |
|---|---|---|---|
| 20–24 | 4 | 20 | 100 |
| 15–19 | 8 | 16 | 80 |
| 10–14 | 6 | 8 | 40 |
| 5–9 | 0 | 2 | 10 |
| 0–4 | 2 | 2 | 10 |

9. Six patients had lengths of stay that fall:
   a. Below 14.5 days
   b. At 12 days
   c. Above 9.5 days
   d. Between 9.5 days and 14.5 days
10. Twelve patients had lengths of stay that were greater than:
    a. 14.5 days
    b. 15.0 days
    c. 17.0 days
    d. 19.5 days
11. Twenty-eight patients had lengths of stay below:
    a. 20.0 days
    b. 19.5 days
    c. 17.0 days
    d. 14.5 days
12. The cumulative frequency value of "8" means that 8 cases fall below:
    a. 19.5 days
    b. 14 days
    c. 12 days
    d. 10 days

13. Eighty percent of the patients discharged had lengths of stay that fell below:
    a. 19.5 days
    b. 19.0 days
    c. 17.0 days
    d. 14.5 days
14. Which of the following is not a measure of spread?
    a. Mode
    b. Range
    c. Standard deviation
    d. Variance
15. Review the following two frequency distributions:

    Distribution 1:
    200, 210, 190, 220, 195

    Distribution 2:
    210, 170, 180, 235, 240

    The standard deviation for Distribution 1 is:
    a. The same as that for Distribution 2
    b. Less than that for Distribution 2

c.  Greater than that for Distribution 2
d.  Not enough information is provided

16. The standard deviation of a frequency distribution is 5. The variance is:
    a.  10
    b.  15
    c.  20
    d.  25

17. In a frequency distribution, the mean is 32. If each score is divided by 2, the mean of the new distribution is:
    a.  64
    b.  32
    c.  16
    d.  Not enough information is provided

18. In the following frequency distribution,

| 4 | 4 | 5 | 7 |
|---|---|---|---|

the number 4 is the:
    a.  Mean
    b.  Mode
    c.  Median
    d.  Range

19. Review the grouped frequency distribution below:

| Class Interval | $f$ |
|---|---|
| 40–44 | 2 |
| 35–39 | 3 |
| 30–34 | 6 |
| 25–29 | 5 |
| 20–24 | 4 |

After the data were grouped into class intervals, it was determined that a value of 35 was really a value of 39. Correcting this error will change the calculated value of:
    a.  The mean
    b.  The median
    c.  The mode
    d.  None of the above

20. A percentile rank may take on any of the following values except:
    a.  37
    b.  50
    c.  87
    d.  103

## Problems

1. Review the data in Table 5-A.2 and Table 5-A.3 and answer the questions that follow. Use an electronic spreadsheet to assist you in preparing the answers.
    a.  What is the mean age of death for men? For women?
    b.  What are the crude modes and median ages of death for men? For women?
    c.  What are the refined mode and the refined median for men? For women?
    d.  Compare and contrast the crude and refined results for each group. Explain any disparities that may exist.
    e.  In analyzing the results of your data for men and women, what conclusions can you draw?

2. Use the data of the ages of 61 patients discharged from DRG 127, "Heart Failure and Shock," that appear in Table 5-A.4 to solve the following:
    a.  Use statistical software to calculate the mean, median, mode, variance, and standard devia-

tion for the ungrouped frequency distribution and to prepare a frequency table.

b. Group ages into class intervals. Prepare a table that displays the frequencies for each class interval, the cumulative frequency, the relative proportion, and the cumulative percentage.

c. Compute the mean, median, mode, variance, and standard deviation for the grouped data.

d. Compare the results of the grouped and ungrouped frequency distributions.

3. The lengths of stay for a group of patients discharged from DRG 127, "Heart Failure and Shock," are presented in Table 5-A.5.

a. Use statistical software to calculate the mean, median, mode, variance, and standard deviation for the ungrouped frequency distribution.

b. Group ages into class intervals. Prepare a table that displays the frequencies for each class interval, the cumulative frequency, the relative proportion, and the cumulative percent.

c. Compute the mean, median, mode, variance, and standard deviation for the grouped data.

d. Compare the results of the grouped and ungrouped frequency distributions.

Table 5-A.2  **Male Deaths Due to Leukemia (ICD-9-CM Codes 200.0–200.9) in the State of Ohio 1998**

| Age Group | Leukemia Deaths in Men | *p* | Cum *p* | *M* | *f(M)* |
|---|---|---|---|---|---|
| 5–14 | 16 | | | | |
| 15–24 | 20 | | | | |
| 25–34 | 27 | | | | |
| 35–44 | 63 | | | | |
| 45–54 | 118 | | | | |
| 55–64 | 194 | | | | |
| 65–74 | 388 | | | | |
| 75–84 | 418 | | | | |
| 85+ | 124 | | | | |
| Total | 1,368 | | | | |

*Source:* CDC Wonder On-Line Database http://woncer.cdc.gov.

Table 5-A.3  **Female Deaths Due to Leukemia (ICD-9-CM Codes 200.0–200.9) in the State of Ohio 1998**

| Age Group | Leukemia Deaths in Men | *p* | Cum *p* | *M* | *f(M)* |
|---|---|---|---|---|---|
| 5–14 | 6 | | | | |
| 15–24 | 10 | | | | |
| 25–34 | 9 | | | | |
| 35–44 | 26 | | | | |
| 45–54 | 61 | | | | |
| 55–64 | 132 | | | | |
| 65–74 | 296 | | | | |
| 75–84 | 463 | | | | |
| 85+ | 194 | | | | |
| Total | 1,197 | | | | |

*Source:* CDC Wonder On-Line Database http://woncer.cdc.gov.

Table 5-A.4   **Ages of 61 Patients Discharged from DRG 127, Heart Failure and Shock**

| | | | | | |
|---|---|---|---|---|---|
| 37 | 51 | 60 | 65 | 75 | 80 |
| 37 | 51 | 60 | 65 | 76 | 80 |
| 39 | 52 | 61 | 66 | 76 | 82 |
| 39 | 53 | 63 | 66 | 77 | 83 |
| 42 | 54 | 63 | 69 | 77 | 83 |
| 47 | 54 | 63 | 70 | 77 | 84 |
| 47 | 56 | 64 | 72 | 78 | 85 |
| 47 | 57 | 64 | 73 | 79 | 86 |
| 49 | 57 | 64 | 73 | 80 | 87 |
| 51 | 59 | 64 | 75 | 80 | 88 |
| | | | | | 88 |

Table 5-A.5   **Lengths of Stay for Patients Discharged from DRG 127, Heart Failure and Shock**

| | | | | | |
|---|---|---|---|---|---|
| 1 | 2 | 3 | 5 | 8 | 14 |
| 1 | 3 | 3 | 5 | 8 | 15 |
| 1 | 3 | 3 | 5 | 8 | 16 |
| 1 | 3 | 3 | 5 | 10 | 17 |
| 1 | 3 | 3 | 5 | 10 | 27 |
| 1 | 3 | 3 | 6 | 10 | 36 |
| 2 | 3 | 4 | 6 | 10 | |
| 2 | 3 | 4 | 6 | 11 | |
| 2 | 3 | 4 | 6 | 11 | |
| 2 | 3 | 4 | 7 | 11 | |
| 2 | 3 | 4 | 8 | 13 | |

**THE NORMAL DISTRIBUTION AND STATISTICAL INFERENCE**

Asymptotic curve
Central Limit Theorem
Confidence interval
Kurtosis
Normal distribution
Point estimate
Sampling methods
   Cluster sampling

Simple random sampling
Stratified random sampling
Systematic sampling
Skewness
Standard error of the mean
Standard normal deviate
Standard normal distribution
Symmetry
z values

**OBJECTIVES**

At the conclusion of this chapter, you should be able to:

1. Define key terms.

2. Describe the characteristics of the normal distribution and the standard normal distribution.

3. Compare and contrast the normal distribution and the standard normal distribution.

4. Explain the Central Limit Theorem.

5. Calculate the standard error of the mean and confidence intervals for samples.

6. Explain how sample size and variation affect the standard error of the mean.

7. Explain the following sampling techniques: simple random sampling, stratified random sampling, systematic sampling, and cluster sampling.

Much of statistical inference is based on the **normal distribution**, also called the Gaussian distribution after Johann Karl Gauss, the person who best described it. The normal distribution is not a single distribution but an infinite number of possible distributions. This is important in statistical inference because the population mean can take on any positive or negative value, and the population standard deviation can take on any positive or negative value. Thus, the normal distribution is the most widely used theoretical distribution; many naturally occurring phenomena—such as blood pressure, height, and weight—approximate the normal distribution.

## CHARACTERISTICS OF THE NORMAL DISTRIBUTION

There are several characteristics of the normal distribution with which you should be familiar. First, the curve is bell-shaped and **symmetrical** about the population mean and is symbolized by $\mu$ (pronounced "mu"). Second, because the distribution is symmetrical approximately 50% of the observations lie above the mean and 50% of the observations lie below the mean. Third, in a normal distribution the mean, median, and mode are all equal. The values of the normal distribution range from minus infinity ($-\infty$) to plus infinity ($+\infty$), and the total area under the curve is equal to 1.00.

As we move out from the center of the normal curve bilaterally, the height of the curve descends gradually at first, then faster, and finally more slowly as it approaches the horizontal axis. Each tail of the curve approaches the $x$-axis but never touches the $x$-axis, no matter how far from center we go. This type of curve is called an **asymptotic curve** because it is considered asymptotic to the horizontal axis.

Figure 6.1 displays the normal distribution and how the values in the distribution are arranged around the population mean, $\mu$. Approximately 68% of the values lie within one standard deviation from the mean ($\mu \pm 1.68\sigma$); 95% of the observations lie within 1.96 standard deviations from the mean ($\mu \pm 1.96\sigma$); and 99% of the observations lie within 2.58 standard deviations of the mean ($\mu \pm 2.58\sigma$). These characteristics of the normal curve are important when making inferences about population parameters from sample statistics. The symbols used to distinguish between population parameters and sample statistics appear in Table 6.1.

In a normal distribution, we know that the population $\mu$ can take on any value, and that the population $\mu$ is the midpoint of the distribution. Compare Figure 6.1 and Figure 6.2. Even though the means for each distribution—6 and 15, respec-

Table 6.1   **Statistical Symbols**

|  | Population Parameter | Sample Statistic |
| --- | --- | --- |
| Mean | $\mu$ | $\overline{X}$ |
| Variance | $\sigma^2$ | $s^2$ |
| Standard Deviation | $\sigma$ | $s$ |

tively—are different, the shapes of the distributions are the same. Any change in $\mu$ without a corresponding change in $\sigma$ does not change the shape of the distribution. However, changes in the variance ($\sigma^2$) do change the shape of the distribution but do not affect the midpoint. Basically, changes in $\sigma$ affect the dispersion of the values in the distribution. Dispersion can affect the skewness of the distribution.

A frequency distribution that is asymmetrical is skewed, and in this case the mean, median, and mode will take on different values. **Skewness** is the horizontal stretching of a frequency distribution to one side or the other so that one tail is longer than the other (the longer tail has more observations). Because the mean is sensitive to extreme values, the mean moves in the direction of the long tail when a distribution is skewed. When the direction of the long tail is to the right, the distribution is said to be positively skewed or skewed to the right. Conversely, when a distribution's long tail is to the left, the distribution is said to be negatively skewed or skewed to the left. We can determine if a distribution is skewed by using a commercial statistical package such as SPSS, or by using an electronic spreadsheet such as Microsoft Excel. An obtained skewness value greater than one is an indication that the distribution differs significantly from normal. Another way to assess the skewness of a distribution is to compare the mean and median. If the mean and median approximate one another, the distribution is probably not significantly skewed. Examples of these statistics appear in Exhibit 6.2.

**Kurtosis** is the vertical stretching of the frequency distribution. If the distribution appears to be more peaked or more flattened than the normal distribution, it is considered to be kurtotic. For a normal distribution, the value of the kurtosis statistic is zero. A positive kurtosis indicates that the frequency distribution has longer tails than the normal distribution and that the observations are clustered toward the center (peakedness). If the kurtosis statistic is negative, the frequency distribution has tails shorter than the normal distribution and there is less clustering of the observations (flattened).

# THE STANDARD NORMAL DISTRIBUTION (z DISTRIBUTION)

Because there are an infinite number of normal distributions—which may have any mean and any standard deviation—the observations in the distribution must be standardized when we want to make comparisons between distributions. When we standardize a frequency distribution, such as one for the variable "age," we are transforming the units of measurement (age) to a unit-free form; that is, the age units become *z* **values**. The *z* distribution is referred to as the **standard normal distribution**; it has a mean of 0 and a standard deviation equal to 1. Also called the **standard normal deviate**, the *z* value is the number of standard deviation units that the observed value lies away from the mean, $\mu$. Transforming

Exhibit 6.1    **Formulae for Transforming Observed Scores into z Scores**

| z Values in a Population | z Value in a Sample |
|---|---|
| $z = (X - \mu)/\sigma$ | $z = (X - \bar{X})/s$ |
| Where $X$ is the value of the observation, $\mu$ is the mean of the population distribution, and $\sigma$ is the standard deviation of the population distribution. | Where $X$ is the value of the observation, $\bar{X}$ is the mean of the sample distribution, and $s$ is the standard deviation of the sample distribution. |

our raw observations to $z$ values makes it possible to make comparisons between distributions.

In the standardized normal distribution, the area between the $z$ values of ±1.0 is 68%, the area between the $z$ values of ±1.96 is 95%, and the area between ±3.0 is 99.7%. Any normal distribution can be transformed into a standard normal distribution through the formulas in Exhibit 6.1. The transformation of a set of observations to $z$ values is a linear transformation that does not change the shape of the distribution. This feature is illustrated in Figure 6.3, where the normal distribution in Figure 6.1 is transformed into a standard normal distribution with a mean equal to 0 and a standard deviation equal to 1.

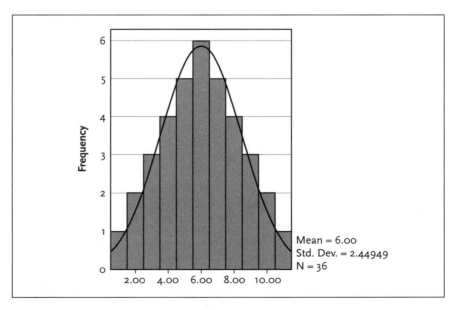

Figure 6.1    **Histogram of Normal Distribution 1**

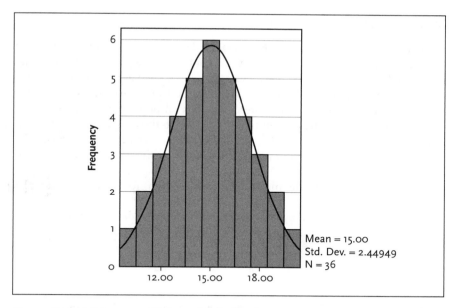

Figure 6.2    **Histogram of Normal Distribution 2**

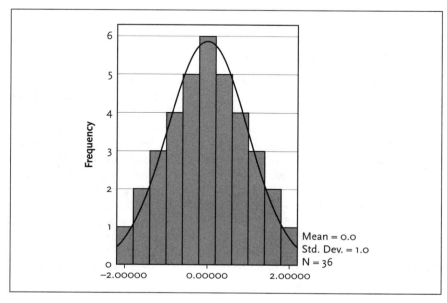

Figure 6.3    **Standard Normal Distribution**

## STATISTICAL INFERENCE

In analyzing health care data, we are usually dealing with data that represent a sample drawn from a larger population. We want to use the sample statistics to describe the larger population. A single sample statistic such as the mean is actually a point estimate. A **point estimate** is a single numerical value computed from the sample that is assumed to best represent the actual population parameter. The properties of the sampling distribution are similar to those of a normal distribution. If the population is normally distributed with a mean $\mu$ and a standard deviation $\sigma$, the sampling distribution of $\bar{X}$ has the following properties:

- It has a mean equal to the mean for the population from which the samples were drawn: $\mu_{\bar{X}} = \mu$
- It has a standard deviation equal to the population standard deviation divided by the square root of the sample size:

$$\sigma_{\bar{X}} = \frac{\sigma}{\sqrt{n}}$$

- It is normally distributed. The sampling distribution of $\bar{X}$ is approximately normal when sampling is from a non-normal population distribution. As the sample size increases, the sample's approximation to normality improves (Central Limit Theorem).

## CENTRAL LIMIT THEOREM

When we draw inferences from our sample, we are assuming that the sample represents a frequency distribution that is normally distributed. When a graph of our sample appears normal, we assume that the population from which the sample was drawn is also normally distributed. This is true regardless of the size of the sample drawn from the same population. However, many populations are not normally distributed. Regardless of the type of population distribution, if sufficiently large the sampling distribution is approximately normal. The **Central Limit Theorem** summarizes the relationship between the shapes of the population distribution and the sampling distribution of the mean, $\bar{X}$.

If repeated random samples of size $N$ are drawn from a population and if a mean is calculated for each sample, the distribution of the sample means approaches the normal distribution as $N$ becomes large. The mean of the sampling distribution will approach the population mean, $\mu$. This is true even if the population distribution is not normal.

The Central Limit Theorem assures us that regardless of the shape of the population distribution, the sampling distribution of $\bar{X}$ approaches normality as the sample size increases. This is true even when data in individual samples are skewed. In reality, the samples do not have to be very large for the sampling distribution of $\overline{X}$ to be approximately normal. In most instances, the approximation to normality is quite rapid as $N$ increases.

These concepts can be illustrated by using the age of nursing home residents' data. In Table 6.2, a frequency distribution of the age of 100 nursing home residents is displayed. The descriptive statistics in Exhibit 6.2 indicate that the mean, median, and mode are similar—76.4, 76.0, and 75.0 years old, respectively. The population standard deviation is 6.2.

Table 6.2  **Frequency Distribution of Age of 100 Nursing Home Residents**

|  |  | Age |  |  |
|  |  | Frequency | % | Valid % | Cumulative % |
|---|---|---|---|---|---|
| Valid | 65.00 | 3 | 3.0 | 3.0 | 3.0 |
|  | 66.00 | 3 | 3.0 | 3.0 | 6.0 |
|  | 67.00 | 4 | 4.0 | 4.0 | 10.0 |
|  | 68.00 | 2 | 2.0 | 2.0 | 12.0 |
|  | 69.00 | 3 | 3.0 | 3.0 | 15.0 |
|  | 70.00 | 3 | 3.0 | 3.0 | 18.0 |
|  | 71.00 | 4 | 4.0 | 4.0 | 22.0 |
|  | 72.00 | 5 | 5.0 | 5.0 | 27.0 |
|  | 73.00 | 4 | 4.0 | 4.0 | 31.0 |
|  | 74.00 | 5 | 5.0 | 5.0 | 36.0 |
|  | 75.00 | 12 | 12.0 | 12.0 | 48.0 |
|  | 76.00 | 5 | 5.0 | 5.0 | 53.0 |
|  | 77.00 | 6 | 6.0 | 6.0 | 59.0 |
|  | 78.00 | 7 | 7.0 | 7.0 | 66.0 |
|  | 79.00 | 4 | 4.0 | 4.0 | 70.0 |
|  | 80.00 | 7 | 7.0 | 7.0 | 77.0 |
|  | 81.00 | 4 | 4.0 | 4.0 | 81.0 |
|  | 82.00 | 4 | 4.0 | 4.0 | 85.0 |
|  | 83.00 | 3 | 3.0 | 3.0 | 88.0 |
|  | 84.00 | 2 | 2.0 | 2.0 | 90.0 |
|  | 86.00 | 3 | 3.0 | 3.0 | 93.0 |
|  | 87.00 | 1 | 1.0 | 1.0 | 94.0 |
|  | 88.00 | 1 | 1.0 | 1.0 | 95.0 |
|  | 89.00 | 1 | 1.0 | 1.0 | 96.0 |
|  | 90.00 | 3 | 3.0 | 3.0 | 99.0 |
|  | 91.00 | 1 | 1.0 | 1.0 | 100.0 |
|  | Total | 100 | 100.0 | 100.0 |  |

Exhibit 6.2 **SPSS Output for Descriptive Statistics, Age of Nursing Home Residents**

| N | Valid | 100 |
|---|---|---|
| | Missing | 0 |
| Mean | | 76.3600 |
| Median | | 76.0000 |
| Mode | | 75.00 |
| Std. Deviation | | 6.23856 |
| Variance | | 38.920 |
| Skewness | | .261 |
| Std. Error of Skewness | | .241 |
| Kurtosis | | −.281 |
| Std. Error of Kurtosis | | .478 |
| Range | | 26.00 |

Exhibit 6.3 **SPSS Output for Descriptive Statistics on Ages of 38 Nursing Home Residents**

| Descriptive Statistics | | |
|---|---|---|
| | Age | Valid N (listwise) |
| N | 38 | 38 |
| Minimum | 65.00 | |
| Maximum | 90.00 | |
| Mean | 75.1842 | |
| Std. Deviation | 6.15500 | |
| Variance | 37.884 | |
| Skewness | .255 | |
| Std. Error | .383 | |
| Kurtosis | −.541 | |
| Std. Error | .750 | |

If we draw a simple random sample of 38 nursing home residents (Table 6.3), we find that the sample distribution is similar to the population distribution. Referring to Exhibit 6.3, we see that the sample mean is 75.2 and the standard deviation is 6.2. The sample distribution does not significantly depart from normality, as indicated by the skewness statistic of 0.255, which is less than one. However, the distribution is flatter than the population distribution, as indicated by the kurtosis statistic of –0.541. The difference between the population parameters and the sample statistics is sampling error. A frequency distribution for the sample is displayed in Table 6.3.

**Table 6.3   Frequency Distribution of Random Sample of Ages of 38 Nursing Home Residents**

|  | Age | Frequency | Percent | Valid Percent | Cumulative Percent |
|---|---|---|---|---|---|
| Valid | 65.00 | 1 | 2.6 | 2.6 | 2.6 |
|  | 66.00 | 2 | 5.3 | 5.3 | 7.9 |
|  | 67.00 | 2 | 5.3 | 5.3 | 13.2 |
|  | 68.00 | 2 | 5.3 | 5.3 | 18.4 |
|  | 69.00 | 1 | 2.6 | 2.6 | 21.1 |
|  | 70.00 | 1 | 2.6 | 2.6 | 23.7 |
|  | 71.00 | 2 | 5.3 | 5.3 | 28.9 |
|  | 72.00 | 3 | 7.9 | 7.9 | 36.8 |
|  | 73.00 | 2 | 5.3 | 5.3 | 42.1 |
|  | 74.00 | 3 | 7.9 | 7.9 | 50.0 |
|  | 75.00 | 2 | 5.3 | 5.3 | 55.3 |
|  | 76.00 | 1 | 2.6 | 2.6 | 57.9 |
|  | 77.00 | 1 | 2.6 | 2.6 | 60.5 |
|  | 78.00 | 3 | 7.9 | 7.9 | 68.4 |
|  | 79.00 | 1 | 2.6 | 2.6 | 71.1 |
|  | 80.00 | 3 | 7.9 | 7.9 | 78.9 |
|  | 81.00 | 2 | 5.3 | 5.3 | 84.2 |
|  | 82.00 | 2 | 5.3 | 5.3 | 89.5 |
|  | 83.00 | 1 | 2.6 | 2.6 | 92.1 |
|  | 84.00 | 1 | 2.6 | 2.6 | 94.7 |
|  | 86.00 | 1 | 2.6 | 2.6 | 97.4 |
|  | 90.00 | 1 | 2.6 | 2.6 | 100.0 |
|  | Total | 38 | 100.0 | 100.0 |  |

## STANDARD ERROR OF THE MEAN

When inferences are made about normally distributed data, conclusions are based on the relationships of the standard deviation and the mean to the normal curve. The mean of the sample may or may not be the same as the population mean. The difference between the sample mean and the population parameter $\mu$ is sampling error. For example, if we draw three different samples from a population, we will get three different means. In addition, if we take many samples from the same population, we will have just as many different means and these means will be normally distributed. The mean of the means will be close to the true population mean.

To determine how close the sample mean is to the population mean, we find the standard deviation of the distribution of means. The standard deviation of the distribution of means is called the **standard error of the mean**, or the standard error. The smaller the standard error, the closer the sample mean is likely to be to the population mean. However, we do not need to draw many samples to calculate the standard error; it can be calculated from a single sample:

$$Standard\ error\ of\ the\ mean = \frac{s}{\sqrt{n}}$$

The standard error is influenced by the standard deviation and the sample size. The greater the dispersion around the mean, the less certain we are about the actual population mean and the greater the standard error of the mean. The larger the sample size, the more confidence we have in the mean and the smaller the standard error of the mean. A smaller standard error yields a more reliable statistic.

The effects of sample size and standard deviation on the standard error are illustrated in the following examples. In a hypothetical frequency distribution on the average age of college graduates, the mean is 22.5 years old and the standard deviation is 3.5. With a sample size of 100, the standard error of the mean is 0.35; if we increase the sample size to 200 and the mean and standard deviation remain the same, the standard error of the mean decreases to 0.25. If the sample size remains at 100 but the standard deviation increases to 5.5, the standard error of the mean increases to 0.55. These data are summarized in Table 6.4.

Table 6.4   **Statistical Comparisons by Sample Size**

|  | Sample 1 | Sample 2 | Sample 3 |
|---|---|---|---|
| N | 100 | 200 | 100 |
| Mean | 22.5 | 22.5 | 22.5 |
| SD | 3.5 | 3.5 | 5.5 |
| SE | .35 | .25 | .55 |

The data in Exhibit 6.4 further illustrate these principles. Using SPSS, three simple random samples were drawn from our population of 100 nursing home residents in which the mean is 76.4 years old and the standard deviation is 6.24.

Exhibit 6.4    **Three Random Samples of Ages of Nursing Home Residents**

| Random Sample 1 | | Random Sample 2 | | Random Sample 3 | |
|---|---|---|---|---|---|
| **Age** | **N** | **Age** | **N** | **Age** | **N** |
| 66 | 1 | 65 | 3 | 65 | 1 |
| 67 | 1 | 66 | 1 | 66 | 3 |
| 68 | 1 | 70 | 2 | 67 | 2 |
| 70 | 1 | 72 | 2 | 68 | 1 |
| 73 | 1 | 73 | 1 | 69 | 2 |
| 75 | 1 | 75 | 3 | 70 | 2 |
| 78 | 1 | 76 | 1 | 71 | 3 |
| 80 | 1 | 77 | 3 | 72 | 1 |
| 81 | 1 | 78 | 1 | 73 | 2 |
| 82 | 1 | 80 | 4 | 74 | 5 |
| 86 | 1 | 81 | 4 | 75 | 2 |
| 89 | 1 | 82 | 2 | 76 | 2 |
| 90 | 1 | 83 | 1 | 77 | 3 |
| | | 84 | 1 | 78 | 4 |
| | | 89 | 1 | 79 | 2 |
| | | 90 | 2 | 80 | 3 |
| | | 91 | 1 | 81 | 3 |
| | | | | 82 | 2 |
| | | | | 83 | 1 |
| | | | | 84 | 1 |
| | | | | 86 | 1 |
| | | | | 88 | 1 |
| | | | | 90 | 1 |
| Total | **13** | | **33** | | **48** |
| Mean | 77.3 | | 77.7 | | 75.5 |
| S.E. Mean | 2.285 | | 1.242 | | 0.874 |
| Variance | 67.90 | | 50.92 | | 36.64 |
| S.D. | 8.24 | | 7.14 | | 6.05 |

*Population Mean = 76.4*

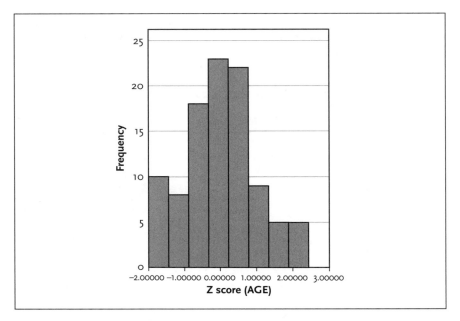

**Figure 6.4** **SPSS Output for Histogram on Ages of 100 Nursing Home Residents**

The sample size in Sample 1 is 13, and the mean, 77.3, is 0.9 units above the population mean. In Sample 2, the sample size is 33, and the mean, 77.7, is 1.3 units above the population mean. The standard deviation for Sample 1 ($s = 8.24$) is greater than that for Sample 2 ($s = 7.14$), indicating more variation and a greater standard error for Sample 1 over Sample 2—8.24 versus 7.14, respectively.

However, when we increase the sample size to 48 the observed mean, 75.5, and the standard deviation, 6.05, are less than in either of the previous two samples. There is also a corresponding decrease in the standard error, which is 0.874 for Sample 3. With each increase in sample size, the standard error is reduced.

## Confidence Intervals

The sample mean, $\overline{X}$, is a point estimate of the population mean, $\mu$. With the additional information of the standard error of the mean, $s_{\overline{X}}$, and our knowledge of the normal curve, we can estimate the limits within which the true population mean probably lies. This is called a **confidence interval** on $\mu$ and gives a range of values that might reasonably contain the true population mean. The confidence interval is represented as

$$a \leq \mu \leq b$$

Using the data from Sample 1 in Exhibit 6.4, we can add and subtract the standard error of the mean from the sample mean:

$$\text{Point estimate} \pm \text{error} = \overline{X}_1 \pm s_{\overline{X}_1} = 77.3 \pm 2.285$$

$$75.0 \leq \mu \leq 79.6$$

The results indicate that the true population mean falls within ±1 standard error on each side of the sample mean. This is interpreted as meaning that if we draw a number of samples from the population, 68% of these sample means will fall between 75.0 and 79.6. From this we can infer that we are 68% confident that the population mean lies within these limits.

But when developing confidence intervals, we generally want to be more confident about the sample statistic. Generally, the confidence intervals are set at 95%. As noted earlier in this chapter, 95% of the area under the standard normal curve lies between ±1.96 standard deviations of the mean. The 95% confidence interval ($CI_{95}$) may be constructed as follows:

$$CI_{95} = \overline{X} \pm 1.96 s_{\overline{X}}$$

Substituting into our formula the $CI_{95}$ for Sample 1 in Exhibit 6.4 yields

$$CI_{95} = 77.3 \pm 1.96(2.285) = 77.3 \pm 4.48$$

Thus, we can say that we are 95% confidant that our true population mean lies between 72.8 and 81.8. This confidence interval is expressed as:

$$72.8 \leq \mu \leq 81.8$$

As you can see from the population data in Exhibit 6.4, the true population mean, 76.4, lies within this band. Note that by increasing the confidence interval from 68% to 95% we have increased the range within which the true mean may fall. Increasing the size of the confidence interval increases our confidence that the true population mean lies within that interval. Correspondingly, we can compute the $CI_{95}$ for Sample 2 and Sample 3:

$$\text{Sample 2: } CI_{95} = 77.7 \pm 1.96(1.242) = 77.7 \pm 2.4343$$
$$75.3 \leq \mu \leq 80.1$$

$$\text{Sample 3: } CI_{95} = 75.5 \pm 1.96(0.874) = 75.5 \pm 1.713$$
$$73.8 \leq \mu \leq 77.2$$

Sample 1 has the greatest variation, as indicated by the standard deviation; thus, it also has the greatest standard error and the widest confidence band.

The general formula for calculating the confidence interval is

$$CI_\mu = \bar{X} \pm \alpha s_{\bar{X}}$$

where $\alpha$ (pronounced alpha) is the confidence coefficient. For the normal distribution with a 95% confidence interval, the confidence coefficient is equal to 1.96; for a confidence interval of 99%, the confidence coefficient is equal to 2.58 (±2.58 standard deviations from the mean).

## SAMPLING METHODS

Before we can make inferences about a population, we must select a sample. Samples should be as representative of the underlying population as possible. If the sample is representative, inferences made from the sample about the population will be correct. There are two general sampling techniques: probability and non-probability sampling. In **probability sampling**, each member of a population has a known probability of being selected for the sample. **Non-probability samples** are those in which members of a sample are deliberately selected for a specified purpose. One example is the selection of patients admitted to the emergency department in January to study the effects of a new anticoagulant. In non-probability sampling, generalization of results to a population is extremely limited. Non-probability sampling is often used in conducting clinical trials.

We will limit our discussion to several methods of probability sampling: simple random sampling, stratified random sampling, systematic sampling, and cluster sampling. In **simple random sampling**, each member of a population has an equal chance of being selected for inclusion in the sample. The selection of one member of the population has no influence on the selection of another. The drawing of numbers in state lotteries is an example of a simple random sample.

Occasionally, we are interested in studying different strata within a population. A **stratum** is a variable by which the population can be subdivided. Common examples in health care include dividing the human population by age or gender, or categorizing acute care facilities by size. Basically, we group the population into subcategories. In **stratified random sampling**, we want to draw a sample so that each stratum within the population is proportionately represented in the sample. Before drawing the sample, we must divide the population into the strata we are interested in studying and then randomly draw the appropriate sample from each stratum. If we are studying a problem where gender is an important variable, we will want a stratified sample that is composed of 50% men and 50% women.

In **systematic sampling**, we select every *k*th member of a population from a list, such as selecting the records of every fifth patient discharged for closed medical record review. If we want to select a sample of 10 from a population of 100, we will select every tenth name from the discharge list. Caution must be exercised with systematic sampling if the list is ordered in any way. For example, if a list of university students is listed by class rank, the resulting sample may not be representative of the population. In systematic sampling, every member of the population does not have an equal chance of being selected for the sample. Selection for inclusion in the sample is dependent upon the first member selected for inclusion in the sample.

In **cluster sampling**, the sampling units are groups rather than individuals. For example, if we want to survey physicians in the state of Ohio, we can define the population as physicians practicing in acute care facilities in the state of Ohio. The units to be sampled are hospitals (clusters); from each hospital included in the sample, a sample of physicians is then surveyed. This is two-stage sampling: We first randomly select hospitals and then randomly select physicians that practice at the hospitals.

## USING COMPUTER SOFTWARE TO SOLVE PROBLEMS

Many commercial computer programs are available that can assist you in solving statistical problems. The advantage of using electronic spreadsheets or a dedicated statistical package is that the data can be entered directly and databases can be designed to help evaluate these problems on a timelier basis. If you will recall from Chapter 4, the more timely the data, the more valuable they are in the decision making process. The health information manager should become proficient not only in data collection but also in the analysis of data so that the data are useful to health care providers, planners, and researchers. In this chapter, we have used examples from both SPSS and Excel.

Selection of statistical computer software is a matter of choice. Dedicated statistical packages such as SPSS are often easier to use in that less manipulation of the data is required. Also, dedicated statistical packages can offer the user more choices in the type of statistical tests that are available, and most include both parametric and non-parametric procedures. Excel does not include options for non-parametric procedures.

## CONCLUSION

The normal and standard normal distributions are theoretical distributions used for testing statistical problems in health care because many naturally occurring phenomena follow the normal distribution. The normal distribution is actually a family of distributions in which the population mean can take on any value. The normal distribution is a symmetrical, bell-shaped distribution where 50% of the observations fall above the mean and 50% of the observations fall below the mean. In the normal distribution, the mean, median, and mode are all equal.

To make comparisons between distributions, the normal distribution can be standardized. The standard normal distribution has many of the same properties as the normal distribution except that in the standard normal distribution, the mean is equal to zero and the standard deviation is equal to one. There is only one standard normal distribution. In the standard normal distribution, 68% of the observations fall between ±1.0 standard deviations of the mean, and 95% of the observations fall between ±1.96 standard deviations of the mean.

The standard normal distribution is important in statistical inference. The standard normal distribution can be used to make comparisons between populations. In statistical testing, we are interested in whether one population is the same as or differs from another population on a variable of interest.

When making comparisons between populations, we must first draw a sample from the population. Probability sampling is the preferred sampling technique. Types of probability sampling include simple random sampling, stratified random sampling, systematic sampling, and cluster sampling. It is important to take care when drawing samples so that we have some level of confidence when making inferences from the sample to the underlying population. In general, the larger the sample size, the more confidence we have in our results.

## References

LaTour, K.M., and Eichenwald-Maki, S. (2006) *Health Information Management: Concepts, Principles, and Practice*, 2nd edition. Chicago: American Health Information Management Association.

Osborn, Carol E. (2006) *Statistical Applications for Health Information Management*, 2nd edition. Boston: Jones and Bartlett Publishers.

# APPENDIX 6-A

## EXERCISES FOR SOLVING PROBLEMS

### Knowledge Questions

1. Define the key terms listed at the beginning of this chapter.
2. Compare the normal distribution with the standard normal distribution.
3. What is the difference between the standard deviation and the standard normal deviate?
4. You have been analyzing discharges by gender from DRG 462, "Rehabilitation," for Critical Care Hospital. Specifically, you are interested in determining if there is a difference in average age by gender. Review the data in Table 6-A.1 and answer the questions that follow.

a. What is the average age for the entire group? For men? For women?
b. Why is the standard error larger for the male group than for the female group?
c. Why is the standard error for the total group smaller than either of the standard errors for the male or female groups?
d. What is the 95% confidence interval for men? For women? For the entire group?
e. What is your interpretation of the 95% confidence interval?

Table 6-A.1   **Mean Age of Patients by Gender, DRG 462, Rehabilitation, Critical Care Hospital, 2006**

|  |  | Female | Male | Total |
|---|---|---|---|---|
|  |  | Age | | |
| N |  | 80 | 88 | 168 |
| Mean |  | 55.467 | 53.947 | 54.671 |
| Std. Deviation |  | 17.5344 | 19.1981 | 18.3856 |
| Std. Error |  | 1.9604 | 2.0465 | 1.4185 |
| 95% Confidence Interval for Mean | Lower Bound | 51.565 | 49.879 | 51.871 |
|  | Upper Bound | 59.370 | 58.015 | 57.472 |
| Minimum |  | 19.4 | 17.5 | 17.5 |
| Maximum |  | 89.1 | 97.6 | 97.6 |

5. The mean length of stay for patients discharged from DRG 005, "Extracranial Vascular Procedures," is 3.33 days. The standard deviation for the group is 3.18, and the number of patients discharged is 21. Calculate the 95% confidence interval for the mean length of stay.

## Multiple Choice

1. In a normal distribution, 68% of the observations fall within:
   a. $\pm 1\sigma$ of the mean
   b. $\pm 2\sigma$ of the mean
   c. $\pm 3\sigma$ of the mean
   d. $\pm 1.5\sigma$ of the mean

2. In a normal distribution, 32% of the scores fall outside:
   a. $\pm 1\sigma$ of the mean
   b. $\pm 2\sigma$ of the mean
   c. $\pm 3\sigma$ of the mean
   d. $\pm 1.5\sigma$ of the mean

3. The normal distribution is:
   a. Continuous
   b. A family of distributions
   c. Symmetrical about the mean
   d. All of the above

4. Which of the following is not a characteristic of the normal curve?
   a. It is unimodal.
   b. It is a discrete distribution.
   c. It is asymptotic to the $x$-axis.
   d. The mean may take on any value.

5. The lengths of stay for DRG 123 were standardized so that comparisons could be made across hospitals. What percentage of the lengths of stay would have a $z$ value greater than or equal to 1.00?
   a. 32%
   b. 16%
   c. 8%
   d. 4%

6. In a standard normal distribution, what percentage of the lengths of stay for DRG 123 would fall above $z = -1.96$?
   a. 99.0%
   b. 97.5%
   c. 95.0%
   d. 68.0%

7. If a distribution has a long tail to the right, it is:
   a. Bimodal
   b. Abnormal
   c. Positively skewed
   d. Negatively skewed

8. In a standard normal distribution, the mean:
   a. Is equal to 0.00
   b. Is equal to $-1.00$
   c. Is equal to $+1.00$
   d. May take on any value

9. A normal distribution has a mean of 20 and a standard deviation of 5. Ninety-five percent of the scores fall between:
   a. 15 and 25
   b. 10 and 30
   c. 5 and 35
   d. Not enough information is provided

10. The standard deviation of a distribution is 24, and the sample size is 9. The standard error of the mean is:
    a. 3
    b. 8
    c. 75
    d. 225

11. A condition that is fundamental to statistical inference is:

a. Random sampling
b. That the population is normally distributed
c. That the mean of the population is known
d. Both (a) and (b)

12. We have drawn a simple random sample of 100 patients who were discharged from Critical Care Hospital in January. Of all the patients discharged during January, 55% were women and 45% were men. To match the population, our sample should contain:
    a. 45 men and 55 women
    b. 50 men and 50 women
    c. 55 men and 45 women
    d. The ratio of men to women in the sample size is not important.

13. You are assisting a physician who is conducting a study on the number of cancer cases at Critical Care Hospital. You jointly decide to take a 5% random sample of the estimated 20,000 charts. This is an example of:
    a. Cluster sampling
    b. Simple random sampling
    c. Stratified random sampling
    d. Two-stage random sampling

14. The physician now decides to draw his 5% sample of cancer cases by selecting every twentieth chart by medical record number. This is an example of:

a. Random cluster sampling
b. Two-stage random sampling
c. Systematic sampling
d. Stratified random sampling

15. You decide to study coding quality by randomly selecting hospitals in your state. From each of the hospitals selected, you review the coded charts of randomly selected coders. This is an example of:
    a. Cluster sampling
    b. Simple random sampling
    c. Stratified random sampling
    d. Two-stage random sampling

## Problems

1. Review the data on length of stay that appear in Table 6-A.2 to answer the questions below.
   a. Using a commercial statistical software package, calculate the average length of stay for men, for women, and for the entire group.
   b. Calculate the standard error of the mean length of stay for men, for women, and for the entire group.
   c. Calculate the 95% confidence interval for length of stay for men, for women, and for the entire group.

Table 6-A.2    **Critical Care Hospital, Length of Stay of Patients by Gender, DRG 127, Heart Failure and Shock, 2006**

|  |  | Gender | | |
|---|---|---|---|---|
|  |  | Female | Male | Total |
| *ALOS* | 1 | 1 | 5 | 6 |
|  | 2 | 1 | 5 | 6 |
|  | 3 | 3 | 13 | 16 |
|  | 4 | 4 | 1 | 5 |
|  | 5 | 0 | 5 | 5 |
|  | 6 | 3 | 1 | 4 |
|  | 7 | 0 | 1 | 1 |
|  | 8 | 2 | 2 | 4 |
|  | 10 | 1 | 3 | 4 |
|  | 11 | 1 | 2 | 3 |
|  | 13 | 1 | 0 | 1 |
|  | 14 | 0 | 1 | 1 |
|  | 15 | 1 | 0 | 1 |
|  | 16 | 0 | 1 | 1 |
|  | 17 | 0 | 1 | 1 |
|  | 27 | 1 | 0 | 1 |
|  | 36 | 1 | 0 | 1 |
| Total |  | 20 | 41 | 61 |

# CHAPTER 7

# HYPOTHESIS TESTING AND STATISTICAL INFERENCE

## KEY TERMS

Alpha level
Alternative hypothesis
Critical region
Degrees of freedom (df)
Effect
Hypothesis testing
Level of significance
Non-critical region
Null hypothesis
One-tailed test

*p* value
Statistical significance
*t* tests
   One-sample *t* test
   *t* statistic
   *t* test for comparison of two
     independent sample means
Two-tailed test
Type I error
Type II error
*z* test

## OBJECTIVES

At the conclusion of this chapter, you should be able to:

1. Define key terms.
2. Explain the differences between the null and alternative hypotheses.
2. Define Type I and Type II errors.
3. Explain the factors that affect Type I and Type II errors.
4. Differentiate between the alpha level and the *p* value.
5. Identify the factors that influence sample size.
6. Calculate one- and two-tailed tests of significance for one and two independent samples using *z*.
7. Compare and contrast the normal distribution and the *t* distribution.
8. Calculate one- and two-tailed tests of significance for one and two independent samples using *t*.
9. Conduct a paired-sample *t* test.
10. Use statistical software to calculate the various *t* tests.

## HYPOTHESIS TESTING AND STATISTICAL SIGNIFICANCE

With statistical inference, we are interested in making generalizations about a particular population from a sample drawn from that population. When we generalize, we are describing the population from our sample statistics. However, we are often interested in determining whether two population means are different with respect to a given variable, such as age, length of stay (LOS), or total charges. To determine whether two means are different, we must first develop a hypothesis and perform a statistical test to determine if the observed differences between the means are statistically significant. We want to know whether the observed difference between the group means is greater than what would be expected by chance alone.

To understand the concept of **statistical significance**, consider the following example. Say that the researcher is interested in determining whether Physician A's practice profile is superior to Physician B's, as indicated by the LOS of their respective patients. The researcher will evaluate the differences between the practice profiles of these two physicians on the basis of the patients' average length of stay (ALOS) for Physician A and Physician B. In addition, the researcher will want to know if the "observed" difference between the two mean LOSs is due to something other than measurement error. The observed differences in the patients' mean LOSs could be due to the following reasons:

- The practice profile of Physician A is actually superior to the practice profile of Physician B.
- Some confounding factor that was not controlled in any way, such as the age or type of patient, could account for the difference.
- Random variation could account for the difference.

Only after the second and third reasons have been ruled out can we say that the practice profile of Physician A is superior to the practice profile of Physician B. To rule out the second reason, we must design a study that does not permit any extraneous factors that may bias the comparison. To rule out the third reason, we test for statistical significance.

Before we select a statistical test for comparing the two means, we must develop a hypothesis for statistical testing. For tests involving the comparison of two or more groups, the null hypothesis states that there is no difference between the population means from which the two samples were drawn. The **null hypothesis** is consistent with the idea that the observed difference between the means of two or more groups is due to random variation in the data. The null hypothesis is expressed as

$$H_0 : \mu_A = \mu_B$$

The interpretation is that the population mean for group A is equal to the population mean for group B.

After we have developed the null hypothesis, we must state the **alternative hypothesis**. The alternative hypothesis states what our theory is or what we expect to happen as a result of the statistical test. The alternative hypothesis may take one of several forms:

$$H : \mu_A \neq \mu_B$$
$$H_A : \mu_A < \mu_B$$
$$H_A : \mu_A > \mu_B$$

In the first example, we are stating that we expect that the two population means will not be equal. We are interested only in whether the observed differences between the two population means are significantly different. In the latter two examples, we are stating a direction in which we expect the population means to differ. In the second example, we are stating that we expect the mean for population A to be significantly less than the mean for population B. And in the third example, we are stating that we expect the mean for population A to be greater than the mean for population B.

For our comparison of the practice profiles of the two physicians, our alternative hypothesis will take the form of the second example: we hypothesized that the ALOS for Physician A is less than the ALOS for Physician B.

## LEVEL OF SIGNIFICANCE

To determine if the ALOS for Physician A is less than that of Physician B, we select an appropriate test of statistical significance and establish an appropriate alpha level, such as $\alpha = 0.05$ or $\alpha = 0.01$. The **alpha ($\alpha$) level** is the maximum probability of rejecting the null hypothesis when it is true; this is referred to as a **Type I error**. If alpha is set at 0.05, we run a 5% risk of error when we reject the null hypothesis—that is, when we state that the means of the two groups are different when they are actually not. A **Type II error** occurs when we accept the null hypothesis when it is false.

The null hypothesis is rejected only if the sample results are so different from the hypothesis that the probability of such a difference occurring by chance alone is very low or insignificant. The lower the significance level—for example, $\alpha = 0.01$—the more the sample data must depart from the null hypothesis to be statistically significant. An alpha set at 0.01 is considered to be stricter than an alpha set at 0.05—that is, it is more difficult to reject the null hypothesis when alpha is set at 0.01.

When we reject the null hypothesis, we actually support what we believe to be true. Rejecting the null hypothesis supports our theory. Failure to reject the null hypothesis does not mean that the null hypothesis is true; it only means that we did not prove that the observed difference between the means of the two groups was statistically significant beyond a reasonable doubt. The level of significance refers to the probability of making a Type I error. For Type I error, the level of significance is designated by $\alpha$, with the level of significance usually set at 0.01 or 0.05. For small sample sizes, alpha is usually set at 0.05; for large sample sizes, alpha is usually set at 0.01. This is because it is easier to achieve statistical significance with large samples. If the significance for $\alpha$ is set at 0.05 and the null hypothesis is rejected, the probability of a Type I error is 5%. In the long run, when drawing multiple samples from the same population, the rejection of a true null hypothesis will occur 5% of the time. Conversely, the sample data will justify accepting the true null hypothesis 95% of the time.

The probability of committing a Type II error is designated by $\beta$ (beta). Type II errors occur only when we incorrectly fail to reject the null hypothesis. Because the level of significance is set to reduce the probability of Type I errors, the probability of a Type II error is increased. However, the probability of making a Type II error decreases as the sample size increases. Table 7.1 shows the probabilities of Type I and Type II errors.

## THE $p$ VALUE

The level of significance is determined before conducting the statistical test or *a priori*. The **$p$ value** is obtained from the statistical test of significance and indicates the probability that the observed difference between the means could have been obtained by chance alone, given random variation and a single test of the null hypothesis. If the obtained $p$ value is 0.03, the correct interpretation is that the probability of obtaining the test statistic at least as extreme as the one calculated is 3%. That is, only 3% of all possible samples will produce a test statistic as extreme as the calculated test statistic if the null hypothesis is true. If the $p$ value obtained from the statistical test is less than or equal to the preset alpha level, the result is considered sufficiently rare so that the null hypothesis is rejected.

Exhibit 7.1 provides an example of a statistical test for the difference between two population means using Excel. In the example, the $z$ test for the difference between two population means was conducted to determine if the ALOS varied by

Table 7.1   **Probabilities of Type I and Type II Errors**

| Action | $H_0$ Is True | $H_0$ Is False |
|--------|--------------|---------------|
| Reject $H_0$ | Type I error $\alpha$ | Correct $1 - \beta$ |
| Accept $H_0$ | Correct $1 - \alpha$ | Type II error $\beta$ |

gender for a particular diagnosis-related group (DRG). In the example, the LOS for males and females discharged from DRG XXX were compared. The mean LOS for men is 4.26 days, and the mean LOS for women is 4.95 days. Prior to conducting the $z$ test, the null and alternative hypotheses were stated and the alpha level was set:

$$H_0 : \mu_A = \mu_B$$
$$H_A : \mu_A \neq \mu_B$$
$$\alpha = 0.05$$

The null hypothesis states that there is no difference between the ALOS for patients by gender for DRG XXX; the alternative hypothesis states that there is a difference between the ALOS of the patients by gender for DRG XXX.

The Excel output provides the calculated $z$ statistic and its corresponding $p$ values, which indicate whether the means of the two groups are significantly different from each other. (Exhibit 7.2 provides an explanation of each row in the Excel output.) In Exhibit 7.1, the calculated value of $z$ is –3.27. Excel provides two other $z$ values: 1.96 and 1.64. These values are interpreted as ±1.96 and ±1.64. These are the critical values of $z$ for both one- and two-tailed tests when alpha is set at 0.05. Recall from Chapter 6 that in the standard normal distribution, 95% of the observations fall between ±1.96 standard deviations of the mean. This means that 5% of the observations fall outside ±1.96 standard deviations. The remaining 5% of the observations are divided between the two tails of the standard normal distribution—2.5% in the left tail and 2.5% in the right tail.

**Exhibit 7.1    *z* Test for the Difference between Population Means, Excel Output**

|  | Male | Female |
|---|---|---|
| Mean | 4.26 | 4.95 |
| Known Variance | 9.60 | 9.00 |
| Observations | 134.00 | 151.00 |
| Hypothesized Mean Difference | 0.50 | |
| $z$ | – 3.27 | |
| P(Z ≤ z) one-tail | 0.000 | |
| z Critical one-tail | 1.64 | |
| P(Z ≤ z) two-tail | 0.001 | |
| z Critical two-tail | 1.96 | |

The critical *z* value for a one-tailed test is ±1.64. In a one-tailed test, we are interested in whether one population mean is greater or less than the other population mean. When alpha equals 0.05, this is interpreted as 95% of observations falling above or below 1.64, depending on the direction of the test. The remaining 5% of the observations are located in either the right tail or the left tail of the standard normal distribution. The calculated value of *z*, −3.27, must equal or exceed the critical value of *z* if we are to reject the null hypothesis.

The Excel output provides two *p* values, one for a one-tailed test and one for a non-directional or two-tailed test. Our alternative hypothesis states that we are interested in whether the mean LOS for men and women for DRG XXX are significantly different. We will use the *p* value for the two-tailed test. The *p* value is 0.0011, which is less than the preset alpha level of 0.05. The interpretation of the *p* value is that the probability of obtaining a *z* statistic as extreme as −3.27, given the corresponding sample size, is 0.11%, or less than 1.0%. Because the *p* value is less

**Exhibit 7.2    Explanation of Excel Output, z Test for the Difference Between Two Population Means**

| | |
|---|---|
| Mean: | The arithmetic mean for each group, male and female |
| Known Variance: | The population variance for each group must be provided in order to conduct the *z* test. |
| Observations: | The sample size for each group. |
| Hypothesized Mean Difference: | When conducting the *z* test, the investigator must specify the difference between the two means that he/she believes to be important. No difference was specified for this example. |
| Z: | The calculated value of *z* (−3.2733) as a result of conducting the statistical test. |
| p(Z ≤ z) one tail: | The *p* value. The probability that the critical value of *z* (1.64) is less than or equal to the calculated value of *z* (−3.2733) for a one-tailed test. |
| z critical one-tail: | The critical value of *z* (1.64) for a one-tailed test when $\alpha = .05$. It should be interpreted as ±1.64 depending on the direction of the test. |
| p(Z ≤ z) two tail: | The *p* value. The probability that the critical value of *z* (1.96) is less than or equal to the calculated value of *z* (−3.2733) for a two-tailed test. |
| z critical two-tail: | The critical value of *z* (1.96) for a two-tailed test when $\alpha = .05$. |

than the previously stated alpha level, we reject the null hypothesis and conclude that the mean LOS for men and women are significantly different from each other. We will discuss one- and two-tailed tests in more detail later in this chapter.

Remember that the *p* value is not the level of significance; the level of significance, or alpha level, is set prior to conducting the statistical test. The *p* value is obtained as a result of the statistical test. The *p* value is the probability of obtaining the resultant test statistic when all possible samples are drawn. The *p* value is a statistic that indicates how rare the particular sample is, whereas the level of significance is an independent criterion for evaluating the sample result and is in no way dependent upon that particular result.

When our statistical analysis results in a non-significant difference, we should evaluate the sample size. When the sample size is small, sampling error is likely to be large, and this often leads to a non-significant test result even when the observed difference is caused by a real effect. There is no way to determine whether a non-significant difference is the result of the small sample size or whether the null hypothesis is correct. It is for this reason that when our statistical test is not significant, we should almost always regard it as inconclusive rather than as an indication of no effect. Alternatively, very large samples are very likely to result in statistical significance. With large samples, the alpha level is set at 0.01, which requires very strong evidence to reject the null hypothesis. Even with an alpha as strict as 0.01, one must judge the practical implications of the findings. The test may result in statistical significance, but does this difference have any practical application? When working with data, one cannot rely solely on the results of statistical tests; the knowledge and judgment of the researcher play a vital role in the interpretation of statistical procedures. We will discuss sample size in relation to Type I and Type II errors in greater detail in a later chapter.

## The Standard Normal Distribution and the Z Test for Comparing Population Means

In our discussion of **hypothesis testing** of the difference between population means, we will be dealing with examples where population parameters are both known and unknown. If population parameters are known and we have sufficiently large samples ($N \geq 30$), the standard normal distribution is used as the basis for statistical decision making in the form of a *z* test. If we are comparing means when population parameters are unknown and if our samples are smaller, the Student's *t* test is used as the basis for statistical decision making. Our discussion will first focus on the use of the *z* test and the standard normal distribution, and then will consider the *t* test and the *t* distribution for comparing sample means to population means and comparing the means of two populations.

Before we conduct a statistical test such as the *z* test, we must develop a hypothesis for the test. We select a statistical test based on our research questions, which are developed into statistical hypotheses. A statistical hypothesis may involve comparing a sample mean to a population mean or comparing two or more sample means drawn from two populations. The hypothesis may be either one-tailed (directional) or two-tailed (non-directional). In a **one-tailed test**, we are seeking to determine if our sample mean, $\overline{X}$, is significantly greater or less than the population parameter $\mu$. If we are interested in determining whether our sample $\overline{X}$ is significantly greater than the population parameter $\mu$, we look for a critical $z$ value in the positive tail of the distribution. Conversely, if we are interested in determining whether our sample $\overline{X}$ is significantly less than the population parameter $\mu$, we look for a critical $z$ value in the negative tail of the distribution. In a one-tailed test with an alpha of 0.05, we look for statistical significance in either the upper or lower tail of the distribution.

In a non-directional or **two-tailed test**, we are interested only in determining whether the sample mean, $\overline{X}$, and the population parameter, $\mu$, are significantly different from each other; the direction of the inequality is not an issue. In this case, both tails of the $z$ distribution are used in the statistical decision making. A two-tailed test divides alpha in half, placing 0.025 in each tail. That is, when alpha is set at 0.05, we look for statistical significance in either the positive or negative tails of the standard normal distribution.

The null and alternative hypotheses can take the following forms:

$$H_0 : \mu_1 = 5.5 \quad \text{or} \quad H_0 : \mu_1 = \mu_2$$
$$H_A : \mu_1 \neq 5.5 \quad \text{or} \quad H_A : \mu_1 \neq \mu_2 \quad \text{(two-tailed tests)}$$
$$H_A : \mu_1 < 5.5 \quad \text{or} \quad H_A : \mu_1 < \mu_2 \quad \text{(one-tailed tests)}$$
$$H_A : \mu_1 > 5.5 \quad \text{or} \quad H_A : \mu_1 > \mu_2 \quad \text{(one-tailed tests)}$$

From our discussion in Chapter 6, we know from the Central Limit Theorem that we can expect that 95% of the sampling means will fall between ±1.96 standard deviations of the true mean, and that 99% of the sampling means will fall between ±2.58 standard deviations of the true mean. For a two-tailed test, these standard deviations correspond to the significance levels of 0.05 and 0.01, respectively. In a one-tailed test, $z = \pm1.64$ when $\alpha = 0.05$, and $z = \pm2.33$ when $\alpha = 0.01$. In a one-tailed test when $\alpha = 0.05$, ±1.65 is required to achieve statistical significance; in a two-tailed test, ±1.96 is required for statistical significance. The critical values for the standard normal distribution are displayed in Table 7.2.

A one-tailed test is considered more "robust" than a two-tailed test because it is easier to achieve statistical significance. When conducting a statistical test, we "calculate" the value of $z$ and compare it to the critical value of $z$. On a one-tailed test when $\alpha = 0.05$, a $z$ value of ±1.65 is required to achieve statistical significance, so our calculated value of $z$ must fall outside ±1.65 to be statistically significant. In a two-tailed test, a $z$ value of ±1.96 is required for statistical significance, so our calculated value of $z$ must fall outside ±1.96 to be statistically significant. In a two-

Table 7.2 **Critical Values for Standard Normal Distributions**

|  | Alpha | Critical Value $z$ |
|---|---|---|
| Two-tailed test | .05 | ±1.95 |
|  | .01 | ±2.58 |
| One-tailed test | .05 | ±1.65 |
|  | .01 | ±2.33 |

tailed test, the space between ±1.96 when $\alpha = 0.05$ is called the **non-critical region**, or the area where we do not reject the null hypothesis. Thus, if the calculated value of $z$ falls between ±1.96, we fail to reject the null hypothesis. Alternatively, the space outside or beyond ±1.96 when $\alpha = 0.05$ is called the **critical region**. If the calculated value of $z$ is greater than or equal to +1.96 or less than or equal to −1.96, we reject the null hypothesis.

When we are conducting either a one- or a two-tailed $z$ test, the population parameters $\mu$ and $\sigma$ are known. In our first example, we will conduct a two-tailed test in which we are interested in whether the hospital's ALOS for patients discharged from hypothetical DRG XXX is different from the national ALOS. The 2003 national mean LOS ($\mu$) for DRG XXX is 6.3 days, and the standard deviation ($\sigma$) is 2.44 days. At Critical Care Hospital in 2003, 104 patients were discharged from DRG XXX with an ALOS of 5.49 days and a standard deviation of 3.44 days. In determining whether the observed difference in the ALOS is statistically significant, we must first state the null and alternative hypotheses and alpha level:

$$H_0 : \mu_1 = \mu_2$$
$$H_A : \mu_1 \neq \mu_2$$
$$\alpha = 0.05$$

The null hypothesis states that the hospital's ALOS is equal to the national ALOS for DRG XXX. The alternative hypothesis states that the hospital ALOS for DRG XXX is significantly different from the national ALOS. Because the alternative hypothesis is one of inequality, we are conducting a two-tailed test. The calculated value of $z$ must fall outside or equal the critical value of $z$, or ±1.96. The $z$ value is calculated as follows:

$$z = \frac{\overline{X} - \mu}{\sigma / \sqrt{n}} = \frac{5.49 - 6.30}{2.44 / \sqrt{104}} = \frac{-0.81}{2.44 / 10.19} = -3.398$$

The results would be reported as

$$z_{calc} = -3.39$$
$$z_{crit} = -1.96$$

Because our calculated value is negative, we refer to the negative tail of the distribution. The calculated value of $z$ ($-3.39$) falls outside the critical value of $z$ ($-1.96$) when $\alpha = 0.05$. We therefore reject the null hypothesis and conclude that the ALOS at Critical Care Hospital is significantly different from the national ALOS for DRG XXX.

In our second example, we will conduct a one-tailed test. The quality improvement team at Critical Care Hospital is interested in determining if the administration of a new antibiotic has had any effect in reducing the ALOS for patients discharged from DRG XXX. (An **effect** is a change in one variable—in this case, the ALOS—that can be associated with another variable—in this case, the antibiotic.) In 2003, the ALOS for the 104 patients discharged from DRG XXX at Critical Care Hospital was 5.49 days, and the standard deviation was 3.44 days. Specifically, we want to know if the antibiotic resulted in a significant reduction of the ALOS.

We will first construct our null and alternative hypotheses. In the null hypothesis, we are assuming that the antibiotic had no effect. If we reject the null hypothesis on the basis of our statistical test, we are saying that the probability of getting such a mean value by random chance is too small for us to believe that the null hypothesis is true. If we fail to reject the null hypothesis, we are stating that the probability associated with the observed mean is large, that such samples are common, and that there is not enough evidence that the antibiotic was effective in reducing the ALOS.

The null and alternative hypotheses are

$$H_0 : \mu_1 = 5.49$$
$$H_A : \mu_1 < 5.49$$
$$\alpha = 0.05$$

The null hypothesis states that the hospital ALOS is equal to 5.49 days, the hospital's ALOS for DRG XXX in 2003. The alternative hypothesis states that the hospital ALOS is significantly less than the 5.49 days.

In this one-tailed test, we are interested in determining if the ALOS for DRG XXX is significantly less than the ALOS prior to the administration of the new antibiotic. Thus, we will look for statistical significance in the negative end of the tail. For a one-tailed test in which alpha is set at 0.05, the critical value of $z$ is $-1.64$, so the calculated value of $z$ must be less than or equal to $-1.64$ for the results to be statistically significant.

Exhibit 7.3   **Descriptive Statistics for Sample from DRG XXX**

|  |  | LOS | Valid N (listwise) |
|---|---|---|---|
| | | **Descriptive Statistics** | |
| N | Statistic | 66 | 66 |
| Minimum | Statistic | 1.00 | |
| Maximum | Statistic | 11.00 | |
| Mean | Statistic | 4.7121 | |
| Std. Deviation | Statistic | 2.6181 | |
| Skewness | Statistic | .601 | |
| | Std. Error | .295 | |
| Kurtosis | Statistic | − .608 | |
| | Std. Error | .582 | |

Since the beginning of the study, 66 patients have been discharged from DRG XXX. The size of the standard deviation indicates that there is quite a bit of variation in the LOS for the 2004 discharges. The descriptive statistics for these 66 discharges appear in Exhibit 7.3. The sample mean for the 66 patients who were treated after implementation of the antibiotic is 4.71 days.

$$z = \frac{\overline{X} - \mu}{\sigma/\sqrt{n}} = \frac{4.72 - 5.49}{2.44/\sqrt{66}} = \frac{-0.78}{2.44/8.12} = -2.59$$

Our calculated value of $z$ is −2.59 and falls in the region of rejection because the critical value of $z$ for a one-tailed test is −1.64 when alpha equals 0.05. Because the calculated value is less than or equal to the critical value of $z$, we reject the null hypothesis and conclude that the new antibiotic may have had an effect on reducing LOS for patients discharged from DRG XXX in 2004. Note that this example is used for illustrative purposes only. Other factors may be at work that account for the reduction in the ALOS.

We can find the critical value of $z$ by referring to a statistical table. Appendix B contains a table for the $z$ scores in the standard normal distribution (Table B.1).

The table contains three columns:

| z | Cum p | Tail p |
|---|---|---|
| 0.00 | 0.5000 | 0.5000 |
| 0.01 | 0.5040 | 0.4960 |
| .. | .. | .. |
| 3.90 | 1.000 | 0.0000 |

The first column contains the values of z from 0.00 to 3.90; these should be read as both positive and negative because the normal distribution is symmetrical. (As you recall, the z score of 0.00 is the mean or center of the distribution.) The second column is the cumulative probability of z from the lower end to the distribution to the location of z in the standard normal distribution. The third column is the tail probability, or the area beyond the location of z in the remaining portion of the distribution. For each value of z, the sum of these two probabilities is equal to 1.0.

To locate the exact probability of a calculated value of z such as −3.39, locate 3.39 in the z column. The third column indicates that the exact p value for a one-tailed test is 0.0003. This is the portion of the standard normal distribution that is in one tail of the distribution beyond the z value of ±3.39. If we are conducting a two-tailed test, we must double the p value to 0.0006.

## The *t* Test

Thus far, we have discussed only the normal and standard normal distributions. There are other distributions from which statistical inferences can be made, one of which is the *t* distribution, sometimes referred to as the Student's *t*. Student's *t* is named for William Gosset, who published under the pseudonym of *Student* and was the first to describe this family of distributions. We conduct a **t test** when the population parameter $\sigma$ is unknown. The $\sigma$ is estimated from the sample statistic *s*. Before conducting the actual *t* test, we will compare the normal distribution with the *t* distribution.

The *t* distribution is used for statistical testing when population parameters are unknown or when the sample size is small. The definition of small varies; some researchers state that a sample size of less than 500 is small, whereas others consider a sample size of less than 90 small. Others have used the various forms of the *t* test with sample sizes of less than 30. With very large samples ($N \geq 1000$), the *t* distribution and the normal distribution are approximately the same.

Both the normal and *t* distributions are symmetrical about the mean. Like the normal distribution, the *t* distribution is actually a family of distributions based on sample size. This additional parameter is referred to as **degrees of freedom (df)** and is calculated by subtracting 1 from the sample size (df = $N - 1$). Exhibit 7.4 provides an explanation of degrees of freedom. The normal distribution is bell-shaped, but the shape of the *t* distribution is related to the number of degrees of freedom. A distribution with a small number of degrees of freedom is flatter; this results in a greater area in the tails of the distribution. Because the *t* distribution is so spread out, it is more difficult to achieve statistical significance with a small sample size.

In the *t* distribution when $\alpha = 0.05$, the critical value required to achieve statistical significance varies with the size of the sample. With the *t* distribution for a sample size of 10 (df = 9) and for a two-tailed test, a value outside or equal to ±2.262 must be obtained to achieve statistical significance, as compared to ±1.96 in the normal distribution. In the *t* distribution with 9 degrees of freedom, 95% of the observations fall between ±2.262 standard deviations of the mean. If the size of the sample is increased from 10 to 20 (df = 19), the critical value required to achieve statistical significance decreases to ±2.093. Thus, the critical value needed to achieve statistical significance decreases as the sample size increases.

As the sample size increases, the *t* distribution becomes less broad and flat and approaches the bell shape of the normal curve. With a sample size of 500, the critical value for the *t* distribution when alpha is set at 0.05 is ±1.965, similar to the critical value of ±1.96 when alpha is set at 0.05 for the normal distribution. To test

---

Exhibit 7.4    **Degrees of Freedom**

---

The term *degrees of freedom* refers to the number of values that are free to vary after certain restrictions have been placed on the data. For example, in any set of interval or ratio level data, we can sum the data to get a total. Assume that for a given frequency distribution, the sum is 100 and there are 10 cases (N = 10). If we arbitrarily assign a value of 10 to the first case, 5 to the second case, 15 to the third, 8 to the fourth, 2 to the fifth, 18 to the sixth, 23 to the seventh, 4 to the eighth, and 6 to the ninth, the cumulated sum will be:

$$10 + 5 + 15 + 8 + 2 + 18 + 23 + 4 + 6 = 91$$

The first nine values sum to 91. For all 10 cases to sum to 100, the 10th case must be equal to 9. Nine scores were arbitrarily set before the 10th was determined. Nine scores were free to vary; thus, we have nine degrees of freedom. Degrees of freedom are the number of elements in a set that can be arbitrarily defined before the rest of the elements in the set are determined.

---

a hypothesis using the *t* distribution, we compare the calculated value of *t* to the critical value of *t* that is contained in the *t* table (Appendix B, Table B.2). Remember that the *t* distribution is actually a family of distributions where the tabled value of *t* is dependent upon the number of degrees of freedom in the sample.

The assumptions for the *t* test are that the samples are drawn randomly and independently from their respective populations and that they are normally distributed. In addition, it is assumed that the population variances of the two groups are approximately equal.

## Two-Tailed *t* Test

In a non-directional *t* test, our question is just whether our sample mean is significantly different from the population mean, regardless of direction. In this case, both tails of the *t* distribution are used in the statistical decision making. A two-tailed *t* test divides alpha in half, placing half in each tail. That is, when alpha is set at 0.05, 2.5% of the area under both the upper and lower tails of the curve is considered when deciding whether to accept the null hypothesis.

Given this information about the *t* test and the *t* distribution, let us work through the same LOS problem that we used with the one-tailed *z* test. To restate our question of interest, we are interested in determining whether the hospital's ALOS for DRG XXX is significantly different from the national ALOS for DRG XXX. The national ALOS is 6.3 days, our hospital mean LOS is 5.49 days, and the standard deviation is 3.44 days. There were 104 discharges from DRG XXX. The first step in the process is to state our null and alternate hypotheses and to set the alpha level at which we will reject our null hypothesis:

$$H_0 : \mu_1 = \mu_2$$
$$H_A : \mu_1 \neq \mu_2$$
$$\alpha = 0.05$$

As with the non-directional *z* test, the null hypothesis states that the hospital ALOS for DRG XXX is equal to the national ALOS for DRG XXX. The alternative hypothesis states that the ALOS for the hospital is significantly different from the national ALOS for DRG XXX. Because we are interested in determining only whether our hospital mean is different from the national mean, the *t* test is a non-directional or two-tailed test. Next, we determine the critical region for rejection of the null hypothesis. For a sample size of 104 (df = 103), the tabled *t* or critical *t* ($t_{0.05}$) value is approximately $\pm 1.98$. Because $H_A$ is non-directional, the critical region consists of all values of $t \geq 1.984$ or $t \leq 1.984$.

To locate the critical value of *t*, we refer to the tabled critical values of the *t* distribution in Appendix B, Table B.2. The first column lists the degrees of freedom and the remaining columns identify the critical values of *t* for alpha levels for both one- and two-tailed tests. Because the table does not list all possible degrees of freedom, we select the row for df = 100 for our problem. For a two-tailed test with alpha set at 0.05, the critical value of $t$ is 1.984. Therefore, our region of rejection for the calculated value of $t$ must equal or fall outside ±1.984.

Using the formula for a **one-sample $t$ test**, we can now calculate $t$:

$$t = \frac{\overline{X} - \mu}{s/\sqrt{N}} = \frac{5.49 - 6.30}{3.44/\sqrt{104}} = \frac{-0.81}{3.44/10.19} = -2.399$$

The results would be reported as

$$t_{\text{calc}} = -2.399$$
$$t_{\text{crit.05}} = -1.984$$

Because our $t_{\text{calc}}$ falls in the region of rejection, we reject the null hypothesis and conclude that our hospital LOS is significantly different from the national ALOS for DRG XXX.

Notice that the formula for $t$ takes the same general form as that for $z$. The only difference is that in $z$, the population parameter $\sigma$ is used in the calculation, whereas in $t$, the population $\sigma$ is estimated from the sample statistic $s$. To calculate the $CI_{95}$, we use the same procedures as presented in Chapter 6, except that we use the critical value of $t_{0.05}$, which for 103 degrees of freedom is 1.98:

$$CI_{95} = \overline{X} \pm t_{\alpha}\left(\frac{s}{\sqrt{N}}\right) = 5.49 \pm 1.98\left(\frac{3.44}{\sqrt{104}}\right) = 5.49 \pm 1.98(0.34) = 5.49 \pm 0.668$$

or

$$[4.82, 6.16]$$

Thus, we are 95% confident that the true population mean lies between 4.82 and 6.16. We can use SPSS to calculate the one-sample $t$ test. When requesting the one-sample $t$ test, the population parameter (i.e., 6.3 days) to which the sample mean is being compared must be specified. The output for the one-sample $t$ test appears in Exhibit 7.5, and an explanation of the SPSS output appears in Exhibit 7.6.

Note that the calculated $t$ for our SPSS output is the same as that calculated with the assistance of a hand-held calculator. (When minor differences occur, they are most likely due to rounding.) The obtained $p$ value is 0.018, which is less than our previously established alpha level of 0.05. SPSS reports results in terms of significance—what we previously described as the $p$ value. The critical value of $t$ for the predetermined alpha level is not reported. The 95% confidence interval of

Exhibit 7.5 **SPSS Output for One-Sample *t* Test**

| One-Sample Statistics | | | One-Sample Test | | | |
|---|---|---|---|---|---|---|
| | | **LOS** | | | | **LOS** |
| N | | 104 | Test Value = 6.3 | t | | −2.399 |
| Mean | | 5.4904 | | df | | 103 |
| Std. Deviation | | 3.44159 | | Sig. (2-tailed) | | .018 |
| Std. Error Mean | | .33748 | | Mean Difference | | −.80962 |
| | | | | 95% Confidence Interval of the Difference | Lower | −1.4789 |
| | | | | | Upper | −.1403 |

Exhibit 7.6 **Output for One-Sample *t* Test**

| Test Value | Population Parameter to Which the Sample Is Compared |
|---|---|
| *t* | The calculated value of *t*. |
| *df* | Degrees of freedom; for the one-sample *t* test the degrees of freedom are equal to $(n − 1)$ |
| Sig two-tailed | For a two-tailed or non-directional statistical test, the *p* value for the calculated value of *t* |
| Mean difference | The **actual** difference between the two population means; the hospital mean is subtracted from the national mean |
| 95% confidence interval of the difference | The interval that covers the true difference between the two population means |

the difference between the means is also provided. The 95% confidence interval of the mean is interpreted as meaning that we are 95% confident that the interval [−0.1403, 1.4789] covers the true difference in the LOS between the hospital mean and the national mean for DRG XXX. In other words, the true difference between the observed means could be as low as −0.1403 and as high as 1.4789. It is calculated as

$$CI_{95} = (\overline{X}_1 - \overline{X}_2) \pm t_\alpha s \sqrt{\tfrac{1}{n_1} + \tfrac{1}{n_2}}$$

## One-Tailed *t* Test

Using the same information for the one-tailed *z* test, we will conduct a one-tailed *t* test. Recall that the quality improvement team is interested in determining if the administration of a new antibiotic resulted in a decrease in the ALOS. As before, the null and alternative hypotheses are

$$H_0 : \mu_1 = 5.49$$
$$H_A : \mu_1 < 5.49$$
$$\alpha = 0.05$$

From the data in Exhibit 7.3, we know that the mean after administration of the antibiotic is 4.7121. The number of discharges is 66. Because this is a one-tailed test, the critical *t* value for an alpha of 0.05 and for 65 degrees of freedom is approximately −1.664. We had to approximate the critical *t* value because our *t* table does not include the critical values of *t* for all possible degrees of freedom. Our table provides the critical values of *t* for 60 and 80 degrees of freedom, so a conservative estimate of the critical *t* for 80 degrees of freedom was selected, −1.664. This is not much different from the critical value of *t* for 60 degrees of freedom, −1.671.

$$t = \frac{\overline{X} - \mu}{s/\sqrt{N}} = \frac{4.71 - 5.49}{2.62/\sqrt{66}} = \frac{-0.78}{2.62/8.124} = -2.41$$

Because our $t_{calc}$, −2.41, is less than or equal to −1.664, we reject the null hypothesis and state that it appears that the new antibiotic may have been effective in reducing the hospital ALOS for DRG XXX. The 95% CI for the mean would be calculated as

$$CI_{95} = \overline{X} \pm t_\alpha \left( \frac{s}{\sqrt{N}} \right) = 4.71 \pm 1.67 \left( \frac{2.62}{\sqrt{66}} \right) = 5.71 \pm 1.67(0.322) = 4.71 \pm 0.54$$

or

$$[4.17, 5.25]$$

We are therefore 95% confident that the interval from 4.17 to 5.25 covers the true LOS for our hospital patients after the administration of the antibiotic.

When we use SPSS for the one-tailed *t* test, the output is the same as that for the two-tailed test, as displayed in Exhibit 7.7. The significance of the *t* statistic or *p* value for a two-sided test is reported. If we are conducting a one-tailed test, we must divide the *p* value when reporting the results. For a one-tailed *t* test, the

Exhibit 7.7   **SPSS Output for One-Sample *t* Test**

| One-Sample Statistics | | | One-Sample Test | | | |
|---|---|---|---|---|---|---|
| | **LOS** | | | | | **LOS** |
| N | 66 | | Test Value = 5.49 | t | | −2.414 |
| Mean | 4.7121 | | | df | | 65 |
| Std. Deviation | 2.61807 | | | Sig. (2-tailed) | | .019 |
| Std. Error Mean | .32226 | | | Mean Difference | | − .77788 |
| | | | | 95% Confidence Interval of the Difference | Lower | −1.4215 |
| | | | | | Upper | −.1343 |

*p* value becomes 0.019/2 = 0.0095, illustrating that it is easier to achieve statistical significance with a one-tailed test than with a two-tailed test.

## The *t* Test for Comparing Two Independent Sample Means

Sometimes we are interested in comparing means from two independent samples—for example, comparing average charges by DRG or average charges by physician. In these examples, we would draw independent random samples from their respective populations. The null hypothesis would state that there was no difference in the population means for the two groups, and the alternative hypothesis would be that there was a difference between the two population means:

$$H_0 : \mu_1 = \mu_2$$
$$H_A : \mu_1 \neq \mu_2$$
$$\alpha = 0.05$$

The formula for the *t* test for the comparison of **two independent sample means** is

$$t = \frac{\overline{X}_1 - \overline{X}_2}{s_p \sqrt{\frac{1}{n_1} + \frac{1}{n_2}}}$$

where $s_p$ is called the pooled standard deviation. The **pooled standard deviation** is an average of the sample variances, $n_1$ and $n_2$. The pooled standard deviation is found by

$$s_p = \sqrt{\frac{(n_1 - 1)s_1^2 + (n_2 - 1)s_2^2}{n_1 + n_2 - 2}}$$

The degrees of freedom for the $t$ test for two independent samples is df = $n_1$ + $n_2$ − 2. Exhibit 7.8 outlines the steps for solving the two-sample $t$ test. The null hypothesis states that the mean charges for Dr. Sparenocost and Dr. Spendtheleast are equal; the alternative hypothesis states that the mean charges for Dr. Spareno-cost and Dr. Spendtheleast are significantly different. We are conducting a one-tailed, non-directional $t$ test. The SPSS output for a two-sample $t$ test appears in Exhibit 7.9.

The results indicate that the calculated value of $t$ (−3.92) fall outside the critical value of $t$ (1.96). We therefore reject the null hypothesis and conclude that the mean charges for each doctor are significantly different from each other. Why is it important to know if the charges of different physicians are significantly different from one another? The results could help us determine if one physician is more cost-effective than another in the delivery of health care services. Some possible questions that could be explored after obtaining this result include: Does one physician order more diagnostic tests than the other? Is the ALOS for the patients of one physician less than that for the other physician? If so, why? Answers to these and other questions can help us to educate physicians on the variations in their practice patterns. This may lead to a more cost-effective delivery of health care services.

It is important to remember that we should be careful in drawing any definitive conclusions before conducting further investigation. In the previous example, the mean charges for one physician were significantly different from the mean charges for the other. When significant results are achieved, the data analyst must conduct further investigation to determine if there is an explanation for the difference. Perhaps the patients of one physician are older and sicker than the other physicians' patients. It would also be important to compare charges between all physicians who treat similar patients.

The results of our hand calculations are the same as the SPSS results. We are interested in the results in the column labeled, "Equal Variances Assumed." SPSS automatically provides the results of Levene's test, which compares the equality of the variances between the groups. One of the assumptions of the $t$ test is that the variances of the populations from which the two samples are drawn are equal. Because the result of the test is not significant, the variances of the two samples are assumed to be equal—therefore we have met the assumption that sample variances are approximately equal and it was appropriate to use the $t$ test. If the result of Levene's test is significant, it means that the variances of the two samples are significantly different and it may not be appropriate to use the $t$ test to test the hypothesis. In this example the result of the test is significant ($p < .05$)–the variances of the two samples are not equal, and we should use caution when evaluating the

Exhibit 7.8 **Calculation of *t* Test for Two Independent Sample Means**

At Critical Care Hospital, the average charge for Dr. Sparenocost (Physician # 1550) is $18,130 (rounded); the average charge for Spendtheleast (Physician # 1510) is $7,049. The question of interest is whether the average charges for Dr. Sparenocost are significantly different from those for Dr. Spendtheleast.

1. State the null and alternative hypotheses, and set the alpha level.

   $H_0 : \mu_A = \mu_B$

   $H_A : \mu_A \neq \mu_B$

   $\alpha = 0.05$

2. Determine the region of rejection for a two-tailed two-sample t test where df $= n_1 + n_2 - 2$ $= (116 + 101) - 2 = 215$, $t_{crit} = \pm 1.96$.

3. Calculate the sample statistics:

   |       | Dr. Sparenocost (#1550) | Spendtheleast (#1510) |
   |-------|-------------------------|------------------------|
   | Mean  | $14,694                 | $5,203                 |
   | S.D.  | $24,685                 | $7,843                 |
   | N     | 101                     | 116                    |

   The pooled standard deviation:

   $$s_p = \sqrt{\frac{(n_1 - 1)s_1^2 + (n_2 - 1)s_2^2}{n_1 + n_2 - 2}}$$

   $$= \sqrt{\frac{(101 - 1)24,685^2 + (116 - 1)7,843^2}{101 + 116 - 2}}$$

   $$= 17,785.4$$

   Calculation of *t*:

   $$= \frac{\$5,203 - \$14,694}{17,785.4\sqrt{(1/116) + (1/101)}}$$

   $$= \frac{-9,491}{2,420.5}$$

   $$= -3.92$$

4. Conclusion: $t_{calc} = -3.92$; $t_{calc} \leq t_{crit}$ (df $= 215$) $= +1.96$. We reject the null hypothesis and conclude that it appears that the average charges for Dr. Sparenocost are significantly different from the average charges for Dr. Spendtheleast.

Exhibit 7.9   **SPSS Output for Two-Sample *t* Test**

**Group Statistics**

| | Charges Physician | |
|---|---|---|
| | **1510** | **1550** |
| N | 116 | 101 |
| Mean | 5203.1953 | 14694.444 |
| Std. Deviation | 7843.4506 | 24685.3201 |
| Std. Error Mean | 728.24611 | 2456.28124 |

**Independent Samples Test**

| | | | Charges | |
|---|---|---|---|---|
| | | | **Equal variances assumed** | **Equal variances not assumed** |
| Levene's Test for Equality of Variances | F | | 6.397 | |
| | Sig. | | .012 | |
| t-test for Equality of Means | t | | −3.921 | −3.705 |
| | df | | 215 | 117.563 |
| | Sig. (2-tailed) | | .000 | .000 |
| | Mean Difference | | −9491.24862 | −9491.24862 |
| | Std. Error Difference | | 2420.53525 | 2561.96407 |
| | 95% Confidence Interval of the Difference | Lower | −14262.26671 | −14564.83023 |
| | | Upper | −4720.23053 | −4417.66700 |

results. It is more difficult to evaluate this assumption when performing these calculations with a hand-held calculator.

Excel may also be used for conducting the *t* test for comparing the means of two independent samples. The Excel output appears in Exhibit 7.10. The interpretation of the output is the same as that outlines in Exhibit 7.2, with the exception of the "pooled variance." The pooled variance is the pooled standard deviation squared, which appears in Exhibit 7.8.

Exhibit 7.10    **Excel Output for Two-Sample *t* Test, Assuming Equal Variances**

|  | 1510 | 1550 |
|---|---|---|
| Mean | 5203.195 | 14694.444 |
| Variance | 61519718.6060 | 609365068.3906 |
| Observations | 116 | 101 |
| Pooled Variance | 316331509.203 | |
| Hypothesized Mean Difference | 0 | |
| df | 215 | |
| t Stat | −3.921 | |
| P(T ≤ t) one-tail | 0.000 | |
| t Critical one-tail | 1.652 | |
| P(T ≤ t) two-tail | 0.000 | |
| t Critical two-tail | 1.971 | |

## CONCLUSION

With statistical inference, we are interested in making generalizations about our population parameters from sample statistics. For example, if we are interested in comparing two population means for significant differences, we must set up a hypothesis. For statistical testing, we set up two hypotheses: the null hypothesis and the alternative hypothesis. The null hypothesis states that there is no difference between the population parameters of interest, and the alternative hypothesis states that there is a statistically significant difference in the population parameters of interest.

After formulating our hypotheses, we must set an alpha level for the rejection of the null hypothesis. For large samples, alpha is usually set at 0.01 because it is easy to achieve statistical significance with large samples; for small samples, alpha is usually set at 0.05 because it is more difficult to achieve statistical significance with smaller samples. The alpha level also indicates the probability of making a Type I error. In a Type I error, we reject the null hypothesis when it is true. A Type II error is made when we fail to reject a null hypothesis that is false.

In this chapter, we have also reviewed statistical procedures for testing hypotheses of the differences between means. We can use the *z* distribution for testing hypotheses involving one and two independent samples. To use the *z* distribution, we must assume that the samples are independent and are normally distributed, and the sample size must be greater than 30. The population parameters $\mu$ and $\sigma$ must be known if we are to use the *z* distribution.

When population parameters are not known, we can use the *t* distribution to test hypotheses of differences between population means. We can use *t* to compare a sample mean with a population mean or to compare the mean of two samples drawn independently from two populations. In using both the *t* and *z* distributions, we are restricted to comparing the means of two samples.

## References

Hall, H.I. (1998) The *z* test. *Quality Resource* 16, 5:7.

Jekel, J.F., et al. (1996) *Biostatistics, Epidemiology, and Preventive Medicine*. Philadelphia: W.B. Saunders.

Katz, D.L. (1997) *Biostatistics, Epidemiology, and Preventive Medicine Review*. Philadelphia: W.B. Saunders.

Osborn, Carol E. (2006) *Statistical Applications for Health Information Management*, 2nd edition. Boston: Jones and Bartlett Publishers.

Schloesser (2000) *Student's t-Test of Difference of Means*. Wellesley College, Psychology Department. (http://www.wellesley.edu/psychology/Psych205/indepttest.html)

# APPENDIX 7-A

## EXERCISES FOR SOLVING PROBLEMS

### Knowledge Questions

1. Define the key terms listed at the beginning of this chapter.
2. You have been analyzing hospital discharges from DRG 15, "Transient Ischemic Attack and Precerebral Occlusions." The ALOS for patients discharged from DRG 15 is 2.2 days. The national length of stay for DRG 15 is 4.1 days. You are interested in determining whether the hospital's length of stay for DRG 15 is significantly different from the national ALOS.
    a. State the null and alternative hypotheses.
    b. Set the alpha level.
3. Explain the differences between the alpha level and the *p* value.
4. What are Type I and Type II errors? What factors contribute to making either a Type I or Type II error?
5. Compare and contrast the *z* distribution with the *t* distribution.
6. Describe situations in which we would use one-tailed tests. Describe situations in which we would use two-tailed tests.
7. What assumptions must be met when using *z* and *t* distributions for hypothesis testing? Why are these assumptions not always strictly followed?
8. In hypothesis testing, what is meant by the term *effect*?

### Multiple Choice

1. The null hypothesis is a statement that is:
    a. Probably true
    b. Considered to be false until proven true
    c. Evaluated statistically as either true or false
    d. All of the above
2. When $\alpha = 0.05$, the null hypothesis will be:
    a. Rejected 5% of the time
    b. Rejected 5% of the time when it is true
    c. Accepted 5% of the time
    d. Accepted 5% of the time when it is false
3. A Type I error occurs when:
    a. We reject the null hypothesis when it is true
    b. We reject the null hypothesis when it is false
    c. We accept the null hypothesis when it is true
    d. We accept the null hypothesis when it is false

4. A Type II error occurs when we:
   a. Use a two-tailed test when a one-tailed test is more appropriate
   b. Use a one-tailed test when a two-tailed test is more appropriate
   c. Reject the null hypothesis when it is true
   d. Accept the null hypothesis when it is false

5. If we change the alpha level for a statistical test from 0.05 to 0.01, we are:
   a. Increasing the risk of making a Type I error
   b. Decreasing the risk of making a Type I error
   c. Decreasing the risk of making a Type II error
   d. Increasing the probability of finding statistical significance

6. In general, large sample sizes:
   a. Reduce the risk of Type I error
   b. Reduce the risk of Type II error
   c. Make it easier to achieve statistical significance
   d. All of the above

7. The $p$ value is the:
   a. Power of a statistical test
   b. Probability that the null hypothesis is true
   c. Probability of making a Type II error
   d. Probability of getting a result as extreme as the one observed if the null hypothesis is true

8. It is easier for a statistical test to achieve statistical significance when we conduct a:
   a. Non-directional test
   b. One-tailed test
   c. Two-tailed test
   d. All of the above

9. If a statistical test is significant at the 0.01 level, it is:
   a. Also significant at the 0.05 level
   b. Not significant at the 0.05 level
   c. Also significant at the 0.001 level
   d. Also significant at the 0.0001 level

For Questions 10 through 13, refer to the problem below:

We are conducting a study of the age of nursing home patients in the county. The null and alternative hypotheses are

$H_0 : \mu = 80$

$H_A : \mu \neq 80$

We have used the $z$ test for evaluating our results when the critical values of $z$ are $\pm 1.96$ where $\alpha = 0.05$, and $\pm 2.58$ where $\alpha = 0.01$.

10. In this case, the null hypothesis is:
    a. Directional
    b. Non-directional
    c. A one-tailed $z$ test
    d. A two-tailed $t$ test

11. If the calculated $z = 2.30$, we would:
    a. Accept the $H_0$ at $\alpha = 0.05$ but reject the $H_0$ at $\alpha = 0.01$
    b. Accept the $H_0$ at $\alpha = 0.05$ and accept the $H_0$ at $\alpha = 0.01$
    c. Reject the $H_0$ at $\alpha = 0.05$ but accept the $H_0$ at $\alpha = 0.01$
    d. Reject the $H_0$ at $\alpha = 0.05$ and reject the $H_0$ at $\alpha = 0.01$

12. If the calculated value of $z = 1.80$, we would:
    a. Accept the $H_0$ at $\alpha = 0.05$ but reject the $H_0$ at $\alpha = 0.01$
    b. Accept the $H_0$ at $\alpha = 0.05$ and accept the $H_0$ at $\alpha = 0.01$
    c. Reject the $H_0$ at $\alpha = 0.05$ but accept the $H_0$ at $\alpha = 0.01$
    d. Reject the $H_0$ at $\alpha = 0.05$ and reject the $H_0$ at $\alpha = 0.01$

13. If the calculated value of $z = -2.80$, we would:
    a. Accept the $H_0$ at $\alpha = 0.05$ but reject the $H_0$ at $\alpha = 0.01$
    b. Accept the $H_0$ at $\alpha = 0.05$ and accept the $H_0$ at $\alpha = 0.01$
    c. Reject the $H_0$ at $\alpha = 0.05$ but accept the $H_0$ at $\alpha = 0.01$
    d. Reject the $H_0$ at $\alpha = 0.05$ and reject the $H_0$ at $\alpha = 0.01$

14. You believe that the hospital's average length of stay for DRG XXX is significantly less than the national average for the same DRG. Which of the following statistical tests would be most appropriate for answering this question?
    a. One-sample directional $t$ test
    b. One-sample non-directional $t$ test
    c. $t$ test for two independent samples
    d. Any of the above

15. In Question 14, the sample size is 100. The number of degrees of freedom for evaluating the statistical significance of the test result is:
    a. 99
    b. 98
    c. 97
    d. Not enough information is provided

## Problems

1. As a health information management DRG analyst, you are interested in comparing the mean LOS for Critical Care Hospital and the national mean for DRG 002, "Craniotomy, Age Greater Than 17 without CC." The hospital mean LOS is 4.17 days, and the standard deviation is 2.57 days. The national average LOS for DRG 002 is 5.2 days. The summary data for Critical Care Hospital appear in Table 7-A.1 and Exhibit 7-A.1.
   a. State the null and alternative hypotheses and the alpha level.
   b. Calculate the difference between the hospital mean and the national mean using the one-sample $t$ test. What is the number of degrees of freedom? What is the resultant $t$ statistic? Is it statistically significant?
   c. What are your conclusions?

2. For the DRG 410, "Chemotherapy without Acute Leukemia as Secondary Diagnosis," you want to determine if there is a difference in the length of stay by two payors, Managed Care and Medicare. The summary data appear in Table 7-A.2 and Table 7-A.3.
   a. State the null and alternative hypotheses and the alpha level.
   b. Use the $t$ test for two independent sample means to determine if the observed difference between the two means is statistically significant. What is the number of degrees of free-

Table 7-A.1    **Frequency Distribution for Length of Stay for DRG 002 in 2003 at Critical Care Hospital (SPSS Output)**

|         |    | Frequency | Percent | Valid Percent | Cumulative Percent |
|---------|----|-----------|---------|---------------|--------------------|
| Valid   | 1  | 2         | 8.7     | 8.7           | 8.7                |
|         | 2  | 4         | 17.4    | 17.4          | 26.1               |
|         | 3  | 6         | 26.1    | 26.1          | 52.2               |
|         | 4  | 2         | 8.7     | 8.7           | 60.9               |
|         | 5  | 4         | 17.4    | 17.4          | 78.3               |
|         | 6  | 2         | 8.7     | 8.7           | 87.0               |
|         | 7  | 1         | 4.3     | 4.3           | 91.3               |
|         | 10 | 1         | 4.3     | 4.3           | 95.7               |
|         | 11 | 1         | 4.3     | 4.3           | 100.0              |
| Total   |    | 23        | 100.0   | 100.0         |                    |

Exhibit 7-A.1    **Length of Stay Statistics for DRG 002 in 2003 at Critical Care Hospital (SPSS Output)**

| | LOS | |
|---|---|---|
| N | Valid | 23 |
|   | Missing | 0 |
| Mean | | 4.17 |
| Std. Error of Mean | | .536 |
| Median | | 3.00 |
| Mode | | 3 |
| Std. Deviation | | 2.570 |

dom, the resultant $t$ statistic, and the significance level?

c. What are your conclusions?

3. You have been monitoring the lengths of stay for two of your physicians who discharge the most patients from DRG 410, "Chemotherapy without Acute Leukemia as a Secondary Diagno-sis." The relevant statistics appear in Table 7-A.4 and Table 7-A.5. You specifically want to know if the observed difference in the lengths of stay for Physician 1460 and Physician 8210 is statistically significant.

a. State the null and alternative hypotheses and the alpha level.

Table 7-A.2    **Frequency Distribution of Length of Stay by Payer, DRG 410, at Critical Care Hospital in 2004 (SPSS Output)**

LOS * Payor Cross-tabulation

| Count | | Payor Managed Care | Medicare | Total |
|---|---|---|---|---|
| LOS | 1 | 12 | 3 | 15 |
| | 2 | 5 | 16 | 21 |
| | 3 | 1 | 5 | 6 |
| | 4 | 13 | 8 | 21 |
| | 5 | 10 | 5 | 15 |
| | 6 | 1 | 0 | 1 |
| | 7 | 1 | 0 | 1 |
| | 8 | 2 | 1 | 3 |
| | 9 | 1 | 1 | 2 |
| | 13 | 1 | 0 | 1 |
| | 14 | 1 | 0 | 1 |
| | 15 | 2 | 1 | 3 |
| | 23 | 1 | 0 | 1 |
| | 54 | 0 | 1 | 1 |
| Total | 51 | 41 | 92 | |

Table 7-A.3    **Mean and Standard Deviation for Length of Stay by Payer, DRG 410, at Critical Care Hospital in 2003 (SPSS Output)**

| Payor | Mean | N | Std. Deviation |
|---|---|---|---|
| Managed care | 4.80 | 51 | 4.382 |
| Medicare | 4.71 | 41 | 8.280 |
| Total | 4.76 | 92 | 6.379 |

b. Use the *t* test for two independent sample means to determine if the observed difference between the two means is statistically significant. What are the number of degrees of freedom, the resultant *t* statistic, and the significance level?

c. What are your conclusions?

Table 7-A.4    **Frequency Distribution of Length of Stay by Physician, DRG 410, in 2003 at Critical Care Hospital (SPSS Output)**

| | | **LOS * Physician Cross-tabulation** | | |
|---|---|---|---|---|
| | | **Physician** | | |
| | | **1460** | **8210** | **Total** |
| LOS | 2 | 13 | 21 | 34 |
| | 3 | 1 | 1 | 2 |
| | 4 | 1 | 0 | 1 |
| | 5 | 1 | 1 | 2 |
| | 13 | 1 | 0 | 1 |
| | 14 | 0 | 1 | 1 |
| | 15 | 1 | 0 | 1 |
| | 23 | 1 | 0 | 1 |
| Total | | 19 | 24 | 43 |

Table 7-A.5    **Mean and Standard Deviation for Length of Stay by Physician, DRG 410, in 2003 at Critical Care Hospital (SPSS Output)**

| | **Report** | | |
|---|---|---|---|
| **Physician** | **Mean** | **N** | **Std. Deviation** |
| 1460 | 4.68 | 19 | 5.812 |
| 8210 | 2.67 | 24 | 2.496 |
| Total | 3.56 | 43 | 4.350 |

**OBJECTIVES**

Upon completion of this chapter, you should be able to:

1. Define key terms.

2. Define the Pearson's $r$ product moment correlation coefficient.

3. Construct scatter diagrams for variables $x$ and $y$.

4. Construct scatter diagrams using commercial statistical software.

5. Interpret the Pearson's $r$.

6. Distinguish between the Pearson's $r$ correlation coefficient and the Spearman's rho correlation coefficient.

7. Compare the Pearson's $r$ with the coefficient of determination.

8. Conduct hypothesis testing for the Pearson's $r$.

9. Conduct the $\chi^2$ test of independence and the $\chi^2$ goodness-of-fit test for given situations.

10. Explain the concept of standardized residuals.

11. Analyze results of the $\chi^2$ test of independence using standardized residuals.

Often we are interested in determining relationships between variables such as age and length of stay (LOS), age and survival time, or type of diet and cholesterol levels. To determine the extent to which two variables are related, we can calculate a correlation coefficient. There are many types of correlation coefficients; in this chapter, we will discuss the Pearson's $r$, or more formally, the **Pearson's $r$ correlation coefficient**, the Spearman's rho, and the $\chi^2$ (pronounced "chi square").

The Pearson's $r$ is a measure of the linear relationship between two variables; it is used when both variables under study fall on the interval or ratio scale of measurement. The Spearman's rho and $\chi^2$ are measures of association for variables that fall on either the nominal or ordinal scales of measurement.

## CHARACTERISTICS OF THE PEARSON'S $r$

To calculate the Pearson's $r$, measures must be taken on two variables, $x$ and $y$—for example, height ($x$) and weight ($y$). These measures are taken in pairs for each member of a sample randomly drawn from a population. The values of the calculated Pearson's $r$ range from −1.0 to +1.0. A correlation coefficient of −1.0 indicates that the two variables have a perfect negative relationship; a correlation coefficient of +1.0 indicates that the two variables have a perfect positive relationship; and a correlation coefficient of 0.0 indicates that there is no relationship between the two variables.

A positive relationship between the two variables means that as the measures on one variable increase, so do the measures on the second variable and, conversely, that as the measures on one variable decrease, so do the measures on the second variable. In other words, the measures on each variable move in the same direction. Thus, we can say that there is a direct relationship between the two variables. A negative relationship means that the observations for the two variables are moving in opposite directions. As measures tend to increase on one variable, they tend to decrease on the second variable. In this situation, we say that there is an inverse relationship between the two variables.

The underlying assumption for the Pearson's $r$ is that the relationship between the two variables is linear. Because relationships between variables are not always linear, one should construct a scatter diagram or scatter plot to assess the type of relationship that exists between the two variables. We can construct a **scatter diagram** by plotting one variable, $x$, on the abscissa (horizontal axis) of a graph and plotting the second variable, $y$, on the ordinate (vertical axis). If the points appear to approximate a straight line, then the two variables are linearly related, and it is appropriate to use the Pearson's $r$. Scatter diagrams displaying positive and negative linear relationships appear in Figure 8.1; a scatter diagram indicating no relationship is also displayed.

To further illustrate, consider a health information management example in which we are interested in determining if there is a relationship between age and total charges for DRG 336, "Transurethral Prostatectomy with CC." The scatter diagram of age ($x$) and total charges ($y$) appears in Figure 8.2.

Examination of the scatter diagram indicates that the relationship between the two variables is negative. Imagine a line drawn through the plots from the upper left corner down to the lower right. The diagram indicates that as age increases, total charges decrease. Therefore, the relationship between the two variables is considered negative. The means and standard deviations for age and charges for DRG 336 appear in Exhibit 8.1. The SPSS output for the Pearson's $r$ verifies that

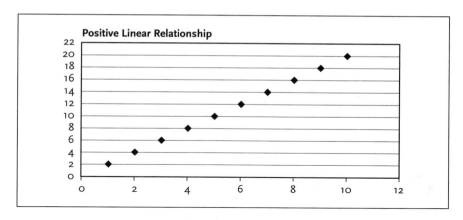

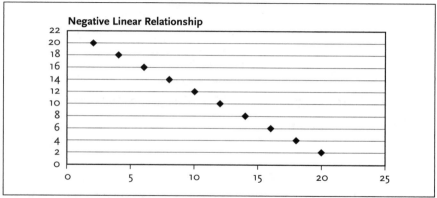

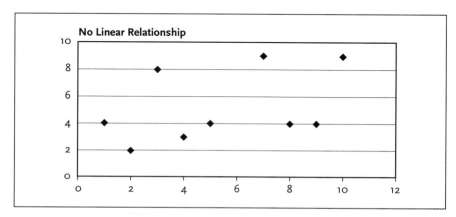

Figure 8.1    **Scatter Diagram of Linear Relationships**

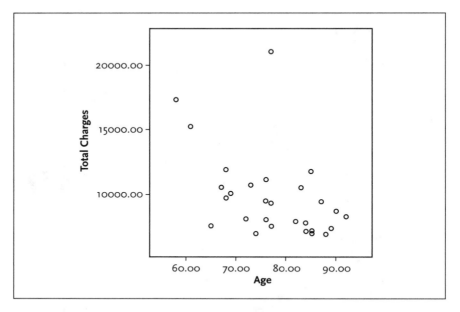

Figure 8.2  **Scatter Diagram, Age and Total Charges for DRG 336 (SPSS Output)**

Exhibit 8.1  **Means and Standard Deviations, Age and Total Charges, DRG 336 (SPSS Output)**

|  |  | **Age** | **Total Charges** |
|---|---|---|---|
| N | Valid | 28 | 28 |
|  | Missing | 0 | 0 |
| Mean |  | 77.4286 | 9803.7500 |
| Median |  | 77.0000 | 9003.5000 |
| Mode |  | 76.00[a] | 6899.00[a] |
| Std. Deviation |  | 9.11827 | 3326.68467 |
| Minimum |  | 58.00 | 6899.00 |
| Maximum |  | 92.00 | 21093.00 |

[a]Multiple modes exist. The smallest value is shown.

Exhibit 8.2    **SPSS Output for Pearson *r*, Age and Total Charges, DRG 336**

|  |  | Age | **Total Charges** |
|---|---|---|---|
| Age | Pearson Correlation | 1 | −.471* |
|  | Sig. (2-tailed) | . | .011 |
|  | N | 28 | 28 |
| Total Charges | Pearson Correlation | −.471* | 1 |
|  | Sig. (2-tailed) | .011 | . |
|  | N | 28 | 28 |

*Correlation is significant at the 0.05 level (2-tailed).

Exhibit 8.3    **Excel Output for Pearson *r*, Age and Total Charges, DRG 336**

|  | Age | Totchg |
|---|---|---|
| Age | 1 |  |
| Totchg | −0.47111 | 1 |

the relationship is negative (Exhibit 8.2). The Pearson's *r* is −0.471, which is statistically significant ($p = 0.011$). The results indicate a moderate negative correlation between our two variables, age and total charges. The SPSS output also displays the Pearson's *r* for each variable with itself—for example, the Pearson's *r* for "total charges" with "total charges" is 1.0. The Excel output for the Pearson's *r* appears in Exhibit 8.3. Excel does not provide the *p* value for the Pearson's *r*.

Both age and charges are variables that fall on the ratio scale of measurement.

## CALCULATION OF THE PEARSON'S *r*

The Pearson's *r* is a sample of the true population correlation value, which is denoted by the symbol $\rho$ (rho) and is subject to sampling variation. When calculating the Pearson's *r*, we are interested in testing the null hypothesis that $\rho = 0$; that is, that the true population correlation is zero. A value of $\rho = 0$ indicates that there is no linear relationship between the two variables of interest; a significant *r* indicates that there is a relationship between the two variables of interest. Just as with *t* tests, the obtained value of *r* is compared to a critical value of *r* to determine its statistical significance. For the Pearson's *r*, the alternative hypothesis is usually a non-directional test.

The null and alternative hypotheses are

$$H_0 : \rho = 0$$
$$H_A : \rho \uparrow 0 \qquad \text{(two-tailed alternative)}$$

The formula for calculating the Pearson's *r* is

$$r = \frac{\sum xy}{\sqrt{\sum x^2 \sum y^2}}$$

Now we will follow the procedure for calculating the Pearson's *r* for the two variables, LOS and total charges for DRG 087, "Pulmonary Edema and Respiratory Failure." It should be obvious that the longer one stays in the hospital, the greater the charges, so one would expect a positive correlation as a result.

We will first construct a scatter diagram to assess the relationship between the two variables. We want to determine whether our assumption of linearity is tenable. The scatter diagram appears in Figure 8.3.

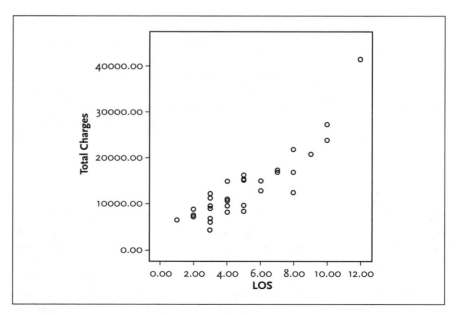

Figure 8.3    **Scatter Diagram, Length of Stay (LOS) and Total Charges for DRG 087**

Examination of the scatter diagram indicates a linear relationship between LOS and total charges; as the LOS increases, so do total charges. We would expect the resultant Pearson's $r$ to be positive. The null and alternative hypotheses are

$$H_0 : \rho = 0$$
$$H_A : \rho > 0$$
$$\alpha = 0.05$$

The null hypothesis states that there is no relationship between LOS and total charges. The alternative hypothesis states that there is a positive relationship between LOS and total charges, so we will be conducting a one-tailed test. We are using a one-tailed test because we expect that the relationship between the two variables will be positive—that is, LOS and total charges will move in the same direction. All cases discharged from DRG 087 are presented in Table 8.1.

Excel was used to prepare the data required for calculating the Pearson's $r$. Before we can calculate the Pearson's $r$, we must first calculate $\Sigma x^2$, $\Sigma y^2$, and $\Sigma xy$ (from Table 8.1):

$$\sum x^2 = \sum X^2 - \sum \frac{X^2}{n} = 1125 - \frac{(173)^2}{34} = 244.74$$

$$\sum y^2 = \sum Y^2 - \sum \frac{Y^2}{n} = 7,915,583,426 - \frac{(457,442)^2}{34} = 1,761,078,032.94$$

$$\sum xy = \sum XY - \sum \frac{XY}{n} = 2,905,363 - \frac{(173)(457,442)}{34} = 577,790.47$$

$$r = \frac{\sum xy}{\sqrt{\sum x^2 \sum y^2}} = \frac{577,790.47}{\sqrt{(244.74)(1,761,078,032.94)}} = 0.88$$

The calculated Pearson's $r$ is 0.88, indicating a strong positive relationship. Referring to Table B.3 in Appendix B, we find that the critical value for $r$ for 32 degrees of freedom, $\alpha = 0.05$ (df $= n - 2$, where $n = $ number of pairs), and for a one-tailed test is 0.287. Because our calculated value for $r$ exceeds the critical value, we reject the null hypothesis and conclude that the relationship between LOS and total charges is statistically significant. The SPSS descriptive statistics and results of Pearson's $r$ appear in Exhibit 8.4. The SPSS calculated Pearson's $r$ matches the results we obtained by using the hand-held calculator.

It is important to remember that two variables' correlation with one another does not necessarily imply causality. We cannot assume that $x$ causes $y$ or vice versa. In this example, we cannot state that long LOS will cause high charges. We

Table 8.1    **Total Charges and Length of Stay (LOS) for Patients Discharged from DRG 087**

| Patient | LOS (X) | Total Charges (Y) | LOS² (X²) | Total Charges² (Y²) | LOS × Charges (XY) |
|---|---|---|---|---|---|
| 1 | 1 | $6,507 | 1 | $42,341,049 | $6,507 |
| 2 | 2 | $8,771 | 4 | $76,930,441 | $17,542 |
| 3 | 2 | $6,971 | 4 | $48,594,841 | $13,942 |
| 4 | 2 | $7,405 | 4 | $54,834,025 | $14,810 |
| 5 | 3 | $11,290 | 9 | $127,464,100 | $33,870 |
| 6 | 3 | $8,944 | 9 | $79,995,136 | $26,832 |
| 7 | 3 | $11,133 | 9 | $123,943,689 | $33,399 |
| 8 | 3 | $4,304 | 9 | $18,524,416 | $12,912 |
| 9 | 3 | $6,702 | 9 | $44,916,804 | $20,106 |
| 10 | 3 | $12,143 | 9 | $147,452,449 | $36,429 |
| 11 | 3 | $5,867 | 9 | $34,421,689 | $17,601 |
| 12 | 3 | $11,061 | 9 | $122,345,721 | $33,183 |
| 13 | 3 | $9,494 | 9 | $90,136,036 | $28,482 |
| 14 | 4 | $10,920 | 16 | $119,246,400 | $43,680 |
| 15 | 4 | $14,917 | 16 | $222,516,889 | $59,668 |
| 16 | 4 | $8,222 | 16 | $67,601,284 | $32,888 |
| 17 | 4 | $10,566 | 16 | $111,640,356 | $42,264 |
| 18 | 4 | $9,389 | 16 | $88,153,321 | $37,556 |
| 19 | 5 | $9,660 | 25 | $93,315,600 | $48,300 |
| 20 | 5 | $15,106 | 25 | $228,191,236 | $75,530 |
| 21 | 5 | $16,289 | 25 | $265,331,521 | $81,445 |
| 22 | 5 | $8,285 | 25 | $68,641,225 | $41,425 |
| 23 | 6 | $12,893 | 36 | $166,229,449 | $77,358 |
| 24 | 6 | $14,840 | 36 | $220,225,600 | $89,040 |
| 25 | 7 | $17,375 | 49 | $301,890,625 | $121,625 |
| 26 | 7 | $16,925 | 49 | $286,455,625 | $118,475 |
| 27 | 8 | $16,892 | 64 | $285,339,664 | $135,136 |
| 28 | 8 | $12,462 | 64 | $155,301,444 | $99,696 |
| 29 | 8 | $16,955 | 64 | $287,472,025 | $135,640 |
| 30 | 8 | $21,754 | 64 | $473,236,516 | $174,032 |
| 31 | 9 | $20,830 | 81 | $433,888,900 | $187,470 |
| 32 | 10 | $23,915 | 100 | $571,927,225 | $239,150 |
| 33 | 10 | $27,245 | 100 | $742,290,025 | $272,450 |
| 34 | 12 | $41,410 | 144 | $1,714,788,100 | $496,920 |
| Total | 173 | $457,442 | 1,125 | $7,915,583,426 | $2,905,363 |

Exhibit 8.4    **SPSS Output for Pearson *r*, DRG 087, Total Charges and Length of Stay**

| Descriptive Statistics | | |
|---|---|---|
| | **Mean** | **Std. Deviation** |
| Total Charges | 13454.1765 | 7305.20369 |
| LOS | 5.0882 | 2.72327 |
| N | 34 | 34 |

| Correlations | | | Total Charges | LOS |
|---|---|---|---|---|
| Total Charges | Pearson Correlation | | 1 | .880* |
| | Sig. (2-tailed) | | . | .000 |
| | N | | 34 | 34 |
| LOS | Pearson Correlation | | .880* | 1 |
| | Sig. (2-tailed) | | .000 | . |
| | N | | 34 | 34 |

*Correlation is significant at the 0.01 level (2-tailed).

Exhibit 8.5    **Excel Output for Pearson *r*, DRG 087, Total Charges and Length of Stay**

| | Length of Stay | Total Charges |
|---|---|---|
| Column 1 | 1 | |
| Column 2 | 0.880 | 1 |

can only state that there is a strong relationship between the two variables. The two variables have a high correlation because they vary together in some systematic way. In the previous example where we were considering the relationship between age and total charges, it would not be logical to conclude that old age causes lower charges. Intuitively, this does not make sense. There must be some other variable at work that results in lower charges for older people.

Just as sample size plays a role in statistical significance when determining the difference between population means, it is also true when calculating the Pearson's *r*. Small values of *r* may be statistically significant when there are many observations, whereas large values of *r* may not be statistically significant when there are a few observations.

From the Pearson's *r*, we can calculate the **coefficient of determination**, $r^2$. The $r^2$ tells us how much of the variation in *y* is accounted for by the *x* variable. In our LOS (*x*) and total charges (*y*) example, $r^2 = 0.88^2 = 0.774$, so we conclude that

77.4% of the variation in total charges for DRG 087 is explained by the patient's LOS. The $r^2$ is a better measure of assessing the strength of a relationship between the two variables $x$ and $y$ than is $r$. The Pearson's $r$ alone can be used to make it seem as if the relationship between the two variables is much greater than it actually is. For example, a Pearson's $r$ equal to 0.50 appears to indicate a fairly strong relationship between two variables, when in fact only $0.50^2 = 25\%$ of the variance is accounted for by the two variables together.

## Parametric Versus Nonparametric Statistical Procedures

The statistical procedures discussed thus far—the $z$ value, the $t$ test, and Pearson's $r$—are called **parametric statistics**. Parametric statistical procedures require certain assumptions about the underlying population, most particularly that the underlying population is normally distributed, that measures are at the interval or ratio level of measurement, and that the samples are randomly drawn and independent.

In contrast, nonparametric procedures have less restrictive assumptions. There are no assumptions that the underlying population distribution is normal and the distributions can take on any shape, so they are not limited to the bell shape of the normal distribution. Thus, nonparametric statistical procedures are often referred to as **distribution-free statistics**. Nonparametric statistics are used most often when sample sizes are small and when variables fall on the nominal or ordinal scales of measurement.

## THE SPEARMAN'S RHO RANK ORDER CORRELATION COEFFICIENT

An alternative to the Pearson's $r$ correlation coefficient is the Spearman's rho rank order correlation coefficient. The **Spearman's rho** is used when at least one of the two variables under study falls on the ordinal scale of measurement. The correlation coefficient obtained from the Spearman's rho procedure is the result of the rankings of the observations, not the actual values of the observations.

To calculate the Spearman's rho, we rank the observations on each variable from lowest to highest. Tied observations are assigned the average of the ranks. If two observations are tied for second position, they actually occupy positions 2 and 3, and both are assigned the average rank of $(2 + 3)/2 = 2.5$. For example, consider the following data set:

| Observed score | 2 | 5 | 5 | 5 | 7 |
|---|---|---|---|---|---|
| Rank | 1 | 2 | 3 | 4 | 5 |

The total number of possible ranks is five, but three subjects have the same observation value of 5, and it is incorrect to assign them different ranks. To obtain the average rank, we sum the ranks 2, 3, and 4 and divide by 3 to obtain the average rank of 3. The assigned ranks become

| Observed score | 2 | 5 | 5 | 5 | 7 |
|---|---|---|---|---|---|
| Rank | 1 | 3 | 3 | 3 | 5 |

Once the ranks have been assigned, the differences between the ranks on the $x$ and $y$ variables are obtained, squared, and summed (Table 8.2). The resulting values are substituted into the following formula:

$$r_{rho} = 1 - \frac{6 \sum D^2}{n(n^2 - 1)}$$

The range for the Spearman's rho is the same as that for the Pearson's $r$, −1.0 to +1.0, and it has the same interpretation.

As an example, consider a hypothetical case of eight subjects who smoke. The $R_1$ column (Table 8.2) indicates the rank for each patient in terms of the number of cigarettes smoked, from least (rank = 1) to greatest (rank = 8). The $R_2$ column indicates the rank for each patient in terms of severity of illness, from least severe

**Table 8.2  Patient Ranks by Smoking and Severity of Illness**

| Patient | Number of Cigarettes Smoked $R_1$ | Severity of Illness $R_2$ | Difference in Ranks $D(R_1 - R_2)$ | $D^2$ |
|---|---|---|---|---|
| 1 | 1 | 2 | −1 | 1 |
| 2 | 2 | 4 | −2 | 4 |
| 3 | 3 | 3 | 0 | 0 |
| 4 | 4 | 1 | 3 | 9 |
| 5 | 5 | 7 | −2 | 4 |
| 6 | 6 | 5 | 1 | 1 |
| 7 | 7 | 8 | −1 | 1 |
| 8 | 8 | 6 | 2 | 4 |
| Total | | | 0 | 24 |

(rank = 1) to most severe (rank = 8). To complete the table, $R_2$ is subtracted from $R_1$ and the difference is squared. The null and alternative hypotheses are

$H_0$ : *There is no relationship between number of cigarettes smoked and severity of illness.*

$H_A$ : *There is a relationship between number of cigarettes smoked and severity of illness.*

$$\alpha = 0.05$$

Notice that the $D$ column sums to zero. This column does not need to be summed, but it does serve as a check on our calculations. The difference between the ranks column should always sum to zero. Substituting our obtained values into the formula:

$$r_{rho} = 1 - \frac{6\sum D^2}{n(n^2-1)} = 1 - \frac{6(24)}{8(64-1)} = 0.71$$

To test the significance of rho, we use the Pearson's $r$ table (Appendix B, Table B.5), where df $= n-2$. However, when the sample size is less than 10 we must use the $t$ distribution where df $= n-2$ (Appendix B, Table B.2). The formula for calculating $t$ is

$$t = \frac{r_{rho}\sqrt{n-2}}{\sqrt{1-r_{rho}^2}}$$

Substituting into the formula,

$$t = \frac{0.71\sqrt{6}}{\sqrt{1-0.71^2}} = \frac{1.74}{0.7} = 2.49$$

For six degrees of freedom, $\alpha = 0.05$, $t_{crit} = 2.447$; because the calculated $t$ (2.49) is greater than the critical $t$, it falls in the region of rejection. We therefore reject the null hypothesis and conclude that there is a statistically significant positive relationship between the number of cigarettes smoked and severity of illness.

The Spearman's rho can also be calculated when one of the variables falls on the interval scale of measurement, but it is first necessary to convert the observations to ranks. As an example, we will calculate the Spearman's rho for a data set in which variable $x$ falls on the ordinal scale of measurement and variable $y$ falls on the interval scale, as in Table 8.3. Variable $y$ must be converted to ranks. The null and alternative hypotheses are

$H_0$ : *There is no relationship between variables* x *and* y.

$H_A$ : *There is a relationship between variables* x *and* y.

$$\alpha = 0.05$$

The calculations for the Spearman's rho are

$$r_{rho} = 1 - \frac{6\sum D^2}{n(n^2-1)} = 1 - \frac{6(11)}{9(81-1)} = 0.91$$

Because we have a sample size that is less than 10, we evaluate the significance of rho by using *t*. Substituting into the formula,

$$t = \frac{0.91\sqrt{7}}{\sqrt{1-0.91^2}} = \frac{2.41}{0.41} = 5.88$$

The critical value of *t* for seven degrees of freedom, $\alpha = 0.05$, is 2.365. Because the calculated *t* is greater than the critical *t*, it falls in the region of rejection. We reject the null hypothesis and conclude that there is a strong positive relationship between variables *x* and *y*.

The SPSS output for the Spearman's rho appears in Exhibit 8.6. SPSS does not require that interval-level data be recoded for the Spearman's rho.

Table 8.3 **Spearmans Rho for Ordinal and Interval Level Data**

| Patient | $X$<br>$R_1$ | $Y$ | $R_2$ | Difference<br>in Ranks<br>$S(R_1-R_2)$ | $D^2$ |
|---------|------|-----|-------|-------------|-------|
| 1 | 8.5 | 135 | 6.5 | 2 | 4 |
| 2 | 8.5 | 120 | 9 | −0.5 | .25 |
| 3 | 6 | 140 | 5 | 1 | 1 |
| 4 | 6 | 130 | 8 | −2 | 4 |
| 5 | 6 | 135 | 6.5 | −0.5 | .25 |
| 6 | 4 | 145 | 4 | 0 | 0 |
| 7 | 3 | 150 | 2.5 | 0.5 | .25 |
| 8 | 1.5 | 150 | 2.5 | −1 | 1 |
| 9 | 1.5 | 160 | 1 | 0.5 | .25 |
| Total | | | | 0 | 11 |

Exhibit 8.6    **SPSS Output for Spearman rho**

**Correlations**

|  |  |  | X | Y |
|---|---|---|---|---|
| Spearman's rho | X | Correlation Coefficient | 1.000 | − .905* |
|  |  | Sig. (2-tailed) | . | .001 |
|  |  | N | 9 | 9 |
|  | Y | Correlation Coefficient | − .905* | 1.000 |
|  |  | Sig. (2-tailed) | .001 | . |
|  |  | N | 9 | 9 |

*Correlation is significant at the 0.01 level (2-tailed).

# CHI-SQUARE ($\chi^2$) TESTS

One of the more commonly used nonparametric tests is the chi-square ($\chi^2$) test. The $\chi^2$ distribution is a positive distribution based on the number of degrees of freedom. There is more than one type of $\chi^2$ test that can be used to analyze frequency data; however, all are based on comparing actual observations with expected frequencies. With frequency data, we are reporting the percentages or frequencies of an independent variable on the variables of interest. **Contingency tables** are used to display frequency data. A two-by-two (2 × 2) contingency table is the simplest form.

In a 2 × 2 table, the distribution of one variable is conditionally dependent, or contingent, upon the other. The table is made up of cells, which are specific locations in the matrix created by the two variables under study. Each cell represents the joint frequencies for the categories on each variable. The categories that make up each variable are dichotomous and must be mutually exclusive. The sums of the rows and columns are placed in the margins and are thus called marginal frequencies. The total for the row and column marginals is the cell in the lower right corner (grand total); this sum is equal to *N*. The basic shell for a 2 × 2 contingency table is presented in Exhibit 8.7.

Contingency tables can be larger than 2 × 2. If there are more than two categories for a given variable, the table is referred to as an R × C table (R = rows, C = columns).

We will now use hypothetical data collected to construct a two-by-two contingency table. A survey was conducted in which data were collected on two variables, professional credential and geographic location. "Credential" has two categories, Registered Health Information Technician (RHIT) and Registered Health Information Administrator (RHIA), and "geographic location" was classi-

Exhibit 8.7    **Shell for a 2 × 2 Contingency Table**

| Variable 2 | Category 1 | Variable 1 | | Total |
| | | Category 1 | Category 2 | |
| | Category 2 | a | b | a + b |
| | | c | d | c + d |
| | | a + c | b + d | a + b + c + d |

*Source:* Adapted from *Principles of Epidemiology: An Introduction to Applied Epidemiology and Biostatistics*, p. 210, 1992, U.S. Department of Health and Human Services, Public Health Service.

fied into two categories, urban/suburban and rural. The question of interest was whether there is a relationship between professional credential and geographic practice location (urban/suburban or rural). The results of the classification appear in Table 8.4. When we read a 2 × 2 contingency table or R × C table, the percentages that appear in the cells represent the percentages of the column totals, e.g., in the "RHIT" column 30/85 = 35.3%.

We will now conduct the $\chi^2$ test of independence on these data.

## THE $\chi^2$ TEST OF INDEPENDENCE

In the $\chi^2$ test of independence, we can determine whether a relationship exists between two variables in a 2 × 2 contingency table or an R × C table. It is one of the most widely used statistics in health care. The question that we are trying to answer is whether the categories of the row variable are distributed differentially across the column variables—that is, how one variable relates to another. If the variables are independent, a change in one variable does not have any effect on the other. We will use the data in Table 8.4 to calculate $\chi^2$.

Table 8.4    **Contingency Table of Professional Credential and Geographic Location**

| Location | Credential | | Total |
| | RHIT | RHIA | |
| Urban/Suburban | 30 | 76 | 106 |
| | (35.3%) | (67.3%) | (53.5%) |
| Rural | 55 | 37 | 92 |
| | (64.7%) | (32.7%) | (46.5%) |
| Total | 85 | 113 | 198 |

The null hypothesis is that the two variables, credential and geographic location, are independent of each other—in other words, that there is no relationship between the two variables. If the null hypothesis is true, we would expect that geographic location would appear in the same proportions in both the RHIT population and the RHIA population. The alternative hypothesis is non-directional and states that there is an association between the two variables of interest.

$H_0$ : *There is no association between credential and geographic location.*

$H_A$ : *There is an association between credential and geographic location.*

$$\alpha = 0.05$$

Exhibit 8.8 summarizes the important aspects of the $\chi^2$ test of independence.

The $\chi^2$ test involves comparing observed frequencies with expected frequencies. In a contingency table, the expected frequencies are the proportion of each category that we would expect to find in each cell by chance over the long run. In our example, there are 198 total observations. Of these 198, 106 (53.5%) practice in urban/suburban areas and 92 (46.5%) practice in rural areas. Therefore, in the long run we would expect these frequencies to occur in each group. In our contingency table, there are 85 RHITs and 113 RHIAs. Therefore, we would expect that 53.5% in each group would be practicing in urban/suburban locations—45.5 RHITs and 60.5 RHIAs. The expected frequencies are generated on this assumption. An easy way to generate the expected frequencies is given by the following formula:

$$\text{Expected frequency} = \frac{\text{row marginal} \times \text{column marginal}}{\text{grand total } (N)}$$

## Exhibit 8.8    $\chi^2$ Test of Independence—Points to Remember

1. The $\chi^2$ statistic is used when both the independent variable and the dependent variable are at the nominal level of measurement and the categories of each variable are mutually exclusive.

2. Data contained in the contingency table or R × C table are frequencies, not scores.

3. Observations must be independent of each other.

4. The total number of observations ($N$) should be greater than 20, and the expected frequency per cell should be equal to or greater than 5. For large tables, 20% of the expected frequencies may be less than 5, but should not be less than 2.

The next step is to subtract the expected cell frequency ($E$) from the observed cell frequency ($O$); this gives the amount of deviation in each cell. The sum of the deviates for both rows and columns is equal to zero. The deviates in each cell are then squared, $(O - E)^2$, and divided by the expected value for each cell, $(O - E)^2/E$. This is similar to the numerator of the variance, $(X - \bar{X})^2$, where $\bar{X}$ is the expected value. But where the denominator for the variance is divided by the degrees of freedom, $n - 1$, the denominator for $\chi^2$ is the expected ($E$) frequency. Therefore, the basic statistical method for measuring variation in a data set is rewritten for $\chi^2$ as the sum of $(O - E)^2$.

The formula for calculating the $\chi^2$ statistic is

$$\chi^2_{calc} = \frac{\sum (O - E)^2}{E}$$

which is defined as the sum of the squared deviations divided by the expected frequency for each cell. To calculate the expected frequency for the first cell ($RHIT \times$ *urban/suburban*), we multiply the column marginal by the row marginal (Table 8.4) and divide by the grand total: $(85 \times 106)/198 = 45.5$. We proceed in the same manner for each cell. The expected frequency for each cell is subtracted from the observed frequency, squared, and divided by the expected frequency. The results for each cell are then summed. For the data in Table 8.4, $\chi^2$ is calculated as:

$$\chi^2_{calc} = \frac{\sum (O - E)^2}{E} = 5.28 + 6.08 + 3.97 + 4.58 = 19.91$$

In our example, the calculated $\chi^2$ is fairly large, indicating that the observed frequencies do differ markedly from the theoretical or expected frequencies. This is verified by comparing the calculated $\chi^2$ with the critical value of $\chi^2$ in Appendix B, Table B.4. In a $2 \times 2$ contingency table, the number of degrees of freedom is equal to 1 (df = 1). In larger tables, the number of degrees of freedom is determined by

$$df = (R - 1) \times (C - 1)$$

Conceptual models for the degrees of freedom in contingency tables and $R \times C$ tables are displayed in Exhibit 8.9.

From Table B.4 in Appendix B, the $\chi^2$ critical for $\alpha = 0.05$ and for one degree of freedom is 3.841. Because the calculated $\chi^2$ is greater than the critical $\chi^2$, we reject the null hypothesis and conclude that the variables—credentials and geographic location—are related or that they vary together in some systematic way.

Exhibit 8.9    **Degrees of Freedom**

In a 2 × 2 contingency table, the best estimate of the expected counts in a distribution is given in the row and column totals. Therefore, the row and column totals are fixed. Once an observed count is entered into a cell in a 2 × 2 table, no other cells are free to vary.

|  | Column 1 | Column 2 | Total |
|---|---|---|---|
| Row 1 | Degree of freedom<br>a | Fixed<br>b | Fixed<br>a + b |
| Row 2 | Fixed<br>c | Fixed<br>d | Fixed<br>c + d |
| Total | Fixed<br>a + c | Fixed<br>b + d | Fixed<br>a + b + c + d<br>(N) |

We can extend this idea to R × C tables. As above, the row and column totals are fixed. Now assume that the last column and the bottom row are never free to vary because they must consist of numbers to make the totals come out right. This is illustrated in the 4 × 3 table below (4 rows, 3 columns):

|  | Column 1 | Column 2 | Column 3 | Total |
|---|---|---|---|---|
| Row 1 | Degree of freedom | Degree of freedom | Fixed | Fixed row total |
| Row 2 | Degree of freedom | Degree of freedom | Fixed | Fixed row total |
| Row 3 | Degree of freedom | Degree of freedom | Fixed | Fixed row total |
| Row 4 | Fixed | Fixed | Fixed | Fixed row total |
| Total | Fixed column total | Fixed column total | Fixed column total | Fixed grand total |

There are several points to remember when calculating $\chi^2$ from a contingency table or the larger R × C table. First, the expected counts for each cell should be 5 or more. For larger tables, 20% of the expected counts could be less than 5 but should not be less than 2. When expected cell counts are less than 5, consider collapsing the number of categories.

The $\chi^2$ test of independence is an example of statistical modeling. **Statistical modeling** is a process by which a model is developed to predict the relationship of one or more dependent variables with an independent variable. On the basis of our results in the previous example, we would expect that for any sample drawn from a population of RHITs and RHIAs, RHIAs would be more likely to practice in urban areas than RHITs.

## EXAMINATION OF RESIDUALS

A large $\chi^2$ often results in statistical significance, indicating an association between the two variables under study. However, this does not always tell us which levels of the variable are contributing the most to the $\chi^2$ statistic. By examining the $\chi^2$ residuals, we can determine which cells are contributing the most to the calculated $\chi^2$.

A **residual** is defined as the difference between the actual frequencies and the expected frequencies in each cell $(O - E)$. SPSS provides unstandardized, standardized, and adjusted residuals for each cell. We most often use the **standardized residuals**, which are obtained by

$$\text{Standardized residual} = \frac{O - E}{\sqrt{E}}$$

If the value of the obtained standardized residual is greater than +2 or less than −2 in any cell, we can conclude that the cell in question is an important contributor to the significance of $\chi^2$. In the SPSS output in Exhibit 8.10, the RHIT cells for geographic location are contributing the most to the calculated $\chi^2$, indicating that the observed frequencies deviate most from the expected frequencies.

## YATES CORRECTION FOR CONTINUITY

Because the $\chi^2$ test is based on comparing the calculated values of $\chi^2$ that form a discontinuous distribution with the theoretical values of $\chi^2$ that form a continuous distribution, many recommend that the **Yates continuity correction** be used when the table numbers are small and df = 1. The only difference in the $\chi^2$ formula is that the 0.5 is subtracted from the absolute value of $(O - E)$ in each cell.

$$\text{Yates } \chi^2 = \frac{\sum \left( |O - E| - 0.5 \right)^2}{E}$$

Obviously, this will reduce the size of the calculated $\chi^2$, thus reducing the chance of finding statistical significance and increasing the probability of making a Type II error—failing to reject the null hypothesis when it is false. Recalculating our credentials and geographic location data using the Yates correction for continuity reduces the value of chi square slightly, $\chi^2 = 18.66$, but it still remains statistically significant.

**Exhibit 8.10   SPSS Output for Chi-Square Procedure, Credential and Geographic Location**

**CREDENTIAL \* GEOGRAPHIC LOCATION Cross-tabulation**

| | | | GEOGRAPHIC LOCATION | | |
|---|---|---|---|---|---|
| | | | URBAN/ SUBURBAN | RURAL | Total |
| CREDENTIAL | RHIT | Count | 30 | 55 | 85 |
| | | Expected Count | 45.5 | 39.5 | 85.0 |
| | | Std. Residual | −2.3 | 2.5 | |
| | RHIA | Count | 76 | 37 | 113 |
| | | Expected Count | 60.5 | 52.5 | 113.0 |
| | | Std. Residual | 2.0 | −2.1 | |
| Total | | Count | 106 | 92 | 198 |
| | | Expected Count | 106.0 | 920. | 198.0 |

## Phi Coefficient

Chi square tells us if there is an association between two variables but it does not tell us the degree of association, as does the Pearson's *r* correlation coefficient. Also, we cannot compare values of $\chi^2$ across samples because the calculated $\chi^2$ is a function of sample size. The **phi** ($\varphi$) coefficient corrects for sample size and measures the degree of association between the two variables under study. The formula for phi is

$$\varphi = \sqrt{\frac{\chi^2}{n}}$$

The phi coefficient is interpreted in the same way as the Pearson's *r*, but the range of phi is 0 to 1. As a general rule, a value less than 0.30 may be interpreted as a trivial association. The phi coefficient for the data in Table 8.4 is calculated as

$$\varphi = \sqrt{\frac{\chi^2}{n}} = \sqrt{\frac{19.91}{198}} = 0.317$$

Therefore, the relationship between credentials and geographic location is not very strong. We can see that phi provides us with more knowledge about our sample profile than $\chi^2$ alone.

## $\chi^2$ Goodness of Fit

In the $\chi^2$ goodness-of-fit test, we are also comparing actual frequencies with expected or theoretical frequencies in a distribution. However, instead of being based on the collected data, as in Table 8.4, the expected counts are based on our knowledge of the population under study. For example, if 75% of the physicians practicing in our hospital are men and 25% are women, we will expect to draw a sample composed of 75% men and 25% women. We know that the drawn sample will not precisely match the proportions in the population, but we want to be assured that the sample proportions are not significantly different from the underlying population proportions. In this procedure, the goal is to determine how well the observed counts in our sample fit the expected counts based on the model—that is, how well the observed count matches a theoretical frequency distribution.

As an example, a researcher received 355 responses to a survey that was mailed to directors of health information management (HIM) centers in acute care facilities across the United States. A $\chi^2$ goodness-of-fit test was conducted to ensure that the respondent profile matched that of the distribution of practitioners in the general HIM population. A variable used to compare the respondent profile to the general population was the hospital bed size (defined by the number of inpatient beds within the facility) with which professionals practiced. The obtained frequency distribution of HIM respondents is compared to the respondent profile in Table 8.5.

Table 8.5 **Hypothetical HIM Population Distribution and Respondent Profile by Hospital Size**

| Hospital Size | HIM Population % 1990 | Respondent % |
|---|---|---|
| < 100 beds | 20.1 | 21.7 |
| 101–300 beds | 38.9 | 41.4 |
| 301–500 beds | 21.9 | 22.3 |
| 501+ beds | 19.0 | 14.6 |

Table 8.6  **Observed (*O*) and Expected (*E*) Frequencies of Respondents by Hospital Bed Size (Hypothetical Data)**

| Hospital Bed Size | *O* | *E* | (*O–E*) | (*O–E*)$^2$ | (*O–E*)$^2$/*E* |
|---|---|---|---|---|---|
| <100 beds | 77 | 71.4 | 5.6 | 31.36 | .44 |
| 101–300 beds | 147 | 138.2 | 8.8 | 77.4 | .56 |
| 301–500 beds | 79 | 77.8 | 1.2 | 1.44 | .02 |
| 501+ beds | 52 | 67.5 | –15.5 | 240.25 | 3.56 |
| Total | 355 | | | | 4.58 |

The null and alternative hypotheses based on the actual HIM frequency distribution are

$$H_0 : p_1 = 0.201, p_2 = 0.389, p_3 = 0.219, p_4 = 0.190$$

$H_A$ : *At least one of the hypothesized proportions is different from the expected value.*

The expected frequencies are generated on the basis of the actual frequency distribution of the characteristic of interest in the general population. In the previous example, 20.1% of the HIM professionals practice in hospitals with fewer than 100 beds; therefore, the expected frequency count for the actual respondents for this category is $355 \times 0.201 = 71.4$. Table 8.6 displays the observed and expected frequencies. If the calculated $\chi^2$ is small, there is close agreement between the observed and expected frequencies. As the discrepancy between the observed and expected frequencies increases, the calculated $\chi^2$ increases, and the more likely we are to reject the null hypothesis and conclude that the population proportions are significantly different from the expected population proportions.

In this example, we are comparing observed frequencies with the expected frequencies across four categories (rows) on the variable hospital bed size. In the one-variable case, the degree of freedom is based on the number of categories ($k$) and is equal to one less than the number of categories ($k - 1$). In this example, $k - 1 = 3$, and for 3 degrees of freedom, the critical value of $\chi^2$ with $\alpha = 0.05$ is 7.82. Because the calculated $\chi^2$ does not equal or exceed the critical value of $\chi^2$, we fail to reject the null hypothesis and conclude that the respondent profile "fits" the population profile. Even though we can generalize our results to our population of interest, it is important to note that the category "501+ beds" contributes the most to the $\chi^2$ statistic. It is this category that deviates the most from the expected frequencies.

The SPSS calculations for the data in Table 8.5 appear in Exhibit 8.11. SPSS reports the values $\chi^2 = 4.575$ and $p = 0.206$. SPSS requires that the expected frequencies for each category be entered into the dialog box. The expected frequen-

Exhibit 8.11 **SPSS Output for Chi-Square Goodness of Fit**

| Hospital Size | | | |
|---|---|---|---|
| | Observed N | Expected N | Residual |
| 6–100 Beds | 77 | 71.4 | 5.6 |
| 101–300 Beds | 147 | 138.2 | 8.8 |
| 301–500 Beds | 79 | 77.8 | 1.2 |
| 501+ Beds | 52 | 67.5 | −15.5 |
| Total | 355 | | |

| Test Statistics | |
|---|---|
| | Hospital Size |
| Chi Square[a] | 4.576 |
| df | 3 |
| Asymp. Sig. | .206 |

[a]0 cells (.0%) have expected frequencies less than 5. The minimum expected cell frequency is 67.5.

cies may be specified as proportions, percentages, or actual values. The assumptions for the $\chi^2$ goodness-of-fit test are summarized in Exhibit 8.12.

## CONCLUSION

In this chapter, we explored various measures of association. We first discussed the Pearson's $r$ correlation coefficient to determine whether there is a relationship between two variables, $x$ and $y$. For the Pearson's $r$, the variables must be at least at the interval scale of measurement; furthermore, it is assumed that the relationship between the two variables is linear. The Pearson's $r$ correlation coefficient ranges from −1.0, indicating a perfect negative correlation, to +1.0, indicating a perfect positive correlation. A correlation coefficient of 0.0 indicates no linear relationship. Prior to calculating the Pearson's $r$, a scatter diagram should be constructed to determine if the relationship between the two variables is linear. The Pearson's $r$ is a parametric statistical procedure.

This chapter also explored two nonparametric procedures that explore relationships between variables: the Spearman's rho correlation coefficient, which is analogous to the Pearson's $r$ product moment correlation coefficient, and the various forms of the $\chi^2$ test.

Exhibit 8.12    **Assumptions for $\chi^2$ Goodness of Fit**

1. Select a criterion upon which to compare the selected sample with the underlying population, such as sex, level of education, or certification.
2. Select the null and alternative hypotheses and the significance level for rejection of the null.
3. The criterion variable must have two or more categories, and the categories must be mutually exclusive and exhaustive.
4. The data contained within the cells are frequencies, not scores.
5. Determine the expected or theoretical frequencies under the assumption that the null hypothesis is true. The expected frequencies are obtained by the researcher's knowledge of the target population. Frequencies must be specified in advance.
6. If categories are dichotomous, the expected frequencies for each cell should be at least 5. If there are more than two categories, no more than 20% of the cells should have frequencies less than 5. If this requirement cannot be met, consider collapsing the categories.
7. Compare the observed frequencies to the expected frequencies for each cell.
8. If the aggregate discrepancy ($\chi^2$ calc) between the observed and expected frequencies is too great to attribute to chance at the selected significance level, reject the null.

Nonparametric procedures are less restrictive than their parametric counterparts. Nonparametric procedures do not make assumptions regarding the underlying population distribution nor do they require large sample sizes. They may be used to analyze data about populations that consist of nominal, ordinal, interval, or ratio data. Many nonparametric tests analyze the ranks or orders of the data set rather than the numerical values of the observations. Nonparametric procedures also are used when sample sizes are small ($\leq 30$) or when there are extreme values in the data set so that the median rather than the mean is more representative of the distribution. Also, when the shape of the distributions is unknown or nonnormal, nonparametric procedures may be more powerful, reducing the chance of committing a Type II error.

## References

Conner-Linton (2003) *Chi Square Tutorial.* Georgetown University, Department of Linguistics. (http://www.georgetown.edu/faculty/ballc/webtools/web_chi_tut.html)

Osborn, Carol E. (2006) *Statistical Applications for Health Information Management,* 2nd edition. Boston: Jones and Bartlett Publishers.

# APPENDIX 8-A

## EXERCISES FOR SOLVING PROBLEMS

### Knowledge Questions

1. Define the key terms listed at the beginning of this chapter.
2. What is the Pearson's $r$? At what levels of measurement must the variables be to use the Pearson's $r$?
3. What is the range for the Pearson's $r$? How is the Pearson's $r$ statistic interpreted? Explain the concepts of positive linear relationship and negative linear relationship.
4. Describe the relationship between the Pearson's $r$ and the coefficient of determination, $r^2$.
5. Describe the circumstances under which it would be appropriate to use the $\chi^2$ test.
6. What questions is a researcher attempting to answer when using the $\chi^2$ goodness-of-fit test?

### Multiple Choice

1. To calculate the Pearson's $r$, the two variables should be:
   a. Normally distributed
   b. Linearly related
   c. Random
   d. All of the above
2. In the scatter diagram below, the Pearson's $r$ can be described as:
   a. Equal to 0.0
   b. Equal to 1.0
   c. Negative
   d. Positive

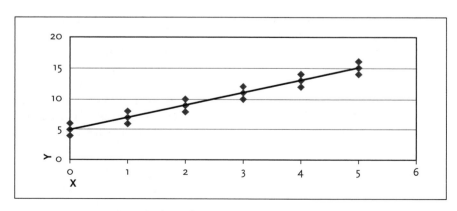

Figure 8-A.1    **Scatter Diagram for Multiple Choice #2**

3. If the Pearson's *r* is equal to 1.0, we can say that:
   a. *x* causes *y*
   b. *y* causes *x*
   c. There is a perfect positive relationship between *x* and *y*
   d. *x* and *y* are negatively correlated

4. Which of the following values for the Pearson's *r* indicates the strongest relationship?
   a. 0.85
   b. 0.76
   c. 0.00
   d. −0.89

5. Which of the following values for the Pearson's *r* indicates the weakest relationship?
   a. 0.85
   b. 0.76
   c. 0.00
   d. −0.89

6. If we cannot predict *y* from *x*, we would conclude that the Pearson's *r* is:
   a. 0.0
   b. Negative
   c. Positive
   d. Not enough information is provided

7. We have calculated a Pearson's *r* for length of stay (*y*) and age (*x*). Our result is *r* = −1.16. We therefore conclude that:
   a. As age increases, the length of stay decreases
   b. As age increases, the length of stay increases
   c. We cannot predict length of stay from age
   d. We have made an error in our calculations

8. We have calculated the Pearson's *r* for length of stay (*x*) and total charges (*y*). Our result is *r* = 0.64. We therefore conclude that:
   a. As length of stay increases, total charges decrease
   b. As length of stay increases, total charges increase
   c. We cannot predict total charges from length of stay
   d. We have made an error in our calculations

9. We use the $\chi^2$ test to determine differences between:
   a. Means
   b. Frequencies
   c. Proportions
   d. Both (b) and (c)

10. You want to compare the number of male and female patients discharged by service at Critical Care Hospital. There are 10 services. For the $\chi^2$ test, the number of degrees of freedom is:
    a. 1
    b. 2
    c. 9
    d. 10

11. In the $\chi^2$ test, if the result is not significant, the:
    a. Observed frequencies are similar to the expected frequencies
    b. Observed frequencies do not match the expected frequencies
    c. Observed and expected frequencies match exactly
    d. All of the above

For Questions 12 through 17, refer to the following R × C table:

Table 8-A.1

|        | Phys A | Phys B | Phys C | Total |
|--------|--------|--------|--------|-------|
| Male   |        |        |        | 60    |
| Female | 10     | 48     |        | 140   |
| Total  | 40     | 60     | 100    | 200   |

12. The observed number of male patients discharged by Physician C is:
    a. 12
    b. 18
    c. 30
    d. Not enough information is provided
13. The expected number of male patients discharged by Physician B is:
    a. 10
    b. 18
    c. 20
    d. Not enough information is provided
14. The observed number of males discharged by Physician A is:
    a. 12
    b. 18
    c. 30
    d. Not enough information is provided
15. The expected number of female patients discharged by Physician A is:
    a. 20
    b. 28
    c. 30
    d. Not enough information is provided
16. The number of degrees of freedom for this problem is equal to:
    a. 2
    b. 4

c. 6
d. 199

17. For the above problem, $\chi^2_{calc}$ is equal to 48.5 and $\chi^2_{crit}$ is equal to 5.99. We therefore:
    a. Reject the null hypothesis
    b. Fail to reject the null hypothesis
    c. Conclude that these physicians have the same number of discharges
    d. Conclude that these physicians prefer to treat men over women
18. The phi coefficient is used to measure the:
    a. Correlation of two ordered variables
    b. Correlation of interval-level variables
    c. Strength of the association between variables in a $2 \times 2$ table
    d. All of the above

## Problems

1. You are assisting Dr. Hartman in studying the number of deaths due to acute myocardial infarctions (AMIs). Dr. Hartman is particularly interested in knowing if more men died from AMIs than women. To answer this question, you review discharges by gender

for DRG 123, "Circulatory Disorders with AMI, Expired." Use the $\chi^2$ test to determine if there is an association between gender and deaths due to AMI at Critical Care Hospital. A frequency distribution of discharges by gender and age from DRG 123 appears in Table 8-A.2.

a. State the null and alternative hypotheses.
b. State the alpha level.
c. What is the result of the $\chi^2$ test?
d. State your conclusions.

2. Using the same information in Table 8-A.1 use the $\chi^2$ test to determine if there is an association between age and gender for discharges from DRG 123. Calculate the phi coefficient.
a. State the null and alternative hypotheses.
b. State the alpha level.

c. What is the result of the $\chi^2$ test?
d. What does the phi coefficient indicate?
e. State your conclusions.

3. You are studying DRG 105, "Cardiac Valve Procedures and other Major Cardiothoracic Procedures without Cardiac Catheterization," for Critical Care Hospital. Using the data provided in Table 8-A.3 calculate the Pearson's $r$ for each of the following pairs:
   • Age and length of stay
   • Total charges and length of stay
   • Age and total charges
a. State the null and alternative hypotheses and alpha level for each.
b. Construct a scatter diagram for each.
c. State your conclusions for each.

Table 8-A.2  **Frequency Distribution of Discharges by Age and Gender, DRG 123 (SPSS Output)**

**Age * Gender Cross-tabulation**

|  |  | Gender | | Total |
|---|---|---|---|---|
|  |  | FEMALE | MALE |  |
| Age | 49 | 0 | 1 | 1 |
|  | 50 | 0 | 1 | 1 |
|  | 61 | 0 | 1 | 1 |
|  | 66 | 0 | 1 | 1 |
|  | 75 | 1 | 0 | 1 |
|  | 76 | 0 | 1 | 1 |
|  | 77 | 0 | 1 | 1 |
|  | 88 | 1 | 0 | 1 |
|  | 88 | 0 | 1 | 1 |
| Total |  | 2 | 7 | 9 |

Table 8-A.3    **Case Summaries for DRG 105, Cardiac Valve Procedures and Other Major Cardiothoracic Procedures without Cardiac Catheterization**

|     | Gender  | Age | LOS | Charges   | Payor          |
| --- | ------- | --- | --- | --------- | -------------- |
| 1   | FEMALE  | 47  | 20  | $91,683   | MEDICAID       |
| 2   | FEMALE  | 75  | 43  | $93,708   | MEDICARE       |
| 3   | FEMALE  | 84  | 7   | $21,446   | MEDICARE       |
| 4   | FEMALE  | 50  | 13  | $37,797   | MEDICARE       |
| 5   | MALE    | 77  | 14  | $54,364   | MEDICARE       |
| 6   | MALE    | 57  | 4   | $17,626   | MEDICARE       |
| 7   | MALE    | 73  | 4   | $12,832   | MEDICARE       |
| 8   | FEMALE  | 56  | 1   | $36,153   | MEDICAID       |
| 9   | MALE    | 69  | 1   | $14,907   | MEDICAID       |
| 10  | FEMALE  | 81  | 23  | $104,148  | MEDICARE       |
| 11  | MALE    | 21  | 5   | $21,423   | MEDICAID       |
| 12  | FEMALE  | 37  | 5   | $24,971   | MEDICAID       |
| 13  | FEMALE  | 69  | 4   | $17,022   | MEDICARE       |
| 14  | FEMALE  | 89  | 17  | $50,652   | MEDICARE       |
| 15  | MALE    | 28  | 35  | $186,496  | MEDICAID       |
| 16  | MALE    | 47  | 6   | $24,441   | MEDICAID       |
| 17  | MALE    | 87  | 11  | $35,349   | MEDICARE       |
| 18  | FEMALE  | 85  | 5   | $22,155   | MEDICARE       |
| 19  | MALE    | 56  | 5   | $24,455   | MANAGED CARE   |
| 20  | MALE    | 45  | 11  | $36,401   | MEDICAID       |
| 21  | MALE    | 82  | 6   | $25,783   | MEDICARE       |
| 22  | FEMALE  | 65  | 10  | $37,055   | MANAGED CARE   |
| 23  | MALE    | 67  | 4   | $19,236   | MEDICARE       |
| 24  | MALE    | 59  | 23  | $60,132   | OTHER          |
| 25  | FEMALE  | 67  | 7   | $35,777   | MEDICARE       |
| 26  | MALE    | 53  | 4   | $19,972   | MANAGED CARE   |
| 27  | MALE    | 71  | 7   | $25,409   | MEDICARE       |
| 28  | FEMALE  | 79  | 6   | $281,140  | MEDICARE       |
| 29  | MALE    | 63  | 1   | $41,283   | MEDICAID       |
| 30  | MALE    | 53  | 19  | $71,439   | MEDICAID       |
| 31  | FEMALE  | 75  | 9   | $33,735   | MEDICARE       |
| 32  | FEMALE  | 68  | 9   | $37,830   | GOV MNGD CARE  |
| 33  | MALE    | 37  | 4   | $22,311   | MEDICAID       |

**Age-adjusted death rate**—The crude death rate is adjusted when the death rates of two populations are to be compared. The death rate is adjusted when population proportions by age are different; this adjustment eliminates the effects of different age distributions in different populations.

**Age-specific death rate (ASDR)**—The total number of deaths for a given age group for a certain time frame divided by the estimated population for the same age group and for the same time frame. The ASDR is usually expressed as the number of deaths per $10^n$, depending on the size of the population.

**Alpha error**—See *Type I error*.

**Alpha level**—The point at which the null hypothesis will be rejected. Set prior (*a priori*) to conducting the research, the alpha level is usually set at 0.05 for small sample sizes and at 0.01 for larger sample sizes.

**Alternative hypothesis**—See *Hypothesis testing*.

**Apparent limits**—See *Class interval*.

**Asymptotic curve**—A property of the normal distribution in which the tails of the curve approach the *x*-axis but never touch it.

**Average daily census**—The mean number of hospital inpatients present in the hospital each day for a given period of time.

**Bar chart**—A graphic technique for displaying discrete or nominal-level data. One or more variables can be displayed on a bar chart; a bar chart that displays two or more variables is called a *grouped bar chart*.

**Bed count day**—A unit of measure that denotes the presence of one inpatient bed (either occupied or vacant) set up and staffed for use in one 24-hour period.

**Bed turnover rate**—A measure of hospital utilization that includes the number of times each inpatient bed changes occupants.

**Beta error**—See *Type II error*.

**Box head**—In a table, the box head contains the column headings.

**Bubble chart**—A type of scatter plot with circular symbols used to compare three variables. The area of the circle indicates the value of a third variable.

**Case fatality rate**—The total number of deaths due to a specific illness during a given time period divided by the total number of cases during the same time period.

**Cause-specific death rate**—The total number of deaths due to a specific cause during a given time interval divided by the estimated mid-interval population.

**Cell**—In a table, a cell is where the row and column variables intersect.

**Census**—The number of inpatients present in a health care facility at any given time.

**Central Limit Theorem**—In a repeated number of random samples of size $N$ drawn from a population, the distribution of the sample means approaches the normal distribution as $N$ becomes large. This occurs even when the population distribution is not normal.

**Chi-square ($\chi^2$) goodness-of-fit test**—A nonparametric test used to determine whether the observed frequencies in a distribution are significantly different from the expected or theoretical frequencies in a distribution based on the researcher's knowledge of a population understudy. The null hypothesis states that there is no difference between the observed and expected frequencies; the alternative hypothesis states that there is a difference between the observed and expected frequencies. The $\chi^2$ goodness-of-fit test is often used to determine whether proportions in a randomly drawn sample are significantly different from the underlying or theoretical population proportions.

**Chi-square ($\chi^2$) test of independence**—A nonparametric test used to determine whether a relationship exists between two variables in a $2 \times 2$ contingency table or an R $\times$ C table. Measures for the variables are nominal or dichotomous. The test uses frequencies of the variables, not the actual observations. The null hypothesis states that there is no relationship between the two variables; thus, they are independent of each other. The alternative hypothesis states that there is a relationship between the two variables.

**Class interval**—A method used to classify interval or ratio level data into categories for analysis. The limits of the class intervals are referred to as either "apparent" or "real." The *apparent limits* are the upper and lower boundaries of the class interval. For example, the upper and lower limits of two successive intervals may be (18, 22) and (23, 27). The *real limits* depict the continuous nature of the frequency distribution, indicating that there are no gaps between successive intervals. For example, the real limits for the previously stated intervals are (17.5, 22.5) and (22.5, 27.5). The upper limit of one class interval is the lower limit for the next class interval.

**Cluster sampling**—A sampling technique in which the sampling units are groups rather than individuals.

**Coefficient of determination**—The square of the Pearson's $r$. The coefficient of determination states how much of the variation in the dependent variable $y$ is explained by the independent variable $x$.

**Confidence interval**—Calculated from the standard error of the mean, this is an estimate of the limits within which the true population mean lies; in other words, the range of values that may reasonably contain the true population mean.

**Confounding**—The relationship between two variables is so close that the effects of either variable cannot be separated from the other.

**Confounding factor**—See *Confounding variable*.

**Confounding variable**—A factor or variable that contributes differentially across the categories or levels of another variable. It is the confusion of two independent variables so that the effect of one variable cannot be differentiated from the effect of the other.

**Contingency coefficient**—A measure of association between two nominal level variables. It is an alternative to the phi coefficient when one variable has more than two categories. The range of the contingency coefficient is 0 to 1.

**Contingency table**—A table that displays the relationship between two variables, whether the distribution of one variable is dependent upon or related to the distribution of a second variable.

**Continuous variable**—A measure taken on the interval or ratio level of measurement.

**Critical region**—In hypothesis testing, the portion of the test statistic distribution that is equal to or beyond the critical value of the test statistic. It is the region of the $z$, $t$, or $\chi^2$ distributions that results in the rejection of the null hypothesis.

**Crude death rate**—The total number of deaths in a given population for a given time period divided by the mid-interval population for the same time period. The crude death rate is usually expressed as the number of deaths per 1000 population.

**Daily inpatient census**—The number of inpatients present at the census-taking time each day, plus any inpatients who were both admitted and discharged after the census-taking time the previous day.

**Degrees of freedom**—The number of observations in a data set that are free to vary after the mean of the distribution has been determined.

**Dichotomous variable**—A variable that falls on the nominal scale of measurement but is limited to only two categories.

**Direct standardization**—When mortality rates of two populations are compared, each population is assigned the same standard population proportion for each age group. The standard population proportion is multiplied by the age-specific death rate for each age group in each population; the sum results in the *age-adjusted death rate*.

**Discrete variable**—A dichotomous or nominal variable whose values are placed into categories.

**Effect**—A change in one variable that can be associated with a change in a second variable.

**Fetal autopsy rate**—The number of autopsies performed on intermediate and late fetal deaths for a given period divided by the total number of intermediate and late fetal deaths for the same period.

**Fetal death (stillborn)**—The death of a product of conception before its complete expulsion or extraction from the mother regardless of the duration of the pregnancy.

**Fetal death rate**—A proportion that compares the number of intermediate and late fetal deaths to the total number of live births and intermediate and late fetal deaths during the same period of time.

**Frequency distribution**—A table or graph that displays the number of times (frequency) a particular observation occurs.

**Gender-specific death rate**—The number of male or female deaths for a given time frame compared to the estimated male or female population total for the same time frame. The gender-specific death rate is usually expressed as the number of deaths per $10^n$, depending on the size of the population.

**Gross autopsy rate**—The number of inpatient autopsies conducted during a given time period divided by the total number of inpatient deaths for the same period.

**Gross death rate**—The number of inpatient deaths that occurred during a given time period divided by the total number of inpatient discharges, including deaths, for the same time period.

**Grouped bar chart**—A *bar chart* in which the bars within a group are adjoining. It is used to illustrate data from a two- or three-variable table when an outcome variable has only two categories.

**Hospital-acquired infection**—An infection acquired by a patient while receiving care or services in a health care organization.

**Hospital autopsy rate**—The total number of autopsies performed by a hospital pathologist for a given time period divided by the number of deaths of hospital patients (inpatients and outpatients) whose bodies were available for autopsy for the same time period.

**Hypothesis testing**—A statement regarding the research question to be tested. There are two forms of the hypothesis: the null hypothesis and the alternative hypothesis. The *null hypothesis* states that there is no difference between the population means or proportions that are being compared, or that there is no association between the two variables that are being compared. The *alternative hypothesis* states that there is a significant difference in the population means or proportions that are being compared, or that there is an association between the two variables that are being compared. The alternative hypothesis usually states what the researcher believes to be true regarding the problem under study.

**Incidence rate**—The number of new cases of a particular disease in a population for a given time period divided by the average population for the same time period.

**Infant mortality rate**—The number of deaths of persons under one year of age during a given time period divided by the number of live births reported during the same time period.

**Inpatient bed occupancy rate (percentage of occupancy)**—The total number of inpatient service days for a given time period divided by the total number of inpatient bed count days for the same time period.

**Inpatient service day**—A unit of measure equivalent to the services received by one inpatient during one 24-hour period.

**Internal consistency**—The extent to which the items on a measuring instrument are consistent with one another. *Cronbach's alpha* is used to evaluate internal consistency.

**Inter-rater reliability**—The percentage of agreement between raters using the same measuring instrument. The *kappa coefficient* is used to measure inter-rater agreement.

**Interval scale**—Similar to the *ratio scale* of measurement but without a true zero. Intervals between successive intervals are equal and continuous.

**Kappa coefficient**—A measure of agreement, beyond what would occur by chance, between two raters on the same measuring instrument. The kappa coefficient ranges from 0.0 to 1.0.

**Kurtosis**—The vertical stretching of a frequency distribution.

**Length of stay (LOS)**—The total number of patient days for an inpatient episode, calculated by subtracting the date of admission from the date of discharge.

**Level of significance (or significance level)**—A cutoff value for evaluating the *p* value that results from a statistical test. This indicates the level of risk that we are willing to take for rejecting the null hypothesis when it is true.

**Line graph**—A graphic technique that consists of a line connecting a series of points on an arithmetic scale. A line graph is often used to display time trends and survival curves, and it does not represent a frequency distribution.

**Maternal mortality rate**—The number of deaths assigned to pregnancy-related causes during a given time period divided by the total number of live births during the same period.

**Mean**—The arithmetic average of the observations in a frequency distribution. A measure of central tendency, it is equal to the sum of the values of the observations in a frequency distribution divided by the total number of observations.

**Measurement**—The process of measuring an attribute or property of a person, object, or event according to a particular set of rules. The set of rules is used to assign numbers to the attribute or property being measured.

**Measures of central tendency**—A single value that summarizes a frequency distribution or illustrates the most typical value in a frequency distribution. Measures of central tendency are the *mean, median,* and the *mode*. The measure selected to represent the dataset depends on the characteristics and shape of the distribution.

**Measures of variation**—Describes how much spread there is in a frequency distribution. Measures of variation include the *range, standard deviation,* and the *variance.*

**Median**—The midpoint of a frequency distribution when the observations have been arranged in order from lowest to highest. A measure of central tendency, it is the point at which 50% of the observations fall above and 50% of the observations fall below.

**Mode**—The most frequently occurring observation in a frequency distribution; a measure of central tendency.

**Mortality rate**—See *Crude death rate.*

**Neonatal mortality rate**—The number of deaths of newborns under 28 days of age during a given time period divided by the number of live births during the same time period.

**Net autopsy rate**—The ratio of inpatient autopsies compared to the inpatient deaths calculated by dividing the total number of inpatient autopsies performed by the hospital pathologist for a given time period by the total number of inpatient discharges minus the number of deaths that occurred less than 48 hours after admission for the same time period.

**Net death rate**—The total number of inpatient deaths minus the number of deaths that occurred less than 48 hours after admission for a given time period divided by the total number of inpatient discharges minus the number of deaths that occurred less that 48 hours after admission for the same time period.

**Newborn**—An inpatient who was born in a hospital at the beginning of the current inpatient hospitalization.

**Newborn autopsy rate**—The number of autopsies performed on newborns who died during a given time period divided by the total number of newborns who died during the same time period.

**Nominal scale**—A level of measurement in which the frequencies of observations on variables are placed into categories.

**Non-critical region**—In hypothesis testing, the area of the test statistic distribution that is between the critical values of the test statistic. If the calculated value of the test statistic falls within this region, we fail to reject the null hypothesis.

**Nonparametric statistical tests**—Tests used to determine statistical significance when the underlying population distribution does not meet the assumptions of the normal distribution or when sample sizes are small.

**Normal distribution**—A continuous frequency distribution characterized by a bell-shaped curve. A normal distribution is symmetrical, with 50% of the values falling above the mean and 50% of the values falling below the mean.

**Null hypothesis**—See *Hypothesis testing*.

**One-sample *t* test**—See t *tests*.

**100% component bar chart**—A *bar chart* in which all bars in the chart are of the same height. A variant of the stacked bar chart, each bar displays the variable categories as percents of the total number. Each bar is like its own *pie chart*.

**One-tailed test (directional test)**—In hypothesis testing, a test in which the researcher is trying to determine if the sample mean is greater than or less than the population parameter.

**Ordinal scale**—A scale of measurement in which measures are placed into ordered categories or measures are ranked in some predetermined order, such as lowest score on a test to highest score on a test. The width between categories or ranks may not be equal.

***p* value**—The result of a statistical test that indicates the probability that the observed differences between the means could have been obtained by chance alone.

**Parametric statistical tests**—Statistical tests of significance used when the underlying population distributions are assumed to be normal.

**Pearson's *r* correlation coefficient**—A measure of the strength of the linear association between two variables that fall on the interval or ratio level of measurement. The Pearson's *r* correlation coefficient has a range of $-1.0$ to $+1.0$. A negative correlation indicates that the variables change in opposite directions to one another, a positive correlation indicates that the variables change in the same direction, and a correlation of zero indicates that there is no relationship between the two variables.

**Percentile rank**—The proportion of scores in a distribution that a specific score is greater than or equal to. For example, if a hospital ranks in the 98th percentile in terms of severity of illness, it means that the hospital has a patient population sicker than or equal to 98% of the hospitals ranked.

**Phi coefficient**—A measure that indicates the degree of association between two nominal level variables. The range of the phi coefficient is 0 to 1, and it has the same interpretation as the *Pearson's* r *correlation coefficient.*

**Pie chart**—A graphic technique in which the proportions of a nominal variable are displayed as "pieces" of the pie.

**Point estimate**—The numerical value calculated from a sample that is assumed to best represent the population parameter.

**Point prevalence rate**—The number of current cases, both new and old, of a specified disease at a given point in time compared to the estimated population at the same point in time. The point prevalence rate is usually expressed as the number of cases per $10^n$, depending on the size of the population.

**Polarization**—The maximum spread or variability in a frequency distribution.

**Population**—All members of a group that are under study; the group to which the sample results are able to be generalized. Members of the group share some measurable characteristic.

**Population parameter**—A measure that results from the compilation of data from a population.

**Postneonatal mortality rate**—The number of deaths of persons aged 28 days up to and not including one year during a given time period divided by the number of live births for the same time period.

**Postoperative infection rate**—The number of infections that occur in clean surgical cases for a given time period divided by the total number of operations for the same time period.

**Prevalence rate**—The number of cases of a particular disease in a population for a given time period divided by the population for the same time period.

**Proportion**—A particular type of ratio. In a proportion, the numerator is always included in the denominator.

**Proportionate mortality ratio (PMR)**—The total number of deaths due to a specific cause during a given time period divided by the number of deaths due to all causes. Proportionate mortality is not a rate because the denominator is the number of deaths during the time period, not the population size during the time period.

**Quartiles**—The four equal parts into which a frequency distribution is divided: 25%, 50%, 75%, and 100%.

**Race-specific death rate**—The number of deaths in a specific ethnic group for a given time frame compared to the estimated population total for the same ethnic group for the same time frame. The race-specific death rate is usually expressed as the number of deaths per $10^n$, depending on the size of the population.

**Range**—The difference between the smallest and largest values in a frequency distribution; a measure of variability.

**Rate**—A measure used to compare an event over time. It is a comparison of the number of times an event did happen (numerator) to the number of times an event could have happened (denominator). Rates are expressed as the event of interest per 100, 1000, 10,000, or 100,000 cases.

**Ratio**—A comparison of categories of dichotomous variables either to each other (e.g., male discharges to female discharges), or of one category to the whole (e.g., male discharges to total discharges).

**Ratio scale**—The highest level of measurement; intervals between successive intervals are equal and continuous. This is a measurement scale with a true zero.

**Real limits**—See *Class interval*.

**Reliability**—A characteristic of a measuring instrument that results in consistent measures over repeated trials. Measurement results are approximately the same on repeated trials.

**Sample**—Items drawn from a population for a study; a subset of the population under study. Ideally, members of the sample are drawn randomly and independently from the population of interest.

**Sampling method**—The process of selecting individuals from a larger group or population in such a way that the resultant sample is representative of the underlying population.

**Scales of measurement**—*Nominal, ordinal, interval,* and *ratio scales* of measurement. The level at which data are collected determines the types of statistics that can be used to describe the population under study.

**Sample statistic**—The measures that result from the analysis of data compiled from samples.

**Scatter diagram**—A graphic representation of the *x* and *y* variables. The *x* variable is plotted on the horizontal axis and the *y* variable is plotted on the vertical axis. It is used to assess the linearity of the relationship between variables *x* and *y* when conducting either the Pearson's *r* or simple linear regression. If the two variables appear to approximate a straight line, the variables are linearly related.

**Simple random sampling**—A sampling technique in which each member of a population has an equal chance of being included in the sample.

**Skewness**—The horizontal stretching of a frequency distribution.

**Spearman's rho**—The nonparametric counterpart of the Pearson's *r* used when one of the variables is ordered. The interpretation of the Spearman's rho is the same as that for the Pearson's *r*.

**Stability**—A type of reliability in which the same or similar results are obtained on repeated measures by administering the same instrument to the same group on two different occasions to obtain a reliability coefficient that ranges from 0.0 (no reliability) to 1.0 (perfect reliability).

**Stacked bar chart**—A type of *bar chart* in which the categories of a nominal level variable are stacked like building blocks on top of one another to form a single bar. The bar represents the total number of cases that occurred in the category and the segments represent the frequencies within the category.

**Standard deviation**—The square root of the variance. A measure of variability, it describes the deviation from the mean in terms of the original unit of measurement (e.g., height, age, blood pressure).

**Standard error of the mean**—A measure of how close the sample mean is to the population mean. It is influenced by the sample size and standard deviation.

**Standard mortality ratio (SMR)**—The actual number of deaths in a group or population under study compared to the expected number of deaths based on standard population death rates applied to the study group or population. This measure is always multiplied by 100.

**Standard normal deviate**—In the standard normal distribution, the distance between the observed value and the mean. It is also referred to as the *z* score or *z* value.

**Standard normal distribution**—A normal distribution with a mean equal to 0 and a standard deviation equal to 1.

**Standardized residuals**—In the $\chi^2$ test of independence, a residual is the difference between the observed cell frequencies and the expected cell frequencies. To obtain the standardized residual, the differences between the observed and expected cell frequencies for each cell are divided by the square root of the expected cell frequencies. An obtained standardized residual of greater than +2 or less than –2 is an indication that the cell in question is an important contributor to the calculated $\chi^2$.

**Statistical significance**—In hypothesis testing, a condition in which a statistical test results in a *p* value that is less than or equal to the preset alpha level. This is usually set at 0.05 for small samples and 0.01 for large samples. The interpretation of the *p* value is that the result obtained would occur by chance no more than 5 out of 100 times when $p = 0.05$, or 1 out of 100 times when $p = 0.01$.

**Stratified random sampling**—A sampling technique in which each stratum within a population is proportionately represented in the sample.

**Stem-and-leaf plots**—A visual display that organizes data to show its shape and distribution, using two columns with the stem in the left column and all leaves associated with that stem in the right column. The "leaf" is the first digit of the number and the other digits form the "stem."

**Stub**—The row captions in a table.

**Symmetry**—A property of the normal distribution in which 50% of the observations fall above the mean and 50% of the observations fall below the mean.

**Systematic sampling**—A sampling technique in which every *k*th member of a population is selected for inclusion in the sample.

*t* **statistic**—A statistic that follows the *t* distribution; see *t* test.

*t* **test**—A parametric statistical test that compares the difference between the means of two groups. The *t* test can be used when comparing a single sample mean to a known population parameter (independent sample *t* test), when comparing the means of two independent samples (*t* test for two independent samples), or when comparing the means of matched pairs (paired *t* test).

**Table**—A set of data arranged in rows and columns.

**Table shell**—A form prepared prior to the collection of data to show how the data will be organized and displayed after data collection. Table shells are complete except for the actual data, showing titles, headings, and categories.

**Test-retest reliability**—See *Stability*.

**Timeliness**—The collection, analysis, and reporting of data or information within a time frame useful for decision making.

**Total length of stay (discharge days)**—The sum of the days of stay of any group of inpatients discharged during a given time period.

**Trimmed mean**—The calculation of the mean or a frequency distribution after the elimination (trimming) of outliers from the distribution.

**Two-tailed test (nondirectional test)**—In hypothesis testing, a test in which the researcher is interested in determining whether the sample mean and the population parameter are significantly different from each other; the direction of the inequality is not an issue.

**Type I error**—The rejection of the null hypothesis when it is true; also called *alpha error*.

**Type II error**—The failure to reject the null hypothesis when it is false; also called *beta error*.

**Uniformity**—The even distribution of observations in the categories of a nominal variable.

**Unimodal**—A property of the *normal distribution* in which there is only one mode.

**Validity**—Accuracy in measurement. A valid measuring instrument accurately measures what it is intended to measure.

**Variable**—A characteristic or property that can take on different values.

**Variance**—The average of the squared deviations from the mean. A measure of variability, it measures the variability in original units of measurement squared.

**Vital statistics**—Data related to the crucial events in life: births, deaths, marriages, divorces, fetal deaths, and induced terminations of pregnancy.

**Weighted mean**—A type of mean that takes into account differences in sample size. The weighted mean is equal to the sum of the means multiplied by the number of observations in each sample and divided by the total number of observations in the samples combined.

**Winsorized mean**—A type of mean (average) that has been adjusted for extreme values in the frequency distribution. The most extreme values (highest and lowest) in the distribution are changed to the next less extreme values.

**Yates correction for continuity**—An adjustment made to the $\chi^2$ procedures when the counts in a contingency table are small or when any expected cell count is less than five.

*z* **score**—In the *standard normal distribution*, the number of standard deviation units that the observed value is away from the mean.

*z* **test**—A parametric test of statistical significance. This test is used to make comparisons for two independent population means or two independent population proportions, or for comparing a sample mean to a population mean when the population parameters are known. It is assumed that the population distributions are normal. In a *one-tailed* or *directional z test*, the researcher is trying to determine if the sample mean is significantly less or significantly greater than the population parameter, $\mu$. In a two-tailed or *nondirectional z test*, the researcher is trying to determine if the sample mean is significantly different (either greater than or less) from the population parameter, $\mu$.

*z* **value**—See *z* score.

STATISTICAL TABLES

Table B.1   **Areas under the Normal Curve**

| z | Cum p | Tail p | z | Cum p | Tail p | z | Cum p | Tail p |
|------|--------|--------|------|--------|--------|------|--------|--------|
| 0.00 | 0.5000 | 0.5000 | 0.32 | 0.6255 | 0.3745 | 0.64 | 0.7389 | 0.2611 |
| 0.01 | 0.5040 | 0.4960 | 0.33 | 0.6293 | 0.3707 | 0.65 | 0.7422 | 0.2578 |
| 0.02 | 0.5080 | 0.4920 | 0.34 | 0.6331 | 0.3669 | 0.66 | 0.7454 | 0.2546 |
| 0.03 | 0.5120 | 0.4880 | 0.35 | 0.6368 | 0.3632 | 0.67 | 0.7486 | 0.2514 |
| 0.04 | 0.5160 | 0.4840 | 0.36 | 0.6406 | 0.3594 | 0.68 | 0.7517 | 0.2483 |
| 0.05 | 0.5199 | 0.4801 | 0.37 | 0.6443 | 0.3557 | 0.69 | 0.7549 | 0.2451 |
| 0.06 | 0.5239 | 0.4761 | 0.38 | 0.6480 | 0.3520 | 0.70 | 0.7580 | 0.2420 |
| 0.07 | 0.5279 | 0.4721 | 0.39 | 0.6517 | 0.3483 | 0.71 | 0.7611 | 0.2389 |
| 0.08 | 0.5319 | 0.4681 | 0.40 | 0.6554 | 0.3446 | 0.72 | 0.7642 | 0.2358 |
| 0.09 | 0.5359 | 0.4641 | 0.41 | 0.6591 | 0.3409 | 0.73 | 0.7673 | 0.2327 |
| 0.10 | 0.5398 | 0.4602 | 0.42 | 0.6628 | 0.3372 | 0.74 | 0.7704 | 0.2296 |
| 0.11 | 0.5438 | 0.4562 | 0.43 | 0.6664 | 0.3336 | 0.75 | 0.7734 | 0.2266 |
| 0.12 | 0.5478 | 0.4522 | 0.44 | 0.6700 | 0.3300 | 0.76 | 0.7764 | 0.2236 |
| 0.13 | 0.5517 | 0.4483 | 0.45 | 0.6736 | 0.3264 | 0.77 | 0.7794 | 0.2206 |
| 0.14 | 0.5557 | 0.4443 | 0.46 | 0.6772 | 0.3228 | 0.78 | 0.7823 | 0.2177 |
| 0.15 | 0.5596 | 0.4404 | 0.47 | 0.6808 | 0.3192 | 0.79 | 0.7852 | 0.2148 |
| 0.16 | 0.5636 | 0.4364 | 0.48 | 0.6844 | 0.3156 | 0.80 | 0.7881 | 0.2119 |
| 0.17 | 0.5675 | 0.4325 | 0.49 | 0.6879 | 0.3121 | 0.81 | 0.7910 | 0.2090 |
| 0.18 | 0.5714 | 0.4286 | 0.50 | 0.6915 | 0.3085 | 0.82 | 0.7939 | 0.2061 |
| 0.19 | 0.5753 | 0.4247 | 0.51 | 0.6950 | 0.3050 | 0.83 | 0.7967 | 0.2033 |
| 0.20 | 0.5793 | 0.4207 | 0.52 | 0.6985 | 0.3015 | 0.84 | 0.7995 | 0.2005 |
| 0.21 | 0.5832 | 0.4168 | 0.53 | 0.7019 | 0.2981 | 0.85 | 0.8023 | 0.1977 |
| 0.22 | 0.5871 | 0.4129 | 0.54 | 0.7054 | 0.2946 | 0.86 | 0.8051 | 0.1949 |
| 0.23 | 0.5910 | 0.4090 | 0.55 | 0.7088 | 0.2912 | 0.87 | 0.8078 | 0.1922 |
| 0.24 | 0.5948 | 0.4052 | 0.56 | 0.7123 | 0.2877 | 0.88 | 0.8106 | 0.1894 |
| 0.25 | 0.5987 | 0.4013 | 0.57 | 0.7157 | 0.2843 | 0.89 | 0.8133 | 0.1867 |
| 0.26 | 0.6026 | 0.3974 | 0.58 | 0.7190 | 0.2810 | 0.90 | 0.8159 | 0.1841 |
| 0.27 | 0.6064 | 0.3936 | 0.59 | 0.7224 | 0.2776 | 0.91 | 0.8186 | 0.1814 |
| 0.28 | 0.6103 | 0.3897 | 0.60 | 0.7257 | 0.2743 | 0.92 | 0.8212 | 0.1788 |
| 0.29 | 0.6141 | 0.3859 | 0.61 | 0.7291 | 0.2709 | 0.93 | 0.8238 | 0.1762 |
| 0.30 | 0.6179 | 0.3821 | 0.62 | 0.7324 | 0.2676 | 0.94 | 0.8264 | 0.1736 |
| 0.31 | 0.6217 | 0.3783 | 0.63 | 0.7357 | 0.2643 | 0.95 | 0.8289 | 0.1711 |

(*continues*)

Table B.1  *Continued*

| z | Cum *p* | Tail *p* | z | Cum *p* | Tail *p* | z | Cum *p* | Tail *p* |
|---|---|---|---|---|---|---|---|---|
| 0.96 | 0.8315 | 0.1685 | 1.36 | 0.9131 | 0.0869 | 1.76 | 0.9608 | 0.0392 |
| 0.97 | 0.8340 | 0.1660 | 1.37 | 0.9147 | 0.0853 | 1.77 | 0.9616 | 0.0384 |
| 0.98 | 0.8365 | 0.1635 | 1.38 | 0.9162 | 0.0838 | 1.78 | 0.9625 | 0.0375 |
| 0.99 | 0.8389 | 0.1611 | 1.39 | 0.9177 | 0.0823 | 1.79 | 0.9633 | 0.0367 |
| 1.00 | 0.8413 | 0.1587 | 1.40 | 0.9192 | 0.0808 | 1.80 | 0.9641 | 0.0359 |
| 1.01 | 0.8438 | 0.1562 | 1.41 | 0.9207 | 0.0793 | 1.81 | 0.9649 | 0.0351 |
| 1.02 | 0.8461 | 0.1539 | 1.42 | 0.9222 | 0.0778 | 1.82 | 0.9656 | 0.0344 |
| 1.03 | 0.8485 | 0.1515 | 1.43 | 0.9236 | 0.0764 | 1.83 | 0.9664 | 0.0336 |
| 1.04 | 0.8508 | 0.1492 | 1.44 | 0.9251 | 0.0749 | 1.84 | 0.9671 | 0.0329 |
| 1.05 | 0.8531 | 0.1469 | 1.45 | 0.9265 | 0.0735 | 1.85 | 0.9678 | 0.0322 |
| 1.06 | 0.8554 | 0.1446 | 1.46 | 0.9279 | 0.0721 | 1.86 | 0.9686 | 0.0314 |
| 1.07 | 0.8577 | 0.1423 | 1.47 | 0.9292 | 0.0708 | 1.87 | 0.9693 | 0.0307 |
| 1.08 | 0.8599 | 0.1401 | 1.48 | 0.9306 | 0.0694 | 1.88 | 0.9699 | 0.0301 |
| 1.09 | 0.8621 | 0.1379 | 1.49 | 0.9319 | 0.0681 | 1.89 | 0.9706 | 0.0294 |
| 1.10 | 0.8643 | 0.1357 | 1.50 | 0.9332 | 0.0668 | 1.90 | 0.9713 | 0.0287 |
| 1.11 | 0.8665 | 0.1335 | 1.51 | 0.9345 | 0.0655 | 1.91 | 0.9719 | 0.0281 |
| 1.12 | 0.8686 | 0.1314 | 1.52 | 0.9357 | 0.0643 | 1.92 | 0.9726 | 0.0274 |
| 1.13 | 0.8708 | 0.1292 | 1.53 | 0.9370 | 0.0630 | 1.93 | 0.9732 | 0.0268 |
| 1.14 | 0.8729 | 0.1271 | 1.54 | 0.9382 | 0.0618 | 1.94 | 0.9738 | 0.0262 |
| 1.15 | 0.8749 | 0.1251 | 1.55 | 0.9394 | 0.0606 | 1.95 | 0.9744 | 0.0256 |
| 1.16 | 0.8770 | 0.1230 | 1.56 | 0.9406 | 0.0594 | 1.96 | 0.9750 | 0.0250 |
| 1.17 | 0.8790 | 0.1210 | 1.57 | 0.9418 | 0.0582 | 1.97 | 0.9756 | 0.0244 |
| 1.18 | 0.8810 | 0.1190 | 1.58 | 0.9429 | 0.0571 | 1.98 | 0.9761 | 0.0239 |
| 1.19 | 0.8830 | 0.1170 | 1.59 | 0.9441 | 0.0559 | 1.99 | 0.9767 | 0.0233 |
| 1.20 | 0.8849 | 0.1151 | 1.60 | 0.9452 | 0.0548 | 2.00 | 0.9772 | 0.0228 |
| 1.21 | 0.8869 | 0.1131 | 1.61 | 0.9463 | 0.0537 | 2.01 | 0.9778 | 0.0222 |
| 1.22 | 0.8888 | 0.1112 | 1.62 | 0.9474 | 0.0526 | 2.02 | 0.9783 | 0.0217 |
| 1.23 | 0.8907 | 0.1093 | 1.63 | 0.9484 | 0.0516 | 2.03 | 0.9788 | 0.0212 |
| 1.24 | 0.8925 | 0.1075 | 1.64 | 0.9495 | 0.0505 | 2.04 | 0.9793 | 0.0207 |
| 1.25 | 0.8944 | 0.1056 | 1.65 | 0.9505 | 0.0495 | 2.05 | 0.9798 | 0.0202 |
| 1.26 | 0.8962 | 0.1038 | 1.66 | 0.9515 | 0.0485 | 2.06 | 0.9803 | 0.0197 |
| 1.27 | 0.8980 | 0.1020 | 1.67 | 0.9525 | 0.0475 | 2.07 | 09808 | 0.0192 |
| 1.28 | 0.8997 | 0.1003 | 1.68 | 0.9535 | 0.0465 | 2.08 | 0.9812 | 0.0188 |
| 1.29 | 0.9015 | 0.0985 | 1.69 | 0.9545 | 0.0455 | 2.09 | 0.9817 | 0.0183 |
| 1.30 | 0.9032 | 0.0968 | 1.70 | 0.9554 | 0.0446 | 2.10 | 0.9821 | 0.0179 |
| 1.31 | 0.9049 | 0.0951 | 1.71 | 0.9564 | 0.0436 | 2.11 | 0.9826 | 0.0174 |
| 1.32 | 0.9066 | 0.0934 | 1.72 | 0.9573 | 0.0427 | 2.12 | 0.9830 | 0.0170 |
| 1.33 | 0.9082 | 0.0918 | 1.73 | 0.9582 | 0.0418 | 2.13 | 0.9834 | 0.0166 |
| 1.34 | 0.9099 | 0.0901 | 1.74 | 0.9591 | 0.0409 | 2.14 | 0.9838 | 0.0162 |
| 1.35 | 0.9115 | 0.0885 | 1.75 | 0.9599 | 0.0401 | 2.15 | 0.9842 | 0.0158 |

Table B.1   *Continued*

| z | Cum p | Tail p | z | Cum p | Tail p | z | Cum p | Tail p |
|---|---|---|---|---|---|---|---|---|
| 2.16 | 0.9846 | 0.0154 | 2.56 | 0.9948 | 0.0052 | 2.96 | 0.9985 | 0.0015 |
| 2.17 | 0.9850 | 0.0150 | 2.57 | 0.9949 | 0.0051 | 2.97 | 0.9985 | 0.0015 |
| 2.18 | 0.9854 | 0.0146 | 2.58 | 0.9951 | 0.0049 | 2.98 | 0.9986 | 0.0014 |
| 2.19 | 0.9857 | 0.0143 | 2.59 | 0.9952 | 0.0048 | 2.99 | 0.9986 | 0.0014 |
| 2.20 | 0.9861 | 0.0139 | 2.60 | 0.9953 | 0.0047 | 3.00 | 0.9987 | 0.0013 |
| 2.21 | 0.9864 | 0.0136 | 2.61 | 0.9955 | 0.0045 | 3.01 | 0.9987 | 0.0013 |
| 2.22 | 0.9868 | 0.0132 | 2.62 | 0.9956 | 0.0044 | 3.02 | 0.9987 | 0.0013 |
| 2.23 | 0.9871 | 0.0129 | 2.63 | 0.9957 | 0.0043 | 3.03 | 0.9988 | 0.0012 |
| 2.24 | 0.9875 | 0.0125 | 2.64 | 0.9959 | 0.0041 | 3.04 | 0.9988 | 0.0012 |
| 2.25 | 0.9878 | 0.0122 | 2.65 | 0.9960 | 0.0040 | 3.05 | 0.9989 | 0.0011 |
| 2.26 | 0.9881 | 0.0119 | 2.66 | 0.9961 | 0.0039 | 3.06 | 0.9989 | 0.0011 |
| 2.27 | 0.9884 | 0.0116 | 2.67 | 0.9962 | 0.0038 | 3.07 | 0.9989 | 0.0011 |
| 2.28 | 0.9887 | 0.0113 | 2.68 | 0.9963 | 0.0037 | 3.08 | 0.9990 | 0.0010 |
| 2.29 | 0.9890 | 0.0110 | 2.69 | 0.9964 | 0.0036 | 3.09 | 0.9900 | 0.0010 |
| 2.30 | 0.9893 | 0.0107 | 2.70 | 0.9965 | 0.0035 | 3.10 | 0.9900 | 0.0010 |
| 2.31 | 0.9896 | 0.0104 | 2.71 | 0.9966 | 0.0034 | 3.11 | 0.9991 | 0.0009 |
| 2.32 | 0.9898 | 0.0102 | 2.72 | 0.9967 | 0.0033 | 3.12 | 0.9991 | 0.0009 |
| 2.33 | 0.9901 | 0.0099 | 2.73 | 0.9968 | 0.0032 | 3.13 | 0.9991 | 0.0009 |
| 2.34 | 0.9904 | 0.0096 | 2.74 | 0.9969 | 0.0031 | 3.14 | 0.9992 | 0.0008 |
| 2.35 | 0.9906 | 0.0094 | 2.75 | 0.9970 | 0.0030 | 3.15 | 0.9992 | 0.0008 |
| 2.36 | 0.9909 | 0.0091 | 2.76 | 0.9971 | 0.0029 | 3.16 | 0.9992 | 0.0008 |
| 2.37 | 0.9911 | 0.0089 | 2.77 | 0.9972 | 0.0028 | 3.17 | 0.9992 | 0.0008 |
| 2.38 | 0.9913 | 0.0087 | 2.78 | 0.9973 | 0.0027 | 3.18 | 0.9993 | 0.0007 |
| 2.39 | 0.9916 | 0.0084 | 2.79 | 0.9974 | 0.0026 | 3.19 | 0.9993 | 0.0007 |
| 2.40 | 0.9918 | 0.0082 | 2.80 | 0.9974 | 0.0026 | 3.20 | 0.9993 | 0.0007 |
| 2.41 | 0.9920 | 0.0080 | 2.81 | 0.9975 | 0.0025 | 3.21 | 0.9933 | 0.0007 |
| 2.42 | 0.9922 | 0.0078 | 2.82 | 0.9976 | 0.0024 | 3.22 | 0.9994 | 0.0006 |
| 2.43 | 0.9925 | 0.0075 | 2.83 | 0.9977 | 0.0023 | 3.23 | 0.9994 | 0.0006 |
| 2.44 | 0.9927 | 0.0073 | 2.84 | 0.9977 | 0.0023 | 3.24 | 0.9994 | 0.0006 |
| 2.45 | 0.9929 | 0.0071 | 2.85 | 0.9978 | 0.0022 | 3.25 | 0.9994 | 0.0006 |
| 2.46 | 0.9931 | 0.0069 | 2.86 | 0.9979 | 0.0021 | 3.26 | 0.9994 | 0.0006 |
| 2.47 | 0.9932 | 0.0068 | 2.87 | 0.9979 | 0.0021 | 3.27 | 0.9995 | 0.0005 |
| 2.48 | 0.9934 | 0.0066 | 2.88 | 0.9980 | 0.0020 | 3.28 | 0.9995 | 0.0005 |
| 2.49 | 0.9936 | 0.0064 | 2.89 | 0.9981 | 0.0019 | 3.29 | 0.9995 | 0.0005 |
| 2.50 | 0.9938 | 0.0062 | 2.90 | 0.9981 | 0.0019 | 3.30 | 0.9995 | 0.0005 |
| 2.51 | 0.9940 | 0.0060 | 2.91 | 0.9982 | 0.0018 | 3.31 | 0.9995 | 0.0005 |
| 2.52 | 0.9941 | 0.0059 | 2.92 | 0.9982 | 0.0018 | 3.32 | 0.9995 | 0.0005 |
| 2.53 | 0.9943 | 0.0057 | 2.93 | 0.9983 | 0.0017 | 3.33 | 0.9996 | 0.0004 |
| 2.54 | 0.9945 | 0.0055 | 2.94 | 0.9984 | 0.0016 | 3.34 | 0.9996 | 0.0004 |
| 2.55 | 0.9946 | 0.0054 | 2.95 | 0.9984 | 0.0016 | 3.35 | 0.9996 | 0.0004 |

*(continues)*

Table B.1    *Continued*

| z | Cum p | Tail p | z | Cum p | Tail p | z | Cum p | Tail p |
|---|-------|--------|---|-------|--------|---|-------|--------|
| 3.36 | 0.9996 | 0.0004 | 3.43 | 0.9997 | 0.0003 | 3.50 | 0.9998 | 0.0002 |
| 3.37 | 0.9996 | 0.0004 | 3.44 | 0.9997 | 0.0003 | 3.60 | 0.9998 | 0.0002 |
| 3.38 | 0.9996 | 0.0004 | 3.45 | 0.9997 | 0.0003 | 3.70 | 0.9999 | 0.0001 |
| 3.39 | 0.9997 | 0.0003 | 3.46 | 0.9997 | 0.0003 | 3.80 | 0.9999 | 0.0001 |
| 3.40 | 0.9997 | 0.0003 | 3.47 | 0.9997 | 0.0003 | 3.90 | 1.0000 | 0.0000 |
| 3.41 | 0.9997 | 0.0003 | 3.48 | 0.9997 | 0.0003 | | | |
| 3.42 | 0.9997 | 0.0003 | 3.49 | 0.9998 | 0.0002 | | | |

*Source:* Copyright © Dr. Victor Bissonnette.

Table B.2    **Critical Values of the *t* Distribution**

| | Two-Tailed Testing/One-Tailed Testing | | | | | |
|---|-------|-------|-------|-------|-------|-------|
| | 0.2 | 0.1 | 0.05 | 0.02 | 0.01 | 0.001 |
| df | 0.1 | 0.05 | 0.025 | 0.01 | 0.005 | 0.0005 |
| 5 | 1.476 | 2.015 | 2.571 | 3.365 | 4.032 | 6.869 |
| 6 | 1.440 | 1.943 | 2.447 | 3.143 | 3.707 | 5.959 |
| 7 | 1.415 | 1.895 | 2.365 | 2.998 | 3.499 | 5.408 |
| 8 | 1.397 | 1.860 | 2.306 | 2.896 | 3.355 | 5.041 |
| 9 | 1.383 | 1.833 | 2.262 | 2.821 | 3.250 | 4.781 |
| 10 | 1.372 | 0.812 | 2.228 | 2.764 | 3.169 | 4.587 |
| 11 | 1.363 | 1.796 | 2.201 | 2.718 | 3.106 | 4.437 |
| 12 | 1.356 | 1.782 | 2.179 | 2.681 | 3.055 | 4.318 |
| 13 | 1.350 | 1.771 | 2.160 | 2.650 | 3.012 | 4.221 |
| 14 | 1.345 | 1.761 | 2.145 | 2.624 | 2.977 | 4.140 |
| 15 | 1.341 | 1.753 | 2.131 | 2.602 | 2.947 | 4.073 |
| 16 | 1.337 | 1.746 | 2.120 | 2.583 | 2.921 | 4.015 |
| 17 | 1.333 | 1.740 | 2.110 | 2.567 | 2.898 | 3.965 |
| 18 | 1.330 | 1.734 | 2.101 | 2.552 | 2.878 | 3.922 |
| 19 | 1.328 | 1.729 | 2.093 | 2.539 | 2.861 | 3.883 |
| 20 | 1.325 | 1.725 | 2.086 | 2.528 | 2.845 | 3.850 |
| 21 | 1.323 | 1.721 | 2.080 | 2.518 | 2.831 | 3.819 |
| 22 | 1.321 | 1.717 | 2.074 | 2.508 | 2.819 | 3.792 |
| 23 | 1.319 | 1.714 | 2.069 | 2.500 | 2.807 | 3.768 |
| 24 | 1.318 | 1.711 | 2.064 | 2.492 | 2.797 | 3.745 |
| 25 | 1.316 | 1.708 | 2.060 | 2.485 | 2.787 | 3.725 |
| 26 | 1.315 | 1.706 | 2.056 | 2.479 | 2.779 | 3.707 |

Table B.2    *Continued*

| df | Two-Tailed Testing/One-Tailed Testing | | | | | |
|---|---|---|---|---|---|---|
| | 0.2 | 0.1 | 0.05 | 0.02 | 0.01 | 0.001 |
| | 0.1 | 0.05 | 0.025 | 0.01 | 0.005 | 0.0005 |
| 27 | 1.314 | 1.703 | 2.052 | 2.473 | 2.771 | 3.690 |
| 28 | 1.313 | 1.701 | 2.048 | 2.467 | 2.763 | 3.674 |
| 29 | 1.311 | 1.699 | 2.045 | 2.462 | 2.756 | 3.659 |
| 30 | 1.310 | 1.697 | 2.042 | 2.457 | 2.750 | 3.646 |
| 40 | 1.303 | 1.684 | 2.021 | 2.423 | 2.704 | 3.551 |
| 50 | 1.299 | 1.676 | 2.009 | 2.403 | 2.678 | 3.496 |
| 60 | 1.296 | 1.671 | 2.000 | 2.390 | 2.660 | 3.460 |
| 80 | 1.292 | 1.664 | 1.990 | 2.374 | 2.639 | 3.416 |
| 100 | 1.290 | 1.660 | 1.984 | 2.364 | 2.626 | 3.390 |
| 120 | 1.289 | 1.658 | 1.980 | 2.358 | 2.617 | 3.373 |
| ∞ | 1.282 | 1.645 | 1.960 | 2.327 | 2.576 | 3.291 |

*Source:* Copyright © Dr. Victor Bissonnette.

Table B.3    **Critical Values of *r***

| df | Two-Tailed Testing/One-Tailed Testing | | | | | |
|---|---|---|---|---|---|---|
| | 0.2 | 0.1 | 0.05 | 0.02 | 0.01 | 0.001 |
| | 0.1 | 0.05 | 0.025 | 0.01 | 0.005 | 0.0005 |
| 3 | 0.687 | 0.805 | 0.878 | 0.934 | 0.959 | 0.991 |
| 4 | 0.608 | 0.729 | 0.811 | 0.882 | 0.917 | 0.974 |
| 5 | 0.551 | 0.669 | 0.754 | 0.833 | 0.875 | 0.951 |
| 6 | 0.507 | 0.621 | 0.707 | 0.789 | 0.834 | 0.925 |
| 7 | 0.472 | 0.582 | 0.666 | 0.750 | 0.798 | 0.898 |
| 8 | 0.443 | 0.549 | 0.632 | 0.715 | 0.765 | 0.872 |
| 9 | 0.419 | 0.521 | 0.602 | 0.685 | 0.735 | 0.847 |
| 10 | 0.398 | 0.497 | 0.576 | 0.658 | 0.708 | 0.823 |
| 11 | 0.380 | 0.476 | 0.553 | 0.634 | 0.684 | 0.801 |
| 12 | 0.365 | 0.458 | 0.532 | 0.612 | 0.661 | 0.780 |
| 13 | 0.351 | 0.441 | 0.514 | 0.592 | 0.641 | 0.760 |
| 14 | 0.338 | 0.426 | 0.497 | 0.574 | 0.623 | 0.742 |
| 15 | 0.327 | 0.412 | 0.482 | 0.558 | 0.606 | 0.725 |
| 16 | 0.317 | 0.400 | 0.468 | 0.543 | 0.590 | 0.708 |
| 17 | 0.308 | 0.389 | 0.456 | 0.529 | 0.575 | 0.693 |

*(continues)*

Table B.3    *Continued*

| df | Two-Tailed Testing/One-Tailed Testing | | | | | |
|---|---|---|---|---|---|---|
| | 0.2 | 0.1 | 0.05 | 0.02 | 0.01 | 0.001 |
| | 0.1 | 0.05 | 0.025 | 0.01 | 0.005 | 0.0005 |
| 18 | 0.299 | 0.378 | 0.444 | 0.516 | 0.561 | 0.679 |
| 19 | 0.291 | 0.369 | 0.433 | 0.503 | 0.549 | 0.665 |
| 20 | 0.284 | 0.360 | 0.423 | 0.492 | 0.537 | 0.652 |
| 21 | 0.277 | 0.352 | 0.413 | 0.482 | 0.526 | 0.640 |
| 22 | 0.271 | 0.344 | 0.404 | 0.472 | 0.515 | 0.629 |
| 23 | 0.265 | 0.337 | 0.396 | 0.462 | 0.505 | 0.618 |
| 24 | 0.260 | 0.330 | 0.388 | 0.453 | 0.496 | 0.607 |
| 25 | 0.255 | 0.323 | 0.381 | 0.445 | 0.487 | 0.597 |
| 26 | 0.250 | 0.317 | 0.374 | 0.437 | 0.479 | 0.588 |
| 27 | 0.245 | 0.311 | 0.367 | 0.430 | 0.471 | 0.579 |
| 28 | 0.241 | 0.306 | 0.361 | 0.423 | 0.463 | 0.570 |
| 29 | 0.237 | 0.301 | 0.355 | 0.416 | 0.456 | 0.562 |
| 30 | 0.233 | 0.296 | 0.349 | 0.409 | 0.449 | 0.554 |
| 40 | 0.202 | 0.257 | 0.304 | 0.358 | 0.393 | 0.490 |
| 50 | 0.181 | 0.231 | 0.273 | 0.322 | 0.354 | 0.443 |
| 60 | 0.165 | 0.211 | 0.250 | 0.295 | 0.325 | 0.408 |
| 80 | 0.143 | 0.183 | 0.217 | 0.257 | 0.283 | 0.357 |
| 100 | 0.128 | 1.164 | 0.195 | 0.230 | 0.254 | 0.321 |
| 120 | 0.117 | 0.150 | 0.178 | 0.210 | 0.232 | 0.294 |
| 140 | 0.108 | 0.139 | 0.165 | 0.195 | 0.216 | 0.273 |
| 160 | 0.101 | 0.130 | 0.154 | 0.183 | 0.202 | 0.256 |
| 180 | 0.095 | 0.122 | 0.146 | 0.172 | 0.190 | 0.242 |
| 200 | 0.091 | 0.116 | 0.138 | 0.164 | 0.181 | 0.230 |
| 300 | 0.074 | 0.095 | 0.113 | 0.134 | 0.148 | 0.188 |
| 400 | 0.064 | 0.082 | 0.098 | 0.116 | 0.128 | 0.164 |
| 500 | 0.057 | 0.073 | 0.088 | 0.104 | 0.115 | 0.146 |

Table B.4    **Critical Values of the $\chi^2$ Distribution**

| df | Two-Tailed Testing/One-Tailed Testing | | | | |
|---|---|---|---|---|---|
| | 0.10 | 0.05 | 0.02 | 0.01 | 0.001 |
| | 0.05 | 0.025 | 0.01 | 0.005 | 0.0005 |
| 1 | 2.706 | 3.841 | 5.412 | 6.635 | 10.827 |
| 2 | 4.605 | 5.991 | 7.824 | 9.210 | 13.815 |
| 3 | 6.251 | 7.185 | 9.837 | 11.345 | 16.268 |
| 4 | 7.779 | 9.488 | 11.668 | 13.277 | 18.465 |
| 5 | 9.236 | 11.070 | 13.388 | 15.086 | 20.517 |
| 6 | 10.645 | 12.592 | 15.033 | 16.812 | 22.457 |
| 7 | 12.017 | 14.067 | 16.622 | 18.475 | 24.322 |
| 8 | 13.362 | 15.507 | 18.168 | 20.090 | 26.125 |
| 9 | 14.684 | 16.919 | 19.679 | 21.666 | 27.877 |
| 10 | 15.987 | 18.307 | 21.161 | 23.209 | 29.588 |
| 11 | 17.275 | 19.675 | 22.618 | 24.725 | 31.264 |
| 12 | 18.549 | 21.026 | 24.054 | 26.217 | 32.909 |
| 13 | 19.812 | 22.362 | 25.742 | 27.688 | 34.528 |
| 14 | 21.064 | 23.685 | 26.873 | 29.141 | 36.123 |
| 15 | 22.307 | 24.996 | 28.259 | 30.578 | 37.697 |
| 16 | 23.542 | 26.296 | 29.633 | 32.000 | 39.252 |
| 17 | 24.769 | 27.587 | 30.955 | 33.409 | 40.790 |
| 18 | 25.989 | 28.869 | 32.346 | 34.805 | 42.312 |
| 19 | 27.204 | 30.144 | 33.687 | 36.191 | 43.820 |
| 20 | 28.412 | 31.410 | 35.020 | 37.566 | 45.315 |
| 21 | 29.615 | 32.671 | 36.343 | 38.932 | 46.797 |
| 22 | 30.813 | 33.924 | 37.659 | 40.289 | 48.268 |
| 23 | 32.007 | 35.172 | 38.968 | 41.638 | 49.728 |
| 24 | 33.196 | 36.415 | 40.270 | 42.980 | 51.178 |
| 25 | 34.382 | 37.652 | 41.566 | 44.314 | 52.620 |
| 26 | 35.563 | 38.885 | 42.856 | 45.642 | 54.052 |
| 27 | 36.741 | 40.133 | 44.140 | 46.963 | 55.476 |
| 28 | 37.916 | 41.337 | 45.419 | 48.278 | 56.893 |
| 29 | 39.087 | 42.557 | 46.693 | 49.588 | 58.302 |
| 30 | 40.256 | 43.733 | 47.962 | 50.892 | 59.703 |

## CHAPTER 1

## Knowledge Questions

1. See Glossary.
2. **Rates, ratios, and proportions** are all calculated from data that have two possible categories, such as "outcome at discharge: alive/dead." All three frequency measures are based on the same formula, $(x/y) \times 10^n$.

   In a **ratio**, the variable of interest is divided into two categories. The ratio can be expressed as the relationship of one category to another, such as the number of patients discharged alive compared to the number of patients who expired. If in the month of October 100 patients were discharged from the hospital alive and 10 patients expired, the ratio is 100:10, or 10:1. The interpretation is that for every 10 patients who were discharged alive, one died. In this example, the numerator and denominator are completely independent of each another.

   A ratio can also be expressed in terms of a part to the whole, as when we compare the number of deaths to the total number of discharges, including deaths. In this example, the numerator is included in the denominator. Continuing with our example, for the month of October the **proportion** of patients who were discharged alive is expressed as $100/(100 + 10) = 0.909$. From this example, we can see that a proportion is a type of ratio. In a proportion, the numerator is included in the denominator.

   A **rate** is a frequency measure used to measure an event over time. We basically take the result of our proportion and multiply by $10^n$, where $n$ is equal to 100, 1000, or 10,000. Hospital rates are expressed as the rate per 100 cases; larger population rates are calculated as the rate per 1000, 10,000, or 100,000, with the multiple of 10 that results in a whole number chosen as the multiplier. From the previous example, the hospital death rate for the month of October is calculated as [10 deaths/(10 deaths + 100 live discharges)] = $(10/110) \times 100 = 9.1\%$, or 9.1 deaths per 100 cases.

## Multiple Choice

1. a. Ratio
2. c. Proportion
3. c. Rate

4. b. Daily inpatient census.
5. b. Intra-hospital transfer from MICU to medicine
6. b. Inpatient service day
7. a. Deaths of hospital inpatients only
8. b. Deliveries
9. d. $378 - (18 + 1) + (22 + 2) = 383$
10. d. $(15/238) \times 100 = 6.3\%$
11. d. $(520 \times 14) + (475 \times 17) = 15,355$
    $(13,050/15,355) \times 100 = 85.0\%$
12. c. $10,215/31 = 329.5 \approx 330$
13. b. $9763/1575 = 6.2$

## Problems

1. Average daily census:      $12,220/31 = 394$
   Inpatient bed occupancy rate:      $425 \times 31 = 13,175$
   $(12,220/13,175) \times 100 = 92.8\%$
2. Gross death rate:      $19/(19 + 522) \times 100 = 3.5\%$
   Net death rate:      $(19 - 9)/(541 - 9) \times 100 = 1.9\%$
3. C-section rate:      $7/150 \times 100 = 4.7\%$
4. Average daily census:      $67,106/365 = 183.9$
   Average length of stay:      $68,012/9488 = 7.2$ days
   Inpatient bed occupancy rate:      $(165 \times 175) + (200 \times 200) = 68,875$
   $(67,106/68,875) \times 100 = 97.4\%$
5. $31/(1000 + 31) \times 100 = 3.0\%$
6. $(5/20) \times 100 = 25.0\%$
7. $(122/822) \times 100 = 14.8\%$

8.

Table C.1   **Dr. Green's Discharges by DRG, General Medicine Service, 20XX**

| DRG | DRG Title | RW | N | N*DRG |
|---|---|---|---|---|
| 079 | Respiratory Infections & Inflammations Age > 17 w/CC | 1.5974 | 2 | 3.1948 |
| 085 | Pleural Effusion w/CC | 1.1927 | 1 | 1.1927 |
| 087 | Pulmonary Edema | 1.3430 | 3 | 4.0290 |
| 089 | Simple Pneumonia & Pleurisy Age > 17 w/CC | 1.0463 | 1 | 1.0463 |
| 121 | Circulatory Disorders w/AMI & Major Complications, Discharged Alive | 1.6169 | 1 | 1.6169 |
| 130 | Peripheral Vascular Disorders w/CC | .9505 | 1 | 0.9505 |
| 143 | Chest Pain | .5480 | 1 | 0.5480 |
| 174 | GI Hemorrhage w/CC | 1.0025 | 2 | 2.0050 |
| 182 | Esophagitis, Gastroenteritis & Miscellaneous Digestive Disorders Age > 17 w/CC | .8223 | 2 | 1.6446 |
| 240 | Connective Tissue Disorder w/CC | 1.3153 | 1 | 1.3153 |
| 243 | Medical Back Problems | .7525 | 1 | 0.7525 |
| 316 | Renal Failure | 1.2987 | 1 | 1.1287 |
| 395 | Red Blood Cell Disorders Age > 17 | .8307 | 1 | 0.8307 |
| 416 | Septicemia Age > 17 | 1.5918 | 1 | 1.5918 |
| 450 | Poisoning & Toxic Effects of Drugs Age > 17 w/o CC | .4246 | 1 | 0.4246 |
| 475 | Respiratory System Diagnosis w/Ventilator Support | 3.6000 | 1 | 3.6000 |
| | | | 21 | 26.0414 |

CMI = 26.041/21 = 1.2401

9. a. 24:20, or 6:5, or 1.2:1
   b. 7/44 = 0.16
      11/44 = 0.25
   c. (15/61) × 100 = 24.6%
   d. (5/51) × 100 = 9.8%

# CHAPTER 2

## Knowledge Questions

1. See Glossary.
2. To adjust the crude mortality rate by age, first calculate the age-specific death rate (ASDR) for each age group in the two populations that are being compared. Second, combine the two populations by age groups. Third, multiply the ASDR for each population age group by the combined population total

for each group. This result is the expected number of deaths for each age group for each population. Finally, sum the ASDRs for each age group in each population; this result is the age-adjusted mortality rate for each group.

3. The **direct method** of standardization is used when we are comparing mortality rates in two large populations. The ASDRs for each population are used in calculating the adjusted rate.

In the **indirect method**, we are usually comparing a small population with a larger population, such as a county death rate to a state death rate for a particular illness. To make the comparison, we select the ASDR for the larger population and multiply the ASDR by the population size for each age group in the smaller population. This results in an expected death rate for each age group in the smaller population. These expected rates are summed and compared to the rate for the larger population.

We then calculate the **standard mortality ratio** (SMR), which compares the actual number of deaths to the expected number of deaths in the smaller population. The SMR is interpreted as a rate less than or greater than that for the standard population. If the SMR is greater than 100, the mortality rate in the smaller population is greater than in the larger population; if the SMR is less than 100, the mortality rate is less than that for the larger population.

4. The **neonatal mortality rate** is the number of deaths of newborns under 28 days of age for a given time period compared to the number of live births for the same time period.

The **post-neonatal mortality rate** is the number of deaths of infants of age 28 days up to and not including one year of age for a given time period compared to the number of live births for the same time period.

The **infant mortality rate** is the number of deaths of infants under one year of age for a given time period compared to the number of live births for the same time period. The infant mortality rate combines the neonatal and post-neonatal mortality rates.

5. The **incidence rate** is the total number of new cases of a particular disease during a given time interval. The **prevalence rate** is the number of both new and existing cases of a particular disease during a given time interval. The prevalence rate reports all cases that exist during a given time period; the incidence rate reports only new cases during a given time period.

## Multiple Choice

1. a. Crude death rate
2. b. $(20 + 55 + 155)/(15{,}000 + 17{,}000 + 6000) \times 1000 = 6.1$ per 1000
3. b. $(155/6000) \times 1000 = 25.8$ per 1000
4. b. Neonatal mortality rate
5. b. Cause-specific death rate
6. b. National Centers for Health Statistics

7. b. Centers for Disease Control and Prevention
8. c. $(25/75) \times 100 = 33.3\%$
9. d. HIV infection
10. b. Prevalence rate

## Problems

1. a. There were a total of 44 MICU deaths—24 men and 20 women; the ratio is 24:20, or 6:5. The interpretation is that for every six male deaths, there were five female deaths.
   b. Seven of the patients who died were admitted from the ED; the proportion of patients who were admitted from the ED is 7/44, or 0.16.

      Eleven of the patients who died were transfers from other hospitals; the proportion of patients who were transfers from other hospitals is 11/44, or 0.25.
   c. Fifteen patients who died in the MICU fell into DRG 475. The case fatality rate is $(15/61) \times 100 = 24.6\%$.
   d. Five patients who died in the MICU fell into DRG 483. The case fatality rate is $(5/51) \times 100 = 9.8\%$.

## Table C.2    Critical Care Hospital, Deaths in the MICU by DRG

| DRG | DRG Title | Adm Source | Gender | LOS |
|-----|-----------|------------|--------|-----|
| 001 | Craniotomy Age >17 W Cc | SNF | Male | 2 |
| 014 | Intracranial Hemorrhage & Stroke W Infarct | Other | Male | 3 |
| 014 | Intracranial Hemorrhage & Stroke W Infarct | Emerdept | Female | 3 |
| 020 | Nervous System Infection Except Viral Meningitis | Other | Female | 15 |
| 075 | Major Chest Procedures | Hospital | Male | 6 |
| 105 | Cardiac Valve & Oth Major Cardiothoracic Proc W/O Card Cath | Hospital | Female | 23 |
| 123 | Circulatory Disorders W Ami, Expired | Hospital | Male | 7 |
| 123 | Circulatory Disorders W Ami, Expired | Other | Male | 1 |
| 123 | Circulatory Disorders W Ami, Expired | Other | Male | 4 |
| 123 | Circulatory Disorders W Ami, Expired | Emerdept | Male | 5 |
| 172 | Digestive Malignancy W Cc | Emerdept | Male | 1 |
| 172 | Digestive Malignancy W Cc | Physician | Male | 1 |
| 188 | Other Digestive System Diagnoses Age >17 W Cc | SNF | Female | 1 |
| 191 | Pancreas, Liver & Shunt Procedures W Cc | Hospital | Male | 9 |
| 202 | Cirrhosis & Alcoholic Hepatitis | Physician | Female | 15 |
| 202 | Cirrhosis & Alcoholic Hepatitis | Other | Male | 1 |

(*continues*)

Table C.2 *Continued*

| DRG | DRG Title | Adm Source | Gender | LOS |
|---|---|---|---|---|
| 202 | Cirrhosis & Alcoholic Hepatitis | Emerdept | Male | 24 |
| 205 | Disorders Of Liver Except Malig,Cirr,Alc Hepa W Cc | Physician | Male | 20 |
| 331 | Other Kidney & Urinary Tract Diagnoses Age >17 W Cc | Physician | Male | 44 |
| 357 | Uterine & Adnexa Proc For Ovarian Or Adnexal Malignancy | Physician | Female | 24 |
| 416 | Septicemia Age >17 | Hospital | Female | 4 |
| 416 | Septicemia Age >17 | Other | Male | 2 |
| 449 | Poisoning & Toxic Effects Of Drugs Age >17 W Cc | Other | Male | 1 |
| 473 | Acute Leukemia W/O Major O.R. Procedure Age >17 | Physician | Male | 5 |
| 475 | Respiratory System Diagnosis With Ventilator Support | Physician | Male | 25 |
| 475 | Respiratory System Diagnosis With Ventilator Support | Physician | Female | 1 |
| 475 | Respiratory System Diagnosis With Ventilator Support | Hospital | Female | 1 |
| 475 | Respiratory System Diagnosis With Ventilator Support | Other | Female | 1 |
| 475 | Respiratory System Diagnosis With Ventilator Support | Hospital | Female | 21 |
| 475 | Respiratory System Diagnosis With Ventilator Support | Other | Male | 5 |
| 475 | Respiratory System Diagnosis With Ventilator Support | Hospital | Female | 8 |
| 475 | Respiratory System Diagnosis With Ventilator Support | Emerdept | Female | 10 |
| 475 | Respiratory System Diagnosis With Ventilator Support | Clinic | Male | 13 |
| 475 | Respiratory System Diagnosis With Ventilator Support | SNF | Female | 1 |
| 475 | Respiratory System Diagnosis With Ventilator Support | Emerdept | Male | 5 |
| 475 | Respiratory System Diagnosis With Ventilator Support | Clinic | Female | 4 |
| 475 | Respiratory System Diagnosis With Ventilator Support | Emerdept | Male | 3 |
| 475 | Respiratory System Diagnosis With Ventilator Support | Other | Female | 12 |
| 475 | Respiratory System Diagnosis With Ventilator Support | Other | Female | 5 |
| 483 | Trac W Mech Vent 96+Hrs Or Pdx Except Face, Mouth & Neck Dx | Hospital | Female | 30 |
| 483 | Trac W Mech Vent 96+Hrs Or Pdx Except Face, Mouth & Neck Dx | Hospital | Male | 19 |
| 483 | Trac W Mech Vent 96+Hrs Or Pdx Except Face, Mouth & Neck Dx | Hospital | Male | 22 |
| 483 | Trac W Mech Vent 96+Hrs Or Pdx Except Face, Mouth & Neck Dx | Physician | Female | 46 |
| 483 | Trac W Mech Vent 96+Hrs Or Pdx Except Face, Mouth & Neck Dx | Other | Female | 28 |

2. a. $(4832/7358) \times 100 = 65.6$ per 100 cases
   b. $(947/11,140,950) \times 100,000 = 8.5$ per 100,000

Table C.3   **AIDS Cases in Ohio 1981–1995**

| Year of Diagnosis | Total No. of New Cases | Cases Dead |
|---|---|---|
| 1981 | 2 | 2 |
| 1982 | 7 | 7 |
| 1983 | 27 | 25 |
| 1984 | 58 | 56 |
| 1985 | 120 | 113 |
| 1986 | 211 | 198 |
| 1987 | 401 | 374 |
| 1988 | 540 | 482 |
| 1989 | 631 | 537 |
| 1990 | 682 | 577 |
| 1991 | 763 | 644 |
| 1992 | 775 | 587 |
| 1993 | 1935 | 908 |
| 1994 | 947 | 259 |
| 1995 | 259 | 63 |

US DHHS, Public Health Service, CDC, National Center for HIV, STD, and TB Prevention, AIDS Public Information Data Set, CDC WONDER On-line Database, wonder.cdc.gov

3. a. See table.
   b. White crude death rate:  $(202,362/27,841,516) \times 100 = 0.73\%$
      Black crude death rate:  $(18,885/2,579,673) \times 100 = 0.73\%$
   c. White ASDR:  $(221,111.98/30,421,189) \times 100 = 0.73\%$
      Black ASDR:  $(222,704.26/30,421,189) \times 100 = 0.73\%$
   d. There does not appear to be a difference in the age-adjusted rates for the two groups.

Table C.4  **Age Specific Mortality Rates, State of California, 2003**

| Age | (a) White Pop | (b) Deaths per 1,000 | (c) White ASDR | (d) Black Pop | (e) Deaths per 1,000 | (f) Black ASDR | (g) Comb Pop Tot | (h) Expected No. of Deaths, Whites (g × c) | (I) Expected No. of Deaths, Blacks (g × f) |
|---|---|---|---|---|---|---|---|---|---|
| <1 | 429,511 | 2,130 | 0.50% | 37,591 | 408 | 1.09% | 467,102 | 2,316.42 | 5,069.77 |
| 1-4 | 1,627,070 | 439 | 0.03% | 157,710 | 70 | 0.04% | 1,784,780 | 481.55 | 792.18 |
| 5-9 | 2,046,063 | 282 | 0.01% | 223,448 | 35 | 0.02% | 2,269,511 | 312.80 | 355.49 |
| 10-14 | 2,157,618 | 373 | 0.02% | 249,464 | 53 | 0.02% | 2,407,082 | 416.13 | 511.40 |
| 15-19 | 1,958,101 | 1,201 | 0.06% | 217,838 | 206 | 0.09% | 2,175,939 | 1,334.61 | 2,057.69 |
| 20-24 | 1,984,041 | 1,640 | 0.08% | 189,934 | 305 | 0.16% | 2,173,975 | 1,797.00 | 3,491.01 |
| 25-34 | 4,059,559 | 3,398 | 0.08% | 366,264 | 614 | 0.17% | 4,425,823 | 3,704.58 | 7,419.39 |
| 35-44 | 4,301,525 | 7,415 | 0.17% | 414,771 | 1,263 | 0.30% | 4,716,296 | 8,129.99 | 14,361.37 |
| 45-54 | 3,723,683 | 14,523 | 0.39% | 327,883 | 2,542 | 0.78% | 4,051,566 | 15,801.80 | 31,410.84 |
| 55-64 | 2,462,805 | 20,348 | 0.83% | 192,067 | 2,819 | 1.47% | 2,654,872 | 21,934.88 | 38,966.01 |
| 65-74 | 1,535,605 | 31,716 | 2.07% | 116,784 | 3,326 | 2.85% | 1,652,389 | 34,128.03 | 47,059.92 |
| 75-84 | 1,127,540 | 58,993 | 5.23% | 63,582 | 4,197 | 6.60% | 1,191,122 | 62,319.62 | 78,625.07 |
| 85+ | 428,395 | 59,904 | 13.98% | 22,337 | 3,047 | 13.64% | 450,732 | 63,027.46 | 61,484.55 |
| Total | 27,841,516 | 202,362 | 0.73% | 2,579,673 | 18,885 | 0.73% | 30,421,189 | 221,111.98 | 222,704.26 |

*Source:* Data from Centers for Disease Control and Prevention, CDC Wonder Data Base, http://wonder.cdc.gov

4.

Table C.5  **Critical Care Hospital, Hip Replacement Surgery**

| Age Group | No. of Patients | No. of Patients with Complications | Complication Rate | County Complication Rate | Expected Number of Complications |
|---|---|---|---|---|---|
| ≥ 65 | 170 | 17 | 10.00% | 8.0% | 13.60 |
| < 65 | 42 | 2 | 4.76% | 3.0% | 1.26 |
| Total | 212 | 19 | 8.96% | | 14.86 |

Observed complication rate is $(19/212) \times 100 = 8.96\%$

Expected complication rate is $(14.86/212) \times 100 = 7.01\%$

SMR $= 0.0896/0.0701 = 1.28$

The complication rate for Critical Care Hospital is 28% higher than the county rate.

5.    Table C.6    **Mortality Rates for CVAs, State versus City General Hospital**

| Severity of Illness | State Mortality Rate | Hospital Discharges for CVA | Observed Deaths | Expected Deaths |
|---|---|---|---|---|
| 1 | 4.2 | 55 | 2 | 2.31 |
| 2 | 5.9 | 116 | 8 | 6.84 |
| 3 | 7.8 | 195 | 20 | 15.21 |
| 4 | 20.9 | 147 | 29 | 30.72 |
| 5 | 34.6 | 62 | 32 | 21.45 |
|  |  | 575 | 91 | 76.53 |

a. Observed mortality rate is $(91/575) \times 100 = 15.8\%$
b. Expected mortality rate is $(76.53/575) \times 100 = 13.3\%$
c. SMR $= 0.158/0.133 = 1.19$
d. After indirect standardization, the mortality rate for CGH is 19% higher than the expected mortality rate.

## Online Activities

1. 299,479
2. $25,996
3. 7.3 days
4. 18.6%
5. 65–84
6. $25,996 \times 299,479 = \$7,785,256,084$

Table C.7 **HCUP Query, Outcomes by Patient Characteristics for DRG 416, Septicemia, Age > 17, 2002**

| Age Group | Total Number of Discharges | ALOS | Average Charges | Discharge Status | | | | | | |
|---|---|---|---|---|---|---|---|---|---|---|
| | | | | In-Hospital Deaths | Routine Discharges | Short-Term Hospital | Other Institution | Home Health Care | Against Medical Advice | Missing Discharge Status |
| Total | 299,479 | 7.3 | $25,996 | 55,657 (18.6%) | 107,531 (35.9%) | 9,442 (3.2%) | 93,435 (31.2%) | 30,650 (10.2%) | 1,658 (0.6%) | 849 (0.3%) |
| 18–44 | 26,210 | 6.9 | $26,610 | 2,019 (7.7%) | 15,731 (60.0%) | 1,282 (4.9%) | 3,341 (12.7%) | 2,961 (11.3%) | 802 (3.1%) | |
| 45–64 | 63,372 | 7.4 | $29,356 | 8,803 (13.9%) | 31,905 (50.3%) | 2,906 (4.6%) | 11,898 (18.8%) | 7,109 (11.2%) | 571 (0.9%) | |
| 65–84 | 148,087 | 7.5 | $26,322 | 28,334 (19.1%) | 48,879 (33.0%) | 4,413 (3.0%) | 50,139 (33.9%) | 15,502 (10.5%) | 220 (0.1%) | 460 (0.3%) |
| 85+ | 61,801 | 6.9 | $21,556 | 16,501 (26.7%) | 11,006 (17.8%) | 841 (1.4%) | 28,057 (45.4%) | 5,078 (8.2%) | ★ | 173 (0.3%) |

*Source:* Agency for Healthcare Research and Quality http://www.ahrq.gov/hcupnet

# CHAPTER 3
## Knowledge Questions

1. See Glossary.
2. When considering a table, chart, or graph, one should ask:
   - Is the graphic technique chosen the most appropriate for the data to be displayed?
   - Will the graphic technique chosen allow the reader to think about what the data convey?
   - Will the graphic technique chosen avoid distortion of the data?
   - Will the graphic technique chosen encourage the reader to make comparisons, if appropriate?
   - Does the graphic technique reveal data at several levels, if appropriate?
   - Is the purpose of the table, chart, or graph clear?
   - Does the table, chart, or graph relate to the written/oral descriptions of the data set?
3. The title for a table, chart, or graph should be as complete as possible. It should answer the following questions:
   - What are the data? (counts, percentages)
   - To whom does the data relate? (men and women with a certain condition, diseases by race)
   - Where are the data from? (hospital, community, state, county)
   - When? To what time frame does the data apply? (day, week, month, year)
4. When constructing a bar chart, one should consider:
   - The bar categories should be arranged in some logical order, such as by year or in alphabetical order.
   - All bars should be of the same width.
   - The length of the bars should be proportionate to the frequency of the variable represented.
   - Avoid using more than three bars within a group of bars.
   - Include a legend.
5. In a **stacked bar chart**, the segments of the bar for each data category are stacked like building blocks on top of one another to form a single bar. The bar represents the total number of cases in the data category; the segments of the bar represent the frequency of certain types of cases within the category.

   In a **100% component bar chart**, all bars in the display are of the same height, with each representing 100% of the cases in the category. The bar is divided into segments that represent the percentage of certain types of cases within categories. For example, a 100% component chart can display types of cancer by site; the segments within each bar may represent the percentage of men and women affected by that particular type of cancer.

   The stacked bar chart displays frequencies; the 100% component bar chart displays percentages.

6. A **scatter diagram** is a graphic representation of the relationship between two variables, $x$ and $y$. The $x$ variable is plotted on the horizontal axis and the $y$ variable is plotted on the vertical axis. It is used to assess the linearity of the relationship between variables $x$ and $y$ when conducting either the Pearson's $r$ or simple linear regression. If the two variables appear to approximate a straight line, the variables are linearly related.

A **bubble chart** is a type of scatter plot with circular symbols used to compare three variables. As with a scatter diagram, one variable is plotted on the horizontal axis and one variable is plotted on the vertical axis. The size of the circle indicates the value of a third variable.

## Multiple Choice

1. a. Bar graph
2. c. Line graph
3. b. Percentage of discharges by religion
4. b. Two-variable bar chart
5. d. Scatter diagram

## Problems

1. Actual admissions did not quite meet the budgeted projections except for Psychiatry Service and "other adult." The differences do not appear to be significant.

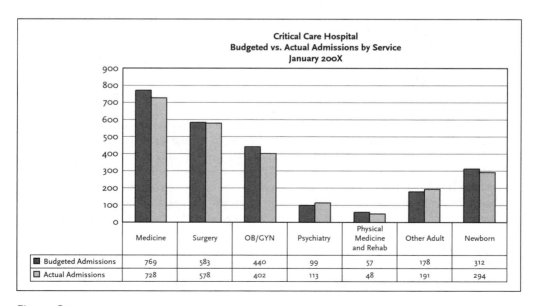

| | Medicine | Surgery | OB/GYN | Psychiatry | Physical Medicine and Rehab | Other Adult | Newborn |
|---|---|---|---|---|---|---|---|
| Budgeted Admissions | 769 | 583 | 440 | 99 | 57 | 178 | 312 |
| Actual Admissions | 728 | 578 | 402 | 113 | 48 | 191 | 294 |

Figure C.1

2.

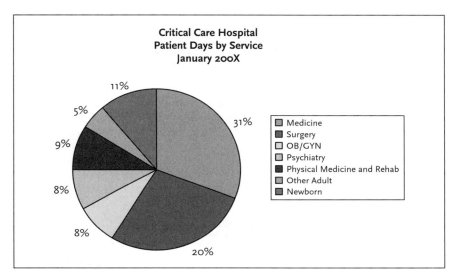

Figure C.2

3.

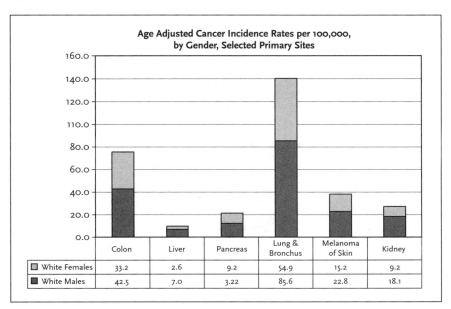

Figure C.3

4.   Table C.8   **Critical Care Cancer Research Institute Discharges, Discharge Service Days, and Average Length of Stay January 200X**

| Service | Discharges | Discharge Days | ALOS |
|---|---|---|---|
| Medicine | 198 | 1,313 | 6.6 |
| Surgery | 152 | 947 | 6.2 |
| Gyn | 74 | 328 | 4.4 |
| ENT | 48 | 290 | 6.0 |

5.

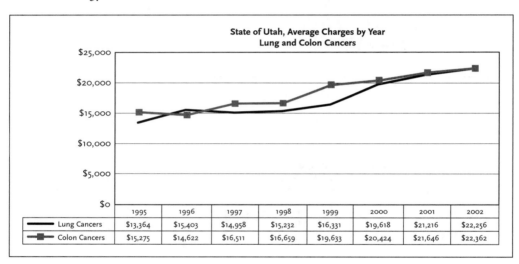

**State of Utah, Average Charges by Year**
**Lung and Colon Cancers**

| | 1995 | 1996 | 1997 | 1998 | 1999 | 2000 | 2001 | 2002 |
|---|---|---|---|---|---|---|---|---|
| Lung Cancers | $13,364 | $15,403 | $14,958 | $15,232 | $16,331 | $19,618 | $21,216 | $22,256 |
| Colon Cancers | $15,275 | $14,622 | $16,511 | $16,659 | $19,633 | $20,424 | $21,646 | $22,362 |

Figure C.4

6.

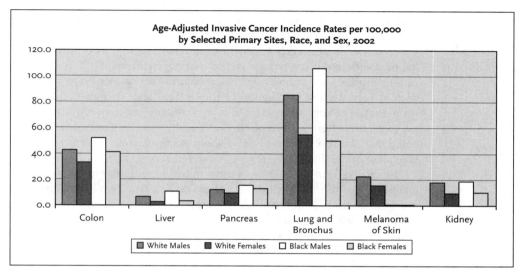

**Age-Adjusted Invasive Cancer Incidence Rates per 100,000 by Selected Primary Sites, Race, and Sex, 2002**

Figure C.5

# CHAPTER 4
## Knowledge Questions

1. See Glossary.
2. The measurement process involves assigning numbers to characteristics or properties that we are interested in studying. The numbers must be assigned according to a defined set of rules. The scale of measurement upon which the property falls also must be considered. For example, eye color, a property that falls on the nominal scale of measurement, must have numbers assigned by a defined coding scheme. We might assign the number "1" for brown eyes, the number "2" for blue eyes, and so on.
3. To have confidence in the data that we collect, we must assess the validity and reliability of the measures. **Validity** tells us that we are truly measuring the characteristic or property of interest, and **reliability** tells us that the measurement results are consistent over time or repeated measures.
4. This is a problem with aspects of **reliability**. In this case, it is a matter of **stability**, or **test-retest** reliability. If we obtain a different result each time a property is measured, we cannot be confident in our results.
5. **Stability** is an aspect of reliability in which we expect to obtain similar or consistent results each time a property is measured. We can determine the

stability of a measuring instrument by administering the instrument on two separate occasions to the same group of individuals.

**Internal consistency** is an aspect of reliability that tells us how well the items on an instrument "fit" together. **Inter-rater agreement** is the extent to which two evaluators agree on their assessment of a property of interest. The **kappa coefficient** is used to assess inter-rater agreement.

6. In the **nominal** scale of measurement, measures are organized into categories such as race, gender, or religion. In the **ordinal** scale of measurement, the properties of interest are presented in rank order—highest to lowest or lowest to highest. Diseases are often classified by stage, with the lowest stage being the least severe form of the disease and the highest stage the most severe form of the disease.

The **interval** and **ratio** scales of measurement are similar in that they have a defined unit of measure; however, there is not a true zero (or absence of a characteristic) on the interval scale of measurement. A common example of a property that falls on the interval scale is the Fahrenheit scale—absence of temperature is not represented on this scale. For the ratio scale, zero represents the absence of the characteristic of interest. On the Kelvin scale, absolute zero is the total absence of temperature.

7. **Discrete** variables have gaps between successive measures, or the gaps between measures are not equal. Discrete variables fall on the nominal and ordinal scales of measurement. We cannot multiply or divide variables that are discrete. In contrast, **continuous** variables fall on the interval and ratio scales of measurement. The term *continuous* implies that there are no gaps between successive numbers. Results of these measures may be fractional, such as a weight of 125.3 lbs. We can use multiplication and division with continuous variables.

## Multiple Choice

1. a. Nominal
2. c. Ratio
3. b. Ordinal
4. b. Discrete
5. d. Interval (no true zero)
6. b. Ordinal
7. a. Age
8. c. DRG assignment upon discharge

## Problems

1. For continuous data, the measure of central tendency that is most often reported is the mean. However, depending on the research question and the research results, the median and/or mode may be reported.

Exhibit C.1 **Selected Data Elements from Case Mix Assessment Tool for Behavioral Health Care**

| Data Element | Measurement Scale Discrete/Continuous Variable | Measure of Central Tendency |
|---|---|---|
| Gender:<br>1—Male<br>2—Female | Discrete | Mode |
| Number of Psychiatric Admissions | Continuous | Mean* |
| Number of Medications | Continuous | Mean |
| Legal Status<br>1—Voluntary<br>2—Involuntary<br>3—Criminal court hold | Discrete | Mode |
| Unable to control substance abuse within past 30 days<br>0—no<br>1—yes | Discrete | Mode |
| Activities of daily living<br>0—Independent<br>1—Setup help only<br>2—Supervision<br>3—Limited assistance<br>4—Extensive assistance<br>5—Maximal assistance<br>6—Total dependence | Discrete | Mode |
| White Blood Count: criteria—range 3.8–10.8 | Continuous | Mean |
| Number of falls in last 30 days | Continuous | Mean |

*Source:* Federal Register, Volume 68, No. 229, Friday, November 28, 2003, p. 66975.

 2. C-section rate at City Hospital: $(34/200) \times 100 = 17.0\%$
 C-section rate at County Hospital: $(54/1100) \times 100 = 4.9\%$
 The C-section rate at City Hospital exceeds the national benchmark. The comparison should be made on the basis of the percentage of C-sections performed out of the total number of deliveries rather than the actual number of C-sections.

3. a. $$\frac{\text{Total number of maternal readmissions within 14 days of delivery for the period} \times 100}{\text{Total number of maternal admissions (OB delivered and OB undelivered) for the period}}$$

   b. $$\frac{\text{Total number of maternal deaths within 42 days postpartum for the period} \times 100}{\text{Total number of maternal discharges (OB delivered and OB undelivered) for the period}}$$

   c. $$\frac{\text{Total number of maternal discharges (delivered) with blood loss greater than 500 ml for the period} \times 100}{\text{Total number of maternal discharges for the period}}$$

# CHAPTER 5
## Knowledge Questions

1. See Glossary.
2. A **population** is a group of individuals or objects that are of interest to the researcher. A **population parameter** is a "number" that describes the population. The "number" is calculated from all members of the defined population.

   A **sample** is a subgroup of a population that is randomly drawn. A **sample statistic** is calculated from the population subgroup. Inferences to the population are made from sample statistics.
3. The **mean** is the arithmetic average of a frequency distribution. All observations in the frequency distribution are used to calculate the mean; the mean is considered a non-resistant statistic because it is influenced by the extreme values in the distribution. The mean is appropriate for interval and ratio level data.

   The **median** is the "middlemost" value in a frequency distribution. Fifty percent of the observations in the distribution lie above the median and 50% lie below the median. The median is considered a resistant statistic because it is not influenced by extreme values in the distribution. The median is appropriate for ordinal, interval, and ratio level data.

   The **mode** is the most frequently occurring value in a frequency distribution. The mode is considered a resistant statistic because it is not influenced by extreme values in the distribution. A limitation of the mode is that a frequency distribution can have more than one mode; a frequency distribution may be bimodal or multi-modal. The mode can fluctuate widely from sample to sample. For nominal level data, the mode is the most frequently occurring category. The mode is the only measure of central tendency appropriate for nominal level data. The mode may also be reported for ordinal, interval, and ratio level data.

4. Polarization, individuality, and uniformity refer to the amount of variability in a frequency distribution. **Polarization** refers to the maximum spread or dispersion within a distribution. Polarization is used to describe the maximum variation for interval and ratio level data.

   Uniformity and individuality are terms used to describe variation in nominal level data. **Uniformity** describes a frequency distribution in which there is an even distribution of cases in all categories of the nominal variable. When each category occurs just one time, the term **individuality** is used to describe the lack of variation within the distribution.

5. Measures of central tendency and variation are calculated from each observation in an ungrouped frequency distribution. Statistics calculated from an ungrouped frequency distribution are more precise than statistics calculated from a grouped frequency distribution.

   In a grouped frequency distribution, the frequency distribution is divided into class intervals. It is assumed that the observations are distributed evenly throughout each class interval, even though this may not be the case. Statistics calculated from a grouped frequency distribution will vary depending upon how the distribution is grouped. Because the midpoints of the class intervals and not each observation in the distribution are used to calculate the statistics that describe the grouped frequency distribution, these statistics will be less precise.

## Multiple Choice

1. a. $(60 \times 0.67) + (70 \times 0.33) = 63.3$; or $[(60 \times 40) + (70 \times 20)]/60 = 63.3$
2. c. 8

| $X$ | $X - \bar{X}$ | $(X - \bar{X})^2$ |
|---|---|---|
| 8 | $8 - 10 = -2$ | 4 |
| 12 | $12 - 10 = 2$ | 4 |
| | | 8 |

3. d. $50 - 25 = 25$
4. a. Be equal
5. c. $10.5 - 4.5 = 6.0$
6. b. 7.5
7. c. 8.0
8. a. 0.5–3.5
9. d. Between 9.5 days and 14.5 days
10. a. 14.5 days

11. d. 14.5 days
12. a. 14.5 days
13. a. 19.5 days
14. a. Mode
15. b. Less than that for Distribution 2
    Range of Distribution 1 = 220 − 190 = 30
    Range of Distribution 2 = 240 − 170 = 70
    In general, the greater the range in a data set, the greater the variance and standard deviation. The calculated standard deviation for Distribution 1 is 12.04 and the standard deviation for Distribution 2 is 31.5.
16. d. $5^2 = 25$
17. c. 16
    When a value on the interval or ratio scale of measurement is multiplied or divided by a constant, the ratios among the values in the distribution remain the same (Chapter 4).
18. b. Mode (the most frequently occurring observation)
19. d. None of the above (because 39 falls into the same class interval as 35)
20. d. 103

## Problems

Table C.9    **Male Deaths Due to Leukemia (ICD-9-CM Codes 200.0–200.9) in the State of Ohio 1998**

| Age Group | Leukemia Deaths in Men | $p$ | Cum $p$ | $M$ | $f(M)$ |
|---|---|---|---|---|---|
| 5–14 | 16 | 0.012 | 0.012 | 9.5 | 152.00 |
| 15–24 | 20 | 0.015 | 0.026 | 19.5 | 390.00 |
| 25–34 | 27 | 0.020 | 0.046 | 29.5 | 796.50 |
| 35–44 | 63 | 0.046 | 0.092 | 39.5 | 2,488.50 |
| 45–54 | 118 | 0.086 | 0.178 | 49.5 | 5,841.00 |
| 55–64 | 194 | 0.142 | 0.320 | 59.5 | 11,543.00 |
| 65–74 | 388 | 0.284 | 0.604 | 69.5 | 26,966.00 |
| 75–84 | 418 | 0.306 | 0.909 | 79.5 | 33,231.00 |
| 85+ | 124 | 0.091 | 1.000 | 89.5 | 11,098.00 |
| Total | 1,368 | 1.000 | | | 92,506.00 |

*Source:* CDC Wonder On-Line Database http://woncer.cdc.gov

| | | |
|---|---|---|
| Mean | 67.6 | |
| Crude Mode | 79.5 | |
| Crude Median | 69.5 | |

Table C.10  **Female Deaths Due to Leukemia (ICD-9-CM Codes 200.0–200.9) in the State of Ohio 1998**

| Age Group | Leukemia Deaths in Women | $p$ | Cum $p$ | $M$ | $f(M)$ |
|---|---|---|---|---|---|
| 5–14 | 6 | 0.005 | 0.005 | 9.5 | 57.00 |
| 15–24 | 10 | 0.008 | 0.013 | 19.5 | 195.00 |
| 25–34 | 9 | 0.008 | 0.021 | 29.5 | 265.50 |
| 35–44 | 26 | 0.022 | 0.043 | 39.5 | 1,027.00 |
| 45–54 | 61 | 0.051 | 0.094 | 49.5 | 3,019.50 |
| 55–64 | 132 | 0.110 | 0.204 | 59.5 | 7,854.00 |
| 65–74 | 296 | 0.247 | 0.451 | 69.5 | 20,572.00 |
| 75–84 | 463 | 0.387 | 0.838 | 79.5 | 36,808.50 |
| 85+ | 194 | 0.162 | 1.000 | 89.5 | 17,363.00 |
| Total | 1,197 | 1.000 | | | 87,161.50 |

*Source:* CDC Wonder On-Line Database http://woncer.cdc.gov

| | |
|---|---|
| Mean | 72.82 |
| Crude Mode | 79.5 |
| Crude Median | 79.5 |

1. a. The mean age of death for men is $92,506/1368 = 67.6$ years; the mean age for women is $87,161.5/1197 = 72.8$ years.
   b. The crude mode for men is 79.5 years; the crude mode for women is 79.5 years (the midpoints of the most frequently occurring intervals). The crude median for men is 69.5 years; the crude median for women is 79.5 years.
   c. The refined mode for men:

$$Mode = 74.5 + \frac{10(418-388)}{(418-388)+(418-124)} = 74.5 + \frac{300}{324} = 75.4$$

The refined median for men:

$$M_D = 64.5 + \frac{10(684-438)}{388} = 64.5 + 6.3 = 70.8$$

The refined mode for women:

$$Mode = 74.5 + \frac{10(463-296)}{(463-296)+(463-194)} = 74.5 + 3.8 = 78.3$$

The refined median for women:

$$M_D = 74.5 + \frac{10(598.5 - 540)}{463} = 74.5 + 1.3 = 75.8$$

d. The crude median for men (69.5) is similar to the refined median (70.8). However, the crude mode for men (79.5) is somewhat higher than the refined mode (75.4). This is because there are more observations in the interval that falls below the interval containing the mode than the interval that falls above the interval containing the mode—388 and 124, respectively. The mode is pulled in the direction of the interval that contains more observations.

The crude median for women (79.5) is somewhat higher than the refined median (75.8). A greater proportion of deaths for women occur before age 74.5 than after age 84.5; thus the median is being pulled in the direction of the lesser age. This result also better matches the mean age of 72.8. The crude mode for women (79.5) is not much different from the refined mode (78.3).

e. Because we do not have information regarding age at diagnosis or survival times, we cannot say that women live longer with the disease than men. We can only conclude that the average age of death due to leukemia is higher for women (72.8) than the average age for men (67.6). For both data sets, the median better represents the most typical age at death because the mean is influenced by extreme values.

2. a.

Table C.11 **Statistics**

| Age | | |
|---|---|---|
| N | Valid | 61 |
| | Missing | 0 |
| Mean | | 65.57 |
| Median | | 65.00 |
| Mode | | 64[a] |
| Std. Deviation | | 14.240 |
| Variance | | 202.782 |

[a]Multiple modes exist. The smallest value is shown.

Table C.12    **Age**

| | | Frequency | Percent | Cumulative Valid Percent | Percent |
|---|---|---|---|---|---|
| Valid | 37 | 2 | 3.3 | 3.3 | 3.3 |
| | 39 | 2 | 3.3 | 3.3 | 6.6 |
| | 42 | 1 | 1.6 | 1.6 | 8.2 |
| | 47 | 3 | 4.9 | 4.9 | 13.1 |
| | 49 | 1 | 1.6 | 1.6 | 14.8 |
| | 51 | 3 | 4.9 | 4.9 | 19.7 |
| | 52 | 1 | 1.6 | 1.6 | 21.3 |
| | 53 | 1 | 1.6 | 1.6 | 23.0 |
| | 54 | 2 | 3.3 | 3.3 | 26.2 |
| | 56 | 1 | 1.6 | 1.6 | 27.9 |
| | 57 | 2 | 3.3 | 3.3 | 31.1 |
| | 59 | 1 | 1.6 | 1.6 | 32.8 |
| | 60 | 2 | 3.3 | 3.3 | 36.1 |
| | 61 | 1 | 1.6 | 1.6 | 37.7 |
| | 63 | 3 | 4.9 | 4.9 | 42.6 |
| | 64 | 4 | 6.6 | 6.6 | 49.2 |
| | 65 | 2 | 3.3 | 3.3 | 52.5 |
| | 66 | 2 | 3.3 | 3.3 | 55.7 |
| | 69 | 1 | 1.6 | 1.6 | 57.4 |
| | 70 | 1 | 1.6 | 1.6 | 59.0 |
| | 72 | 1 | 1.6 | 1.6 | 60.7 |
| | 73 | 2 | 3.3 | 3.3 | 63.9 |
| | 75 | 2 | 3.3 | 3.3 | 67.2 |
| | 76 | 2 | 3.3 | 3.3 | 70.5 |
| | 77 | 3 | 4.9 | 4.9 | 75.4 |
| | 78 | 1 | 1.6 | 1.6 | 77.0 |
| | 79 | 1 | 1.6 | 1.6 | 78.7 |
| | 80 | 4 | 6.6 | 6.6 | 85.2 |
| | 82 | 1 | 1.6 | 1.6 | 86.9 |
| | 83 | 2 | 3.3 | 3.3 | 90.2 |
| | 84 | 1 | 1.6 | 1.6 | 91.8 |
| | 85 | 1 | 1.6 | 1.6 | 93.4 |
| | 86 | 1 | 1.6 | 1.6 | 95.1 |
| | 87 | 1 | 1.6 | 1.6 | 96.7 |
| | 88 | 2 | 3.3 | 3.3 | 100.0 |
| | Total | 61 | 100.0 | 100.0 | |

b. To determine the number of class intervals needed:

$K = 1 + 3.3 \log (n) = 1 + 3.3 \log (61) = 1 + 3.3(1.785) = 1 + 5.89 = 6.89$, or 7 class intervals

To determine the width of the class intervals:

$W = \dfrac{max - min}{k} = \dfrac{88 - 37}{7} = 7.3$ (width of the class intervals is greater than 7, so eight class intervals are used)

Table C.13　**Grouped Data 1**

| Class Interval | f | cf | rel f | Cum % |
|---|---|---|---|---|
| 37–44 | 5 | 5 | 0.082 | 0.082 |
| 45–52 | 8 | 13 | 0.131 | 0.213 |
| 53–60 | 9 | 22 | 0.148 | 0.361 |
| 61–68 | 12 | 34 | 0.197 | 0.557 |
| 69–76 | 9 | 43 | 0.148 | 0.705 |
| 77–84 | 13 | 56 | 0.213 | 0.918 |
| 85–92 | 5 | 61 | 0.082 | 1.000 |
|  | 61 |  | 1.000 |  |

c. $\overline{X} = \dfrac{4014.5}{61} = 65.8$

Table C.14　**Grouped Data 2**

| Class Interval | f | M | fM | f(M²) |
|---|---|---|---|---|
| 37–44 | 5 | 40.5 | 202.50 | 8,201.25 |
| 45–52 | 8 | 48.5 | 388.00 | 18,818.00 |
| 53–60 | 9 | 56.5 | 508.50 | 28,730.25 |
| 61–68 | 12 | 64.5 | 774.00 | 49,923.00 |
| 69–76 | 9 | 72.5 | 652.50 | 47,306.25 |
| 77–84 | 13 | 80.5 | 1,046.50 | 84,243.25 |
| 85–92 | 5 | 88.5 | 442.50 | 39,161.25 |
|  | 61 |  | 4,014.50 | 276,383.25 |

Crude mode = 80.5
Crude median = 64.5

$$Mode = 76.5 + \frac{8(13 - 9)}{(13 - 9) + (13 - 5)} = 76.5 + 2.7 = 79.2$$

$$M_D = 60.5 + \frac{8(30.5 - 22)}{12} = 60.5 + 5.7 = 66.2$$

Variance and standard deviation:

$$\sum x^2 = \sum f(M^2) - \frac{\sum (fM)^2}{n} = 276,383.25 - \frac{(4014.5)^2}{61} = 12,183.082$$

$$s^2 = \frac{\sum x^2}{n-1} = \frac{12,183.082}{61-1} = 203.05$$

$$s = \sqrt{\frac{\sum x^2}{n-1}} = \sqrt{203.05} = 14.2$$

d.  Table C.15  **Grouped and ungrouped frequency distributions**

|  | Ungrouped | Grouped (Raw) | Grouped (Refined) |
|---|---|---|---|
| Mean | 65.6 | 65.8 | 65.8 |
| Median | 65.0 | 64.5 | 66.2 |
| Mode | 64, 80 | 80.5 | 79.2 |
| Variance | 202.782 | | 203.05 |
| S.D. | 14.2 | | 14.2 |

3. a.  Table C.16  **Partial Excel Output for Descriptives**

|  | Column 1 |
|---|---|
| Mean | 6.311475 |
| Median | 4 |
| Mode | 3 |
| Standard Deviation | 6.219703 |
| Sample Variance | 38.6847 |

b. To determine the number of class intervals needed:

$K = 1 + 3.3 \log (n) = 1 + 3.3 \log (61) = 1 + 3.3(1.785) = 1 + 5.89 = 6.89$, or 7 class intervals (eight class intervals were used to cover the entire distribution)

To determine the width of the class intervals:

$$W = \frac{max - min}{k} = \frac{36 - 1}{7} = 5 \ \ \text{(width of the class intervals is 5)}$$

Table C.17 **LOS Class Intervals**

| Class Interval % | $f$ | $cf$ | rel $f$ | Cum |
|---|---|---|---|---|
| 1–5 | 38 | 38 | 0.623 | 0.623 |
| 6–10 | 13 | 51 | 0.213 | 0.836 |
| 11–15 | 6 | 57 | 0.098 | 0.934 |
| 16–20 | 2 | 59 | 0.033 | 0.967 |
| 21–25 | 0 | 59 | 0.000 | 0.967 |
| 26–30 | 1 | 60 | 0.016 | 0.984 |
| 31–35 | 0 | 60 | 0.000 | 0.984 |
| 36–40 | 1 | 61 | 0.016 | 1.000 |
|  | 61 |  | 1.000 |  |

| Class Interval % | $f$ | $M$ | $fM$ | $f(M^2)$ |
|---|---|---|---|---|
| 1–5 | 38 | 3 | 114 | 342 |
| 6–10 | 13 | 8 | 104 | 832 |
| 11–15 | 6 | 13 | 78 | 1,014 |
| 16–20 | 2 | 18 | 36 | 648 |
| 21–25 | 0 | 23 | 0 | 0 |
| 26–30 | 1 | 28 | 28 | 784 |
| 31–35 | 0 | 33 | 0 | 0 |
| 36–40 | 1 | 38 | 38 | 1,444 |
|  | 61 |  | 398 | 5,064 |

c. $\overline{X} = \dfrac{398}{61} = 6.5$

Crude mode = 3

Crude median = 3

$$Mode = 0.5 + \frac{5(38 - 0)}{(38 - 0) + (38 - 13)} = 0.5 + 3.0 = 3.5$$

$$M_D = 0.5 + \frac{5(30.5 - 0)}{38} = 0.5 + 4.0 = 4.5$$

Variance and standard deviation:

$$\sum x^2 = \sum f(M^2) - \frac{\sum (fM)^2}{n} = 5064 - \frac{(398)^2}{61} = 5064 - 2596.79 = 2467.21$$

$$s^2 = \frac{\sum x^2}{n-1} = \frac{2467.21}{61-1} = 41.1$$

$$s = \sqrt{\frac{\sum x^2}{n-1}} = \sqrt{41.1} = 6.4$$

d.      Table C.18    **Chapter 5, Problem 3d**

|  | Ungrouped | Grouped (Raw) | Grouped (Refined) |
|---|---|---|---|
| Mean | 6.31 | 6.5 | 6.5 |
| Median | 4 | 3 | 4.5 |
| Mode | 3 | 3 | 3.5 |
| Variance | 38.7 |  | 41.1 |
| S.D. | 6.2 |  | 6.4 |

# CHAPTER 6

## Knowledge Questions

1. See Glossary.
2. The **normal distribution** is a family of distributions in which the population mean can take on any value. In the normal distribution, the mean, median, and mode are equal. The normal distribution is bell-shaped and symmetrical, with 50% of the observations falling above the mean and 50% falling below the mean. In the normal distribution, 68% of the observations fall between ±1 standard deviation of the mean, 95% of the observations fall within ±1.96 standard deviations of the mean, and 99% of the observations fall between ±2.58 standard deviations of the mean.

   The same characteristics are true of the **standard normal distribution** except that the population mean is always equal to 0 and the standard deviation is equal to 1. The standard normal distribution is a linear transformation of the normal distribution, with the transformed values referred to as $z$ values. As in the normal distribution, 68% of the observations fall between ±1 standard deviation of the mean, 95% of the observations fall within ±1.96 standard deviations of the mean, and 99% of the observations fall between ±2.58 standard deviations of the mean.

3. The **standard deviation** is a measure of variation that is used to describe the number of units that an observation in a normal distribution is from the mean. The **standard normal deviate** is actually a $z$ value in the standard normal distribution but has the same interpretation as the standard deviation. A standard normal deviate is the number of standard deviation units that an observed value lies away from the population mean, $\mu$.

Table C.19    **Mean Age of Patients by Sex, DRG 462, Rehabilitation, Critical Care Hospital, 2006**

|  |  | Age | | |
|---|---|---|---|---|
|  |  | Female | Male | Total |
| N |  | 80 | 88 | 168 |
| Mean |  | 55.467 | 53.947 | 54.671 |
| Std. Deviation |  | 17.5344 | 19.1981 | 18.3856 |
| Std. Error |  | 1.9604 | 2.0465 | 1.4185 |
| 95% Confidence Interval for Mean | Lower Bound | 51.565 | 49.879 | 51.871 |
|  | Upper Bound | 59.370 | 58.015 | 57.472 |
| Minimum |  | 19.4 | 17.5 | 17.5 |
| Maximum |  | 89.1 | 97.6 | 97.6 |

4. a. Mean age for men = 53.9
      Mean age for women = 55.5
      Mean age for entire group = 54.7
   b. The standard error is influenced by sample size and standard deviation—the greater the sample size and the smaller the standard deviation, the smaller the standard error. Although the sample size for men is greater than that for women, the standard deviation is larger for men. The age range for men is 97.6 − 17.5 = 80.1 versus 89.1 − 19.4 = 69.7 for women. There is more variation in the age for men, which is contributing to the larger standard error.
   c. Combining the two groups increases the total $n$, thus resulting in a smaller standard error of the mean.

d. $CI_{95}$ for men = 49.9 to 58.0
$CI_{95}$ for women = 51.6 to 59.4
$CI_{95}$ for entire group = 51.9 to 57.5

e. We are 95% confident that the true population mean lies between 51.9 and 57.5 for all discharges from DRG 462.

5. Standard error of the mean = $\dfrac{s}{\sqrt{n}} = \dfrac{3.18}{\sqrt{21}} = 0.69$

$$CI_{95} = -X \pm 1.96s_{-X} = 3.33 \pm 1.96(0.69) = 3.33 \pm 1.35 = [1.98, 4.68]$$

## Multiple Choice

1. a. $\pm 1\sigma$ of the mean
2. a. $\pm 1\sigma$ of the mean
3. d. All of the above
4. b. It is a discrete distribution.
5. b. 16%
6. b. 97.5%
7. c. Positively skewed
8. a. Is equal to 0.00
9. b. 10 and 30
10. b. 8
11. d. Both (a) and (b)
12. a. 45 men and 55 women
13. b. Simple random sampling
14. c. Systematic sampling
15. d. Two-stage random sampling

**Problems** Table C.20   Critical Care Hospital, Length of Stay
of Patients by Gender, DRG 127, Heart Failure and
Shock, 2006

|  |  | Gender | | |
|---|---|---|---|---|
|  |  | Female | Male | Total |
| *ALOS* | 1 | 1 | 5 | 6 |
|  | 2 | 1 | 5 | 6 |
|  | 3 | 3 | 13 | 16 |
|  | 4 | 4 | 1 | 5 |
|  | 5 | 0 | 5 | 5 |
|  | 6 | 3 | 1 | 4 |
|  | 7 | 0 | 1 | 1 |
|  | 8 | 2 | 2 | 4 |
|  | 10 | 1 | 3 | 4 |
|  | 11 | 1 | 2 | 3 |
|  | 13 | 1 | 0 | 1 |
|  | 14 | 0 | 1 | 1 |
|  | 15 | 1 | 0 | 1 |
|  | 16 | 0 | 1 | 1 |
|  | 17 | 0 | 1 | 1 |
|  | 27 | 1 | 0 | 1 |
|  | 36 | 1 | 0 | 1 |
| Total |  | 20 | 41 | 61 |

1. a.  Referring to the SPSS output below, the mean length of stay is 6.3 days for
the entire group, 5.2 days for men, and 8.7 days for women.

Table C.21   **SPSS Output Report**

| LOS | | | |
|---|---|---|---|
| Gender | Mean | N | Std. Deviation |
| Female | 8.70 | 20 | 8.761 |
| Male | 5.15 | 41 | 4.163 |
| Total | 6.31 | 61 | 6.220 |

  b.  The standard error for the mean length of stay for women is 1.959; for
men, 0.65; and 0.796 for the entire group.

Table C.22  **Calculate the Standard Error**

| LOS | | FEMALE | MALE | Total |
|---|---|---|---|---|
| N | | 20 | 41 | 61 |
| Mean | | 8.70 | 5.15 | 6.31 |
| Std. Deviation | | 8.761 | 4.163 | 6.220 |
| Std. Error | | 1.959 | .650 | .796 |
| 95% Confidence | Lower Bound | 4.60 | 3.83 | 4.72 |
| Interval for Mean | Upper Bound | 12.80 | 6.46 | 7.90 |
| Minimum | | 1 | 1 | 1 |
| Maximum | | 36 | 17 | 36 |

c. Referring to the SPSS output below, the 95% confidence intervals for each group are:

Table C.23  **SPSS output for 95% Confidence Intervals**

| Group | 95% Confidence Interval |
|---|---|
| Entire Group | 4.72 to 7.90 |
| Men | 3.83 to 6.46 |
| Women | 4.60 to 12.8 |

# CHAPTER 7

## Knowledge Questions

1. See Glossary.
2. a. $H_0 : \mu_1 = \mu_2$
   $H_A : \mu_1 \neq \mu_2$
   b. $\alpha = 0.05$
3. The **alpha level**, or level of significance, is set in advance of conducting the statistical test. The alpha level is the level at which we will reject the null hypothesis. The alpha level also states the probability of making a Type I error. The *p* **value** is obtained as a result of conducting the statistical test, and it tells us how rare the result of the statistical test actually is. If the *p* value is less than or equal to the alpha level, we reject the null hypothesis.
4. A **Type I error** occurs when we reject the null hypothesis when it is true; a **Type II error** occurs when we fail to reject the null hypothesis when it is false. The best way to control for Type I error is by increasing the sample size. We

can also control for Type I error by setting a more strict alpha level (i.e., $\alpha = 0.01$) to reduce the risk of rejecting the null hypothesis when it is true.

5. The **z distribution** is the standard normal distribution that is used to evaluate the differences between populations when population parameters are known and when sample sizes are large. The standard normal distribution is bell-shaped and symmetrical.

    The **t distribution** is a family of distributions based on $N - 1$ degrees of freedom. The t distribution is used when making statistical inferences between populations when population parameters are not known and when sample sizes are small. The shape of the t distribution is broad and flat with smaller sample sizes; as the sample size increases, the shape of the t distribution approaches the shape of the normal distribution.

6. We use a one-tailed test when we are interested in determining whether one population mean is significantly greater or less than another population mean. We use a two-tailed test when we are interested in determining whether two population means are significantly different from each other regardless of direction.

7. The assumptions are that the samples are drawn independently and randomly from populations that are normally distributed and that the population variances are approximately equal. This assumption may not be strictly followed because of the Central Limit Theorem. The **Central Limit Theorem** states that even when populations are not normally distributed, the distribution of the sample means approaches the normal distribution as $N$ becomes large. The z and t tests are also considered "robust" procedures in that statistical significance can be achieved despite violations of certain assumptions.

8. An **effect** is a change in one variable that is due to another variable. The variable that displays the effect is referred to as the **dependent variable**. The variable considered to be responsible for the variability in the dependent variable is referred to as the **independent variable**.

## Multiple Choice

1. c. Evaluated statistically as either true or false
2. b. Rejected 5% of the time when it is true
3. a. We reject the null hypothesis when it is true
4. d. Accept the null hypothesis when it is false
5. b. Decreasing the risk of making a Type I error
6. d. All of the above
7. d. Probability of getting a result as extreme as the one observed if the null hypothesis is true
8. b. One-tailed test
9. a. Also significant at the 0.05 level
10. b. Non-directional

11. c. Reject the $H_0$ at $\alpha = 0.05$ but accept the $H_0$ at $\alpha = 0.01$
12. d. Reject the $H_0$ at $\alpha = 0.05$ and reject the $H_0$ at $\alpha = 0.01$
13. b. Reject the $H_0$ at $\alpha = 0.05$ and reject the $H_0$ at $\alpha = 0.01$
14. a. One sample directional $t$ test
15. a. 99

## Problems

1. a. $H_0 : \mu_1 = \mu_2$
   $H_A : \mu_1 \neq \mu_2$
   $\alpha = 0.05$
   b. The SPSS output for the one-sample $t$ test:

Table C.24  **One-Sample Statistics and One-Sample Test**

**One-Sample Statistics**

|     | N | Mean | Std. Deviation | Std. Error Mean |
|-----|---|------|----------------|-----------------|
| LOS | 23 | 4.17 | 2.570 | .536 |

**One-Sample Test**

**Test Value = 5.2**

|     | t | df | Sig. (2-tailed) | Mean Difference | 95% Confidence Interval of the Difference Lower | Upper |
|-----|---|----|-----------------|-----------------|------|------|
| LOS | −1.915 | 22 | .069 | −1.026 | −2.14 | .09 |

   c. The calculated value of $t$ is −1.915, df = 22, $p = 0.069$. The calculated value of $t$ is not statistically significant; we therefore conclude that it appears that the ALOS for DRG 002 for Critical Care Hospital is not significantly different from the national ALOS for DRG 002.

2. a. Table C.25  **Frequency Distribution of Length of Stay by Payer, DRG 410, At Critical Care Hospital in 2004 (SPSS Output)**

LOS * Payor Crosstabulation

| Count | | MANAGED CARE | MEDICARE | Total |
|---|---|---|---|---|
| LOS | 1 | 12 | 3 | 15 |
| | 2 | 5 | 16 | 21 |
| | 3 | 1 | 5 | 6 |
| | 4 | 13 | 8 | 21 |
| | 5 | 10 | 5 | 15 |
| | 6 | 1 | 0 | 1 |
| | 7 | 1 | 0 | 1 |
| | 8 | 2 | 1 | 3 |
| | 9 | 1 | 1 | 2 |
| | 13 | 1 | 0 | 1 |
| | 14 | 1 | 0 | 1 |
| | 15 | 2 | 1 | 3 |
| | 23 | 1 | 0 | 1 |
| | 54 | 0 | 1 | 1 |
| Total | 51 | 41 | 92 | |

Table C.26  **Mean and Standard Deviation for Length of Stay by Payer, DRG 410, At Critical Care Hospital in 2003 (SPSS Output)**

| Payor | Mean | N | Std. Deviation |
|---|---|---|---|
| MANAGED CARE | 4.80 | 51 | 4.382 |
| MEDICARE | 4.71 | 41 | 8.280 |
| Total | 4.76 | 92 | 6.379 |

$H_0 : \mu_1 = \mu_2$
$H_A : \mu_1 \neq \mu_2$
$\alpha = 0.05$

Table C.27    **Group Statistics and Independent Samples Test**

### Group Statistics

| | LOS | |
|---|---|---|
| | **Payor** | |
| | **MANAGED CARE** | **MEDICARE** |
| N | 51 | 41 |
| Mean | 4.80 | 4.71 |
| Std. Deviation | 4.382 | 8.280 |
| Std. Error Mean | .614 | 1.293 |

### Independent Samples Test

| | | | LOS | |
|---|---|---|---|---|
| | | | **Equal variances assumed** | **Equal variances not assumed** |
| Levene's Test for Equality of Variances | | F | .201 | |
| | | Sig. | .655 | |
| *t*-test for Equality of Means | | t | .072 | .067 |
| | | df | 90 | 57.699 |
| | | Sig. (2-tailed) | .943 | .946 |
| | | Mean Difference | .097 | .097 |
| | | Std. Error Difference | 1.345 | 1.431 |
| | 95% Confidence Interval of the Difference | Lower | −2.576 | −2.769 |
| | | Upper | 2.769 | 2.962 |

b.  Because the hypothesis is one of inequality, we conduct a two-tailed *t* test. The calculated *t* is 0.072, df = 92 − 2 = 90, and *p* = 0.943. The calculated value of *t* is not statistically significant.

c.  We fail to reject the null hypothesis. It appears that the observed difference in the average lengths of stay is not statistically significant.

3. a. Table C.28   **Frequency Distribution of Length of Stay by Physician, DRG 410, in 2003 at Critical Care Hospital (SPSS Output)**

| | | LOS * Physician Cross-tabulation | | |
|---|---|---|---|---|
| | | Physician | | |
| | | 1460 | 8210 | Total |
| LOS | 2 | 13 | 21 | 34 |
| | 3 | 1 | 1 | 2 |
| | 4 | 1 | 0 | 1 |
| | 5 | 1 | 1 | 2 |
| | 13 | 1 | 0 | 1 |
| | 14 | 0 | 1 | 1 |
| | 15 | 1 | 0 | 1 |
| | 23 | 1 | 0 | 1 |
| Total | | 19 | 24 | 43 |

Table C.29   **Mean and Standard Deviation for Length of Stay by Physician, DRG 410, in 2003 at Critical Care Hospital (SPSS Output)**

| | | Report | |
|---|---|---|---|
| Physician | Mean | N | Std. Deviation |
| 1460 | 4.68 | 19 | 5.812 |
| 8210 | 2.67 | 24 | 2.496 |
| Total | 3.56 | 43 | 4.350 |

$H_0 : \mu_1 = \mu_2$
$H_A : \mu_1 \neq \mu_2$
$\alpha = 0.05$

Table C.30

**Group Statistics**

| | LOS | |
|---|---|---|
| | **Physician** | |
| | **1460** | **8210** |
| N | 19 | 24 |
| Mean | 4.68 | 2.67 |
| Std. Deviation | 5.812 | 2.496 |
| Std. Error Mean | 1.333 | .510 |

**Independent Samples Test**

| | | LOS | |
|---|---|---|---|
| | | **Equal variances assumed** | **Equal variances not assumed** |
| Levene's Test for | F | 7.743 | |
| Equality of Variances | Sig. | .008 | |
| *t*-test for Equality of | t | 1.535 | 1.413 |
| Means | df | 41 | 23.253 |
| | Sig. (2-tailed) | .133 | .171 |
| | Mean Difference | 2.018 | 2.018 |
| | Std. Error Difference | 1.315 | 1.427 |
| | 95% Confidence Interval — Lower | − .637 | − .934 |
| | of the Difference — Upper | 4.673 | 4.969 |

b. Because the hypothesis is one of inequality, we conduct a two-tailed *t* test. The calculated *t* is 1.535, df = 43 − 2 = 41, *p* = 0.008. The calculated value of *t* is statistically significant.

c. We reject the null hypothesis. It appears that the observed difference in the average lengths of stay is statistically significant.

## CHAPTER 8
### Knowledge Questions

1. See Glossary.
2. The **Pearson's r** is a measure of the linear relationship between two variables. Both variables must be at the interval or ratio level of measurement.
3. The range of the Pearson's $r$ is ±1.0. If the Pearson's $r$ correlation coefficient is either +1.0 or −1.0, the relationship between the two variables is perfect; if the Pearson's $r$ is equal to zero, there is no relationship between the two variables. If the relationship between the two variables is positive, as one variable increases, so does the second. If the relationship is negative, as one variable increases, the second variable decreases.
4. The Pearson's $r$ is a measure of the strength of the relationship between two variables. The coefficient of determination ($r^2$) tells us how much of the variation in one variable is explained by the other.
5. We can use the $\chi^2$ test of independence when we are interested in determining if two variables, such as age and gender, are related. We can use the $\chi^2$ test to compare frequencies on a variable from two or more independent populations. We can use the $\chi^2$ goodness-of-fit test when we want to compare an observed frequency distribution to a theoretical frequency distribution.
6. The researcher may want to use the $\chi^2$ goodness-of-fit test to determine if obtained population proportions in a sample match the proportions in the underlying population. This helps the researcher in assessing whether the results can be generalized to the underlying population as a whole.

### Multiple Choice

1. d. All of the above
2. b. Equal to 1.0
3. d. Positive.
4. d. −0.89
5. c. 0.0
6. a. 0.0
7. d. We have made an error in our calculations
8. b. As length of stay increases, total charges increase.
9. d. Both (b) and (c)
10. c. For the row variable, "services," the number of categories is 10; for the column variable, "gender," the number of categories is two. In the $\chi^2$ test, the degrees of freedom is equal to (R − 1) × (C − 1); therefore (10 − 1) × (2 − 1) = 9.
11. a. Observed frequencies are similar to the expected frequencies.

Table C.31    **R × C table**

| | **Observed Frequencies** | | | |
|---|---|---|---|---|
| | **Phys A** | **Phys B** | **Phys C** | **Total** |
| Male | 30 | 12 | 18 | 60 |
| Female | 10 | 48 | 82 | 140 |
| Total | 40 | 60 | 100 | 200 |

| | **Expected Frequencies** | | | |
|---|---|---|---|---|
| | **Phys A** | **Phys B** | **Phys C** | **Total** |
| Male | 12 | 18 | 30 | 60 |
| Female | 28 | 42 | 70 | 140 |
| Total | 40 | 60 | 100 | 200 |

12. b.  18
13. b.  18
14. c.  30
15. b.  28
16. a.  $df = (R - 1) \times (C - 1) = (2 - 1) \times (3 - 1) = 2$
17. a.  Reject the null hypothesis
18. c.  Strength of the association between variables in a 2 × 2 table

## Problems

1. a.

Table C.32    **Frequency Distribution of Discharges by Age and Gender, DRG 123 (SPSS Output)**

| | | **Age * Gender Cross-tabulation** | | |
|---|---|---|---|---|
| | | **Gender** | | |
| | | **FEMALE** | **MALE** | **Total** |
| Age | 49 | 0 | 1 | 1 |
| | 50 | 0 | 1 | 1 |
| | 61 | 0 | 1 | 1 |
| | 66 | 0 | 1 | 1 |
| | 75 | 1 | 0 | 1 |
| | 76 | 0 | 1 | 1 |
| | 77 | 0 | 1 | 1 |
| | 88 | 1 | 0 | 1 |
| | 88 | 0 | 1 | 1 |
| Total | | 2 | 7 | 9 |

$H_0 : p_1 = p_2$
$H_A : p_1 \neq p_2$

b. $\alpha = 0.05$

c. 
Table C.33

|  | Observed | Expected | Residual |
|---|---|---|---|
| Female | 2 | 4.5 | −2.5 |
| Male | 7 | 4.5 | −2.5 |
| Total | 9 | | |

| Test Statistics | |
|---|---|
|  | **Gender** |
| Chi-Square[a] | 2.778 |
| df | 1 |
| Asymp. Sig. | .096 |

[a]2 cells (100.0%) have expected frequencies less than 5. The minimum expected cell frequency is 4.5.

d. $\chi^2 = 2.778$, df = 1, $p = 0.096$. We fail to reject the null hypothesis and conclude that it appears there is no difference in the proportion of men and women who expired as a result of an acute myocardial infarction. The result of the $\chi^2$ test is not statistically significant. The results should be viewed with caution because of the number of cells that have expected frequency counts of less than five.

2. a. $H_0$ : *There is no association between age and gender for discharges from DRG 123.*
   $H_A$ : *There is an association between age and gender for discharges from DRG 123.*

   b. $\alpha = 0.05$

c.   Table C.34

**Chi-Square Tests**

| | Value | df | Asymp. Sig. (2-sided) |
|---|---|---|---|
| Pearson Chi-Square | 6.107[a] | 7 | .527 |
| Continuity Correction | | | |
| Likelihood Ratio | 6.762 | 7 | .454 |
| Linear-by-Linear Association | 1.604 | 1 | .205 |
| N of Valid Cases | 9 | | |

[a]16 cells (100.0%) have expected counts less than 5. The minimum expected count is .22.

$\chi^2 = 6.107$, df = 7, $p = 0.527$. The result of the $\chi^2$ test is not statistically significant. The results should be viewed with caution because of the number of cells that have expected frequency counts of less than five.

d. Table C.35

**Symmetrical Measures**

| | | Value | Asymp. Std. Error[a] | Approx. T[b] | Approx. Sig. |
|---|---|---|---|---|---|
| Nominal by Nominal | Phi | .824 | | | .527 |
| | Cramer's V | .824 | | | .527 |
| No. of Valid Cases | 9 | | | | |

[a]Not assuming the null hypothesis.
[b]Using the asymptotic standard error assuming the null hypothesis.

The calculated value of $\chi^2$ can tell us whether there is a relationship between two variables, but it does not indicate the strength of the relationship as does the Pearson's *r*. A significant $\chi^2$ can also be a function of sample size. The phi coefficient corrects for sample size and provides a measure of the strength of the relationship between the two variables. In this example, the phi coefficient is 0.824; it indicates that a strong relationship exists, but it is not statistically significant.

e. $\chi^2 = 6.107$, df = 7, $p = 0.527$. We fail to reject the null hypothesis and conclude that it appears that there is no association between age and gender for patients who were discharged from DRG 123.

3. a.

Table C.36    **Case Summaries for DRG 105, Cardiac Valve Procedures and Other Major Cardiothoracic Procedures without Cardiac Catheterization**

|    | Gender | Age | LOS | Charges | Payor |
|----|--------|-----|-----|---------|-------|
| 1  | FEMALE | 47  | 20  | $91,683 | MEDICAID |
| 2  | FEMALE | 75  | 43  | $93,708 | MEDICARE |
| 3  | FEMALE | 84  | 7   | $21,446 | MEDICARE |
| 4  | FEMALE | 50  | 13  | $37,797 | MEDICARE |
| 5  | MALE   | 77  | 14  | $54,364 | MEDICARE |
| 6  | MALE   | 57  | 4   | $17,626 | MEDICARE |
| 7  | MALE   | 73  | 4   | $12,832 | MEDICARE |
| 8  | FEMALE | 56  | 1   | $36,153 | MEDICAID |
| 9  | MALE   | 69  | 1   | $14,907 | MEDICAID |
| 10 | FEMALE | 81  | 23  | $104,148 | MEDICARE |
| 11 | MALE   | 21  | 5   | $21,423 | MEDICAID |
| 12 | FEMALE | 37  | 5   | $24,971 | MEDICAID |
| 13 | FEMALE | 69  | 4   | $17,022 | MEDICARE |
| 14 | FEMALE | 89  | 17  | $50,652 | MEDICARE |
| 15 | MALE   | 28  | 35  | $186,496 | MEDICAID |
| 16 | MALE   | 47  | 6   | $24,441 | MEDICAID |
| 17 | MALE   | 87  | 11  | $35,349 | MEDICARE |
| 18 | FEMALE | 85  | 5   | $22,155 | MEDICARE |
| 19 | MALE   | 56  | 5   | $24,455 | MANAGED CARE |
| 20 | MALE   | 45  | 11  | $36,401 | MEDICAID |
| 21 | MALE   | 82  | 6   | $25,783 | MEDICARE |
| 22 | FEMALE | 65  | 10  | $37,055 | MANAGED CARE |
| 23 | MALE   | 67  | 4   | $19,236 | MEDICARE |
| 24 | MALE   | 59  | 23  | $60,132 | OTHER |
| 25 | FEMALE | 67  | 7   | $35,777 | MEDICARE |
| 26 | MALE   | 53  | 4   | $19,972 | MANAGED CARE |
| 27 | MALE   | 71  | 7   | $25,409 | MEDICARE |
| 28 | FEMALE | 79  | 6   | $281,140 | MEDICARE |
| 29 | MALE   | 63  | 1   | $41,283 | MEDICAID |
| 30 | MALE   | 53  | 19  | $71,439 | MEDICAID |
| 31 | FEMALE | 75  | 9   | $33,735 | MEDICARE |
| 32 | FEMALE | 68  | 9   | $37,830 | GOV MNGD CARE |
| 33 | MALE   | 37  | 4   | $22,311 | MEDICAID |

$H_0 : \rho = 0$

$H_A : \rho \neq 0$

$\alpha = 0.05$

b.

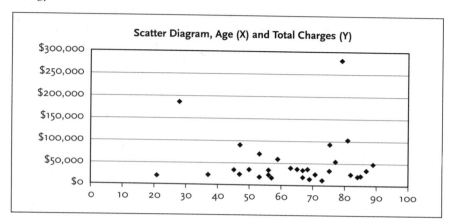

Figure C.6

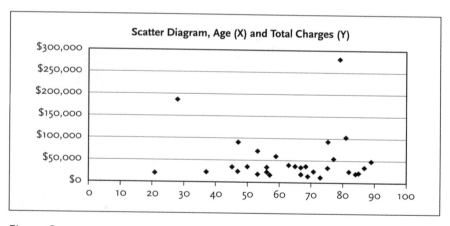

Figure C.7

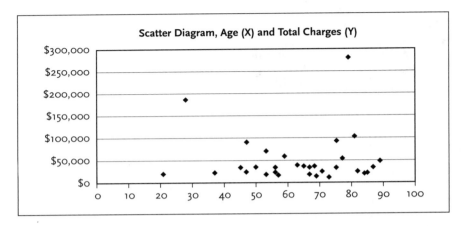

Figure C.8

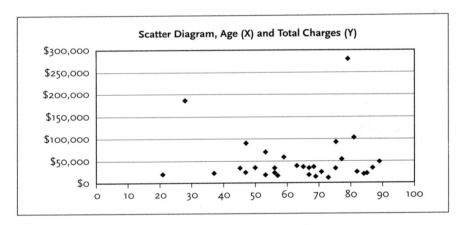

Figure C.9

For the variables age and length of stay, and age and total charges, the regression lines in the scatter plots are flat indicating no relationship. For length of stay and total charges, the regression line originates in the lower left and moves to the upper right, indicating a positive linear relationship. The Pearson's *r* is calculated for each; the results are:

Table C.37

<table>
<tr><th colspan="4">Descriptive Statistics</th></tr>
<tr><th></th><th>Mean</th><th>Std. Deviation</th><th>N</th></tr>
<tr><td>Age</td><td>62.79</td><td>17.315</td><td>33</td></tr>
<tr><td>LOS</td><td>10.39</td><td>9.585</td><td>33</td></tr>
<tr><td>Charges</td><td>49670.7715</td><td>54114.32276</td><td>33</td></tr>
</table>

<table>
<tr><th colspan="5">Correlations</th></tr>
<tr><th></th><th></th><th>Age</th><th>LOS</th><th>Charges</th></tr>
<tr><td>Age</td><td>Pearson Correlation</td><td>1</td><td>−.024</td><td>.009</td></tr>
<tr><td></td><td>Sig. (2-tailed)</td><td>.</td><td>.896</td><td>.961</td></tr>
<tr><td></td><td>N</td><td>33</td><td>33</td><td>33</td></tr>
<tr><td>LOS</td><td>Pearson Correlation</td><td>−.024</td><td>1</td><td>.480*</td></tr>
<tr><td></td><td>Sig. (2-tailed)</td><td>.896</td><td>.</td><td>.005</td></tr>
<tr><td></td><td>N</td><td>33</td><td>33</td><td>33</td></tr>
<tr><td>Charges</td><td>Pearson Correlation</td><td>.009</td><td>.480(**)</td><td>1</td></tr>
<tr><td></td><td>Sig. (2-tailed)</td><td>.961</td><td>.005</td><td>.</td></tr>
<tr><td></td><td>N</td><td>33</td><td>33</td><td>33</td></tr>
</table>

* Correlation is significant at the 0.01 level (2-tailed).

c. For age and length of stay, $r = -0.024$ and $p = 0.896$. We therefore fail to reject the null hypothesis and conclude that it appears that the relationship between age and length of stay is not statistically significant.

For age and total charges, $r = -0.009$ and $p = 0.961$. We therefore fail to reject the null hypothesis and conclude that it appears that the relationship between age and total charges is not statistically significant.

For length of stay and total charges, $r = -0.48$ and $p = 0.005$. We therefore reject the null hypothesis and conclude that it appears that the relationship between length of stay and total charges is statistically significant.